`-DEATH
CIPHERS/CYPHERS
FOR LIFE & DEATH!!!~'

`-DEATH CIPHERS/CYPHERS FOR LIFE & DEATH!!!~'

DWAYNE W. ANDERSON

`-DEATH CIPHERS/CYPHERS FOR LIFE & DEATH!!!~'

iUniverse books may be ordered through booksellers or by contacting:

iUniverse
1663 Liberty Drive
Bloomington, IN 47403
www.iuniverse.com
844-349-9409

Because of the dynamic nature of the Internet, any web addresses or links contained in this book may have changed since publication and may no longer be valid. The views expressed in this work are solely those of the author and do not necessarily reflect the views of the publisher, and the publisher hereby disclaims any responsibility for them.

Any people depicted in stock imagery provided by Getty Images are models, and such images are being used for illustrative purposes only. Certain stock imagery © Getty Images.

ISBN: 978-1-6632-1870-4 (sc)
ISBN: 978-1-6632-1868-1 (hc)
ISBN: 978-1-6632-1869-8 (e)

Library of Congress Control Number: 2021903560

Print information available on the last page.

iUniverse rev. date: 02/17/2021

PREVIOUS BOOKS:

1) The REAL PROPHET of DOOM!...(...!)
2) The REAL PROPHET of DOOM VOL.2 (...!)
3) The REAL PROPHET of DOOM VOL. 3 (...!)
4) The REAL PROPHET of DOOM (KISMET) (INTRODUCTION) PENDULUM FLOW
5) The REAL PROPHET of DOOM (KISMET) (INTRODUCTION) PENDULUM FLOW - (II)
6) The REAL PROPHET of DOOM (KISMET) (INTRODUCTION) PENDULUM FLOW - (III)
7) NEW BOOK - REAL MESSAGES of GOD I, II, & III-!!!~'
8) BOOK TITLE: GOD is The `-MATHEMATICIAN!!!~'
9) The `-GOD `-BOOK of `-NUMEROLOGY!~'
10) DEATH CIPHERS/CYPHERS for LIFE & DEATH!!!~'

WITHOUT a `-DOUBT, OUR LIVES are `-ETCHED; and, `-ARTICULATED in `-TIME' to an `-EVENTUALITY; of `-GOD'S VERY OWN `-PURPOSE, to `-OUR `-VERY `-OWN PURPOSE of `-BEING; in the `-EXISTENCE/ EXPANSE of `-TIME!!!~' OUR `-time OF `-LIVES (BIRTHS, DEATHS, MARRIAGES, CHILDREN, etc.); are `-EXACTLY `-SET by `-GOD!!!~' ALREADY `-PROVEN through `-RECIPROCAL-SEQUENCING-NUMEROLOGY-RSN; and, RECIPROCAL-SEQUENCED-INVERSED-REALITIES-RSIR!!!~' AGAIN; ENJOY the `-READS!!!~'

BULLET POINTS FOR: DEATH CIPHERS/CYPHERS for LIFE & DEATH!!!~'

- *THE LIFE AND DEATH OF CELEBRITIES –*
- *THE LIFE AND DEATH OF SCIENTISTS –*
- *THE LIFE AND DEATH OF COMMON PEOPLE -*
- *READING; and, UNDERSTANDING the`-SCIENCE of `-NUMBERS in the FOCUS of Reciprocal-Sequencing-Numerology-RSN-'*
- *DISCOVERER & FOUNDER of RECIPROCAL SEQUENCING INVERSED REALITIES – EQUATIONS of `-REALITY in LIFE & DEATH - AUTHOR: DWAYNE W. ANDERSON -*

`-DEATH CIPHERS/CYPHERS FOR LIFE & DEATH!!!~'

I've `-CREATED a NEW TYPE of PHILOSOPHY (Reciprocal-Sequencing-Numerology)/ (Reciprocal-Sequenced-Inversed-Realities) that `-PROVES without `-QUESTION the `-PRESENCE of GOD'S EXISTENCE in our DAILY AFFAIRS!!!!!~'

Chadwick Boseman 43 was BORN in 76!~' Birthday 11/29 / Deathday 8/28 = 11 + 29 + 8 + 28 = 76!~' Death/Day # NUMBER = 8 + 28 + 20 + 20 = 76!~' 7 x 6 = 42!~' 7 + 6 = 13 = RECIPROCAL = 31!~' 13 + 31 = 44!~' 42 + 44 = 86 / Divided by 2 = 43 = "AGE of DEATH" for the "BLACK PANTHER"!~'

LOU BROCK 81 = RECIPROCAL = 18 = DAY of BIRTH!~' From BIRTH to DEATH = 81 DAYS!~' DIED at the AGE of 81!~ Birthday = 6/18 = 6(1 + 8) = 69 = RECIPROCAL = 96 = DAY of DEATH = SEPTEMBER 6th!~' Fragmented Birthday # = 37!~' Fragmented Deathday # = 19!~' 37 – 19 = 18 = RECIPROCAL = 81

78Basketball Coach JOHN THOMPSON died at the AGE of 78!~' Death/Day # = 8 + 30 + 20 + 20 = 78!~' Singer HELEN REDDY died at the AGE of 78!~' Death/Day # = 9 + 29 + 20 + 20 = 78!~' American Singer/Songwriter MAC DAVIS died at the AGE of 78!~' Death/Day # = 9 + 29 + 20 + 20 = 78!~'

Attorney MARTIN D. GINSBURG died at the AGE of 78 = RECIPROCAL = 87 = AGE of DEATH of WIFE SUPREME COURT JUSTICE RUTH BADER GINSBURG!~' 8 x 7 or 7 x 8 = 56 = They were MARRIED for 56 YEARS!~' MARTIN'S Birthday # = 67!~' RUTH'S Deathday # = 67!~' MARTIN GINSBURG died on 6(-2-)7!~'

SUPREME COURT JUSTICE RUTH BADER GINSBURG's day OF death = 9/18 = 9 x 18 = 162!~' ATTORNEY MARTIN D. GINSBURG's day OF death = 6/27 = 6 x 27 = 162!~' 162 = 62 + 1 = 63!~' MARTIN'S DEATH/DAY # = 6 + 27 + 20 + 10 = 63!~' 9 + 18 + 6 + 27 = 60 = MARTIN'S BIRTHDAY = 6/10 = 6 x 10 = 60

ATTORNEY MARTIN D. GINSBURG BIRTH/YEAR = 19/32 = 19 + 32 = 51 = RECIPROCAL = 15 = WIFE RUTH BADER GINSBURG'S DAY of BIRTH = 15!~' RUTH BADER GINSBURG's BIRTHDAY = 3/15 = 3 x 15 = 45 = RECIPROCAL = 54 = WAS MARRIED in 54!~' MARTIN'S DEATHDAY 6/27 = 6 + 27 = 33 = RUTH'S BIRTH/YEAR!

Baseball Pitcher BOB GIBSON birth/year = 19/35 = 1 + 9 / 3 – 5 = 10/2 = his DAY of DEATH!~' BOB GIBSON'S BIRTHDAY = 11/9 = 11 + 9 = 20!~' HE died in 20/20!~' DEATH/DAY = 10/2 = 10 x 2 = 20 = DIED in 20/20!~' 11 x 9 = 99!~' 10 x 2 = 20!~' 99 + 20 = 11/9 = BIRTHDAY = NOVEMBER 9th!~'

Two GREATS LOU BROCK was born in the MONTH of 6 and DIED in the MONTH of 9!~' 6/9 = RECIPROCAL = 9/6 = DAY of DEATH for LOU BROCK!~ BOB GIBSON was born in the MONTH of 11 and DIED in the MONTH of 10!~' 11/10 = RECIPROCAL = 10/11 = 10 (1 + 1) = 10/2 = DAY of DEATH for BOB GIBSON!~

EDDIE VAN HALEN deathday # = 10/6/20/20 = 10 + 6 + 20 + 20 = 56 = RECIPROCAL = 65 = AGE of DEATH! BORN in 1955 = 19/55 = (6 =RECIPROCAL= 9) = 1 x 6 / 5 + 5 = 6/10 = RECIPROCAL = 10/6 = DAY of DEATH! VALERIE BERTINELLI birthday = 4/23/19/60 = 4 + 23 + 19 + 60 = 10/6 = DAY of DEATH

BOOK TITLE = "The GOD BOOK of NUMEROLOGY"!~'

AUTHOR: DWAYNE W. ANDERSON....

NEW RELEASE!!!~'

PRESIDENT BILL CLINTON BIRTHDAY # = 8 + 19 + 19 + 46 = 92! PRESIDENT BARACK OBAMA BIRTHDAY # = 8 + 4 + 19 + 61 = 92! PRESIDENT JOE BIDEN BIRTHDAY # = 11 + 20 + 19 + 42 = 92! BEAU BIDEN DIED at the AGE of 46! PRESIDENT JOE BIDEN is the 46th PRESIDENT! 46 + 46 = 92! 42+44+46 = 132!

YESTERDAY = TOMMY "TINY" LISTER DEAD at 62 = 12/10/20/20 = 12+10+20+20 = `-62 = PATTERN within 9 of MY BOOKS! ACTOR RON GLASS BIRTHDAY = 0/71/0 = 71 = AGE of DEATH!~ MOON ASTRONAUT NEIL ARMSTRONG'S BIRTHDAY = 85 = DEATH/ DAY = 2 SURROUNDED by 85 = 82 AGE of DEATH & BIRTHDAY = 825!

PHIL NIEKRO & JON HUBER DIE on 12/26 = 26(-)12 = 14 =RECIPROCAL= 41 = BIRTHDAY of PHIL & AGE of DEATH for JON!~' PHIL NIEKRO BIRTH = 4+1+19+39 = 63 = 6x3 = 18 =RECIPROCAL= 81 = PHIL'S AGE of DEATH!~' 63 x 2 = 126 = 12+16+19+79 = JON HUBER'S BIRTH!~' 12+16 = 28=RECIPROCAL=82 /2=41

CHARLES LANE who STARRED as HOMER BEDLOE on PETTICOAT JUNCTION had a DAY of BIRTH = 26 = FLIP every 2 OVER to a 7 and FLIP every 6 OVER to a 9 & VICE VERSA = 79 = DAY of DEATH for CHARLES = JULY 9th!~' CHARLES died at the AGE of 102 =RECIPROCAL= 201 = DAYS from BIRTH to DEATH!!!~

CHARLES LANE STARRED as HOMER BEDLOE on PETTICOAT JUNCTION & had a BIRTHDAY = 1/26 = 1 + 26 = 27 and DIED IN 2/00/7!~ 41 YEARS before HIS death ON EPISODE 4/12 HE stated HIS AGE of DEATH in the TELEPHONE# 320-555-3270 = 32+70 = 102!~' 3+2+0+5+5+5+3+2+7+0 = 32 = (4x8) = 4x12 = 48!

CHARLES LANE who STARRED as HOMER BEDLOE on PETTICOAT JUNCTION had a DEATH/DAY = 7/9 = 7x9 = 63!~' HIS WIFE ACTRESS RUTH COVELL DIED on 11+30+20+02 = 63!~' FLIP every 6 OVER to a 9 = SHE DIED at the AGE of 93!!!~' 9x3 = 27!~' 11+30 = 41!~' 27+41 = 68 = THE `-MARK!~' 6x8 = 48!!!~'

CHARLES LANE, SMILEY BURNETTE, FRANK CADY; & EDDIE ALBERT from PETTICOAT JUNCTION (ALL) had a `-BIRTHDAY # of (`-51)!!!~' BEA BENADERET had a BIRTH of 4/4 = APRIL 4th!!~' EDGAR BUCHANAN DIED on 4/4!!~' BYRON FOULGER DIED on 4/4/1970 = FINAL EPISODE DATE of PETTICOAT JUNCTION!!!~'

DWAYNE W. ANDERSON

BLUEGRASS GUITARIST TONY RICE BIRTHDAY = 6/8 = DIES at 69!~' TONY RICE DEATHDAY = 12/25! 12 =RECIPROCAL=21! FLIP every 2 OVER to a 7 = 25 = 75! 21 + 75 = 96 =RECIPROCAL= 69 = AGE of DEATH! BIRTHYEAR = 1951 = 1 x 9 / 5 + 1 = 96 =RECIPROCAL= 69!~' DIED 165 DAYS from BIRTH = 69!!!~'

LUKE LETLOW/US REPRESENTATIVE-ELECT DIED (`-23) DAYS after HIS BIRTHDAY!~' DEATH/DAY = 12/29 = 12 + 29 = 41 = LUKE LETLOW'S AGE of DEATH!~' BIRTHDAY = 12/6 = 12 + 6 = 18 =RECIPROCAL= 81!~' DEATHH/DAY # `-NUMBER = 12 + 29 + 20 + 20 = (`-81)!~' BIRTHDAY in REVERSE 79-19-6-12 = 42!~

AMERICAN ACTRESS "GILLIGAN'S ISLAND/MARY ANN SUMMERS" DAWN WELLS `-BIRTHDAY = 10/18 = 10+18 = 28 =RECIPROCAL= (`-82) = DAWN WELL'S AGE of DEATH!!!~' DEATH/DAY # `-NUMBER = 12+30+20+20 = (`-82) = DAWN WELL'S AGE of DEATH!!!~' BIRTHYEAR = 1938 = 1-9 / 3+8 = 811 = 8(1+1) = 82DEATH!~

ALEX TREBEK (GAME SHOW HOST) BIRTH = 7/22/1940; and, DEATH = 11+8+20+20 = 59!~' BIRTHYEAR = 19+40 = 59!~' DEATHDAY = 11/8 = 11x8 = 88!~' BIRTH = 7+22+19+40 = 88!~' YEAR of BIRTH (40) +(20+20 DEATH YEAR) = (80) = AGE of DEATH for AMERICAN-CANADIAN (GAME SHOW HOST) ALEX TREBEK!!!~'

ACTRESS MARY TYLER MOORE BIRTHDAY 12/29!~' 29=RECIPROCAL=92!~' 92 (-) 12 = 80 = AGE of DEATH from BIRTHDAY!~' AMERICAN POLITICIAN (MARCH FONG EU) BIRTHDAY 3/29!~' 29=RECIPROCAL=92!~' 92 + 3 = 95 = AGE of DEATH from BIRTHDAY!~' REREAD the BOOKS!~' CONVERT 3's TO 8's & 8's to 3's!~

CONVERT 3's TO 8's & 8's to 3's!~ MAGICIAN SIEGFRIED FISCHBACHER BORN and DIED on a 13th!~' 13=RECIPROCAL=31!~' 31 = 81 = AGE of DEATH!~' MAGICIAN ROY HORN BIRTHDAY 10/3 = 10+3 = 13!~' MAGICIAN ROY HORN DEATHDAY 5/8 = 5+8 = 13!~' 13x4 = 52 =RECIPROCAL= 25 = 75 = AGE of DEATH RH!~

4

`-DEATH CIPHERS/CYPHERS FOR LIFE & DEATH!!!~'

TELEVISION HOST LARRY KING DIED TODAY at the AGE of 87 on the (23rd = 78) = 1 + 23 + 20 + 21 = 65 = LARRY KING DIED 65 DAYS after HIS LAST BIRTHDAY!~' 65 =RECIPROCAL=56 = (8x7) = 56!~' LARRY KING'S BIRTH = 11 + 19 + 19 + 33 = 82!~' FLIP every 2 OVER to a 7 = 87 = AGE of DEATH!!!~

`-GOD is `-THE `-MATHEMATICIAN!!!~'

AUTHOR/ENGINEER/SINGER/SONGWRITER: DWAYNE W. ANDERSON!!!~'

AMERICAN ACTOR GENE WILDER was `-BORN in (`-**33**); and, `-DIED at the `-AGE of (`-**83**)!!!~' CONVERT 3's TO 8's & 8's to 3's!~'

CANADIAN ACTOR ALAN THICKE was `-BORN in (`-**1947**) = (19 + 47) = (`-**66**) = "FLIP every "**6**" OVER to a "**9**" = (`-**69**)!~' ALAN THICKE `-DIED at the `-AGE of (`-**69**)!!!~'

Major League Baseball `-PLAYER – 3$^{rd}$ BASE PLAYER – Cleveland Indians/Arizona Diamondbacks – ANDY MARTE dies on (**1/22/2017**)!!!!!~' `-HE died in the `-DOMINICAN `-REPUBLIC in an `-Automobile Car Accident!!!!!~' `-HE died at the `-AGE of (`-**33**)!!!!!~' `-HE was born in `-19**83**!!!~'

ANDY MARTE was `-BORN on OCTOBER 21$^{st}$, in `-19**83**!!!!!~'

ANDY MARTE'S `-BIRTHDAY # = `-EQUALS = (10 + 21 + 19 + 83) = `-**133** = (33 x 1) = `-**33** = "ANDY MARTE'S AGE of `-DEATH"!!!~'

ACTOR MIKE CONNERS `-**DIED** on *JANUARY 26$^{th}$* of `-2017!!!~' `-HE was `-BORN on AUGUST 15th in `-1925!!!~' `-HE `-DIED at the `-AGE of (`-**91**)!!!~'

`-**DIED** = 1(26) = / 26 = RECIPROCAL = 62 = 92 = / 92 (-) 1 = (`-**91**)
= AGE of `-**DEATH**!!!~'

GAIL FISHER who played `-HIS `-SECRETARY on "MANNIX"
`-DIED at the `-AGE of (`-**65**) in the `-CALENDAR `-YEAR of (`-
2000)!!!~' `-SHE was `-BORN on AUGUST 18th in `-1935!!!~' `-SHE
`-DIED on DECEMBER 2nd!!!~'

(`-19**3**5) = (9 (-) 3) (1 x 5) = (`-**65**) = "AGE of `-DEATH for GAIL
FISHER"!!!~'

ACTOR JOHN HURT `-DIED on JANUARY 25th within `-2017!!!~'
2(7's) = (`-**77**)!!!~' `-HE was `-BORN on JANUARY 22nd in `-1940!!!~'
`-HE `-DIED at the `-AGE of (`-**77**)!!!~'

`-BORN on a (`-**22**) = "FLIP every (`-**2**) OVER to a (`-**7**)" = (`-**77**) =
"AGE of `-DEATH for ACTOR JOHN HURT"!!!~'

ACTOR RICHARD HATCH `-**DIES** on *FEBRUARY 7th* (`-**2/7**) in
`-2017 / (02/07/20/17)!!!~' `-HE was `-**BORN** on *MAY 21st* in `-1945!!!~'
`-HE `-DIED at the `-AGE of (`-**71**)!!!~'

`-**BIRTH** = (5/21) = (5 + 2) (1) = (`-**71**) = "AGE of `-DEATH for
ACTOR RICHARD HATCH"!!!~'

`-**BORN** on a (`-**21**st) = "FLIP every (`-**2**) OVER to a (`-**7**)" = (`-**71**) =
"AGE of `-DEATH for ACTOR RICHARD HATCH"!!!~'

`-**DIED** in (`-**17**) = RECIPROCAL = (`-**71**) = "AGE of `-DEATH for
ACTOR RICHARD HATCH"!!!~'

SINGER AL JARREAU `-**DIED** on *FEBRUARY 1(2)th* within
`-201(7)!!!~' "FLIP every (`-**2**) OVER to a (`-**7**)"!!!~' `-HE was `-BORN

`-DEATH CIPHERS/CYPHERS FOR LIFE & DEATH!!!~'

on **MARCH 12ᵗʰ** in `-1940!!!~' `-HE `-DIED at the `-AGE of (`-**76**)!!!~'
(7 x 6) = (`-**42**)!!!~' BIRTH: (**3/12**) = (3 + 1) (2) = (`-**42**)!!!~'

`-**DIED** on (**2/12**) = (7/17) = (7) (1 (-) 7) = (`-**76**) = "AGE of `-DEATH
for SINGER AL JARREAU"!!!~'

SINGER BILLY PAUL `-DIED on **APRIL 24ᵗʰ** within `-**2016**!!!~' `-HE
was `-BORN on **DECEMBER 1ˢᵗ** in `-1934!!!~' `-HE `-DIED at the
`-AGE of (`-**81**)!!!~'

`-DEATH = (**4/24**) = (4 + 4) (2) = (`-**82**)!!!~'

`-BIRTH = (**12/1**) = (12 + 1) = (`-**13**) = RECIPROCAL = (`-**31**) = "FLIP
every (`-**3**) OVER to an (`-**8**)" = (`-**81**) = "AGE of `-DEATH for SINGER
BILLY PAUL"!!!~'

`-DEATH/YEAR = (`-2**016**) = (2 + 6) (0 + 1) = (`-**81**) = "AGE of
`-DEATH for SINGER BILLY PAUL"!!!~'

AMERICAN ACTOR SHABBA DOO (ADOLFO GUTIERREZ
QUINONES) `-DIES at the `-AGE of (`-**65**) on (**12/3**0/2020)!!!~'
`-BIRTH = (**5/11/1955**)!!!~' (`-**1955**) = (1 + 5) (9 + 5) = (6) (14) = (6) (1
+ 4) = (`-**65**) = "AGE of `-DEATH for AMERICAN ACTOR SHABBA
DOO"!!!~' `-BIRTH/DAY = (5 x 11) = (`-**55**) = `-BIRTH/YEAR!!!~' (12
x 3) = (`-**36**)!!!~' (5 + 1 + 1 + 1 + 9 + 5 + 5) = (`-**27**)!!!~' (36 + 27) =
(`-**63**)!!!~'

`-**DEATH/DAY** = (12 + 30) = (`-**42**)!!!~' `-**BIRTH/DAY** = (5 x 1 x 1)
= (`-**5**) = (4 + 2) (5) = (`-**65**) = "AGE of `-DEATH for AMERICAN
ACTOR SHABBA DOO"!!!~'

AMERICAN PROFESSIONAL BASEBALL PLAYER HANK AARON
`-DIED on (**1/22/20/21**) = RECIPROCAL = at the -AGE of (`-**86**)!!!~'
BIRTH = (2/5/19**34**)!!!~' PLAYED for (`-**23**) SEASONS!!!~' (`-34) x (`-
2) = (`-**68**) = RECIPROCAL = (`-**86**) = "AGE of `-DEATH for HANK
AARON"!!!~'

ACTRESS CICELY TYSON DIES at (`-**96**) on (**1**/**28**/2021)!!!~' (1 + 28) = (`-**29**)!!!~' `-BIRTH = (1**2**/1**9**/1924) = (1**2**/1**9**) = (29) (1 x 1) = (`-**29**)!!!~' BIRTH/YEAR = (`-**1924**) = (1 x 9) (2 + 4) = (`-**96**) = "AGE of `-DEATH for ACTRESS CICELY TYSON"!!!~' (`-1**9**2**4**) = (`-**92**) = RECIPROCAL = (`-**29**)!!!~' (`-**14**) = RECIPROCAL = (`-**41**) = (20 + 21) = **"YEAR of `-DEATH for ACTRESS CICELY TYSON"!!!~'**

MUSICIAN SOPHIE (SOPHIE XEON) `-**DIES** at the `-**AGE** of (`-**34**) on (**1**/**30**/2021) = (**1** + **30** + 20 + 21) = (`-**72**)!!!~' `-**BORN** on (**9**/**17**/1986) = (9 + 17 + 19 + 86) = (`-**131**) = **"DAY `-AFTER `-DEATH/ DAY (1/30)"!!!~'** (72 + 131) = (`-**203**)!!!~'

`-**BIRTH/DAY** = (**9/17**) = (9 x 17) = (`-**153**) = RECIPROCAL = (35 (-) 1) = (`-**34**) = **"AGE of `-DEATH for MUSICIAN SOPHIE (SOPHIE XEON) (`-34)"!!!~'**

`-**DIED** (`-**135**) `-DAYS after `-**HER** `-**LAST** `-**BIRTH/DAY**!!!~' (365 (-) 135) = (`-**230**)!!!~'

`-**BIRTH** in `-**REVERSE** = (86 (-) 19 (-) 17 (-) 9) = (`-**41**) = **"YEAR of `-DEATH"** = (20 + 21) = (`-**41**)!!!~'

FRAGMENTED `-**BIRTH/DAY #** `-**NUMBER** = (9 + 1 + 7 + 1 + 9 + 8 + 6) = (`-**41**) = **"YEAR of `-DEATH"** = (20 + 21) = (`-**41**)!!!~'

`-**BIRTH/DAY** = (**9/17**) = "FLIP every (`-**9**) over to a (`-**6**)" = (6/17) = (67 x 1) = (`-**67**)!!!~'

`-**BIRTH/YEAR** = (`-**1986**) = (86 (-) 19) = (`-**67**)!!!~'

(**67** (/) `-DIVIDED by (`-**2**) = (`-**33.5**) = (ROUNDED UP) = (`-**34**) = **"AGE of `-DEATH for MUSICIAN SOPHIE (SOPHIE XEON) (`-34)"!!!~'**

`-DEATH CIPHERS/CYPHERS FOR LIFE & DEATH!!!~'

`-AGE of `-DEATH = (`-**34** x 2) = (`-**68**) = RECIPROCAL = (`-**86**) = "**BORN** in (`-**86**)"!!!~'

(`-**34**) = "CONVERT every (`-**3**) to an (`-**8**)" = (`-**84**) = RECIPROCAL = (`-**48**) = (8 x 6) = "**BIRTH/YEAR** (`-**86**)"!!!~'

(`-**34**) = "CONVERT every (`-**3**) to an (`-**8**)" = (`-**84**) = (/) `-DIVIDED by (`-**2**) = (`-**42**) = (6 x 7) = "**BIRTH/DAY** (`-**9/17**)"!!!~'

MUSICIAN SOPHIE (SOPHIE XEON) `-**DIES** at the `-**AGE** of (`-**34**) on (**1/30**/2021) = (**1** + **30** + 20 + 21) = (`-**72**) = (9 x 8) = (9) (1 + 7) = `-**BORN** on (**9/17**/1986)!!!~'

AMERICAN ACTOR DUSTIN DIAMOND `-**DIES** at the `-**AGE** of (`-**44**) on (**2/1**/20**21**) = (**2** + **1** + 20 + **21**) = (`-**44**)!!!~' `-**BORN** on (**1/7**/1977) = (1 + 7 + 19 + 77) = (`-**104**)!!!~' (44 + 104) = (`-**148**)!!!~'

`-**BIRTH/DAY** = (**1/7**) = "FLIP EVERY (`-**7**) OVER to a (`-**2**)" = (**1/2**) = RECIPROCAL = (**2/1**) = `-**DEATH/DAY for AMERICAN ACTOR DUSTIN DIAMOND!!!~'**

`-**DIED** (`-**25**) `-DAYS after `-**HIS** `-**LAST** `-**BIRTH/DAY**!!!~' (`-**24**) DAYS that LIE-IN-BETWEEN = **2**(**4's**) = (`-**44**) = "**AGE of `-DEATH for AMERICAN ACTOR DUSTIN DIAMOND (`-44**)"!!!~' (365 (-) 25) = (`-**340**)!!!~'

FRAGMENTED `-**BIRTH/DAY #** `-**NUMBER** = (1 + 7 + 1 + 9 + 7 + 7) = (`-**32**) = -a PROPHETIC # `-NUMBER!!!~'

FRAGMENTED `-**DEATH/DAY #** `-**NUMBER** = (2 + 1 + 2 + 0 + 2 + 1) = (`-**8**) = (1 + 7) = `-**BIRTH/DAY**!!!~'

(32 (-) 8) = (`-**24**) = **2**(**4's**) = (`-**44**) = "**AGE of `-DEATH for AMERICAN ACTOR DUSTIN DIAMOND (`-44**)"!!!~'

`-**DEATH/DAY** = (**2/1**) = "FLIP every (`-**2**) over to a (`-**7**)" = (**7/1**) =
RECIPROCAL = (**1/7**) = `-**BIRTH/DAY**!!!~'

`-**BIRTH/YEAR** = (`-**77**) = (7 + 7) = (`-**14**) = RECIPROCAL = (`-**41**) =
(20 + 21) = `-**DEATH/YEAR**!!!~'

`-**DEATH/DAY** # `-**NUMBER** = (2 + 1 + 20 + 21) = (`-**44**) = "AGE of
`-**DEATH** for AMERICAN ACTOR DUSTIN DIAMOND (`-**44**)"!!!~'

`-**BIRTH/DAY** # `-**NUMBER** = (1 + 7 + 19 + 77) = (`-**104**) = (14 + 0)
= (`-**14**) = RECIPROCAL = (`-**41**) = (20 + 21) = `-**DEATH/YEAR**!!!~'

AMERICAN ACTRESS CLORIS LEACHMAN `-**DIES** at the `-**AGE**
of (`-**94**) on (**1/27/2021**) = (**1** + **2**7 + 20 + **21**) = (`-**69**)!!!~' `-**BORN** on
(**4/30**/1926) = (4 + 30 + 19 + 26) = (`-**79**)!!!~' (69 + 79) = (`-**148**) =
RECIPROCAL = (`-**841**) = (8 + 1) (4) = (`-**94**) = "AGE of `-**DEATH** for
AMERICAN ACTRESS CLORIS LEACHMAN (`-**94**)"!!!~'

(1 + 27 + 4 + 30) = (`-**62**) = RECIPROCAL = (`-**26**) = `-**BIRTH/
YEAR**!!!~'

`-**DIED** (`-**93**) `-DAYS before `-**HER** `-**NEXT** `-**BIRTH/DAY**!!!~' LEAP
YEAR = (`-**94**) = "AGE of `-**DEATH** for AMERICAN ACTRESS
CLORIS LEACHMAN (`-**94**)"!!!~' (365 (-) 93) = (`-**272**)!!!~'

FRAGMENTED `-**BIRTH/DAY** # `-**NUMBER** = (4 + 3 + 0 + 1 + 9 +
2 + 6) = (`-**25**) = RECIPROCAL = (`-**52**)!!!~'

FRAGMENTED `-**DEATH/DAY** # `-**NUMBER** = (1 + 2 + 7 + 2 + 0 +
2 + 1) = (`-**15**) = RECIPROCAL = (`-**51**)!!!~'

(25 + 15) = (`-**40**)!!!~'

`-DEATH CIPHERS/CYPHERS FOR LIFE & DEATH!!!~'

`-**BIRTH/YEAR** = (`-**26**) = "FLIP every (`-**2**) over to a (`-**7**)" = "FLIP every (`-**6**) over to a (`-**9**)" = (`-**79**) = `-**BIRTH/DAY** # `-NUMBER (`-**79**)!!!~'

`-**BIRTH/YEAR** = (`-**1926**) = (1 x 9) (2 (-) 6) = (`-**94**) = "AGE of `-DEATH for AMERICAN ACTRESS CLORIS LEACHMAN (`-**94**)"!!!~'

AMERICAN RADIO & TELEVISION HOST ALAN COLMES `-*DIED* on *FEBRUARY* **23**ʳᵈ within `-**2017**!!!~' `-HE was `-*BORN* on *SEPTEMBER* **24**ᵗʰ in `-**1950**!!!~' `-HE `-DIED at the `-AGE of (`-**66**)!!!~'

`-**BORN** (**9/24**) = (9) (2 + 4) = (`-**96**) = "FLIP EVERY (`-**9**) OVER to a (`-**6**)" = (`-**66**) = "AGE of `-DEATH for AMERICAN RADIO & TELEVISION HOST ALAN COLMES (`-**66**)"!!!~'

`-**BIRTH/YEAR** = (`-**1950**) = (19 + 50) = (`-**69**) = "FLIP EVERY (`-**9**) OVER to a (`-**6**)" = (`-**66**) = "AGE of `-DEATH for AMERICAN RADIO & TELEVISION HOST ALAN COLMES (`-**66**)"!!!~'

`-**DIED** (**2/23**) = "FLIP EVERY (`-**2**) OVER to a (`-**7**)" = (**7/23**) = (72 (-) 3) = (`-**69**) = "FLIP EVERY (`-**9**) OVER to a (`-**6**)" = (`-**66**) = "AGE of `-DEATH for AMERICAN RADIO & TELEVISION HOST ALAN COLMES (`-**66**)"!!!~'

`-**DEATH/DAY** = (`-**23**ʳᵈ) = "FLIP EVERY (`-**2**) OVER to a (`-**7**)" = (`-**73**)!!!~'

`-**DEATH/YEAR** = (`-**2017**) = (20 + 17) = (`-**37**) = RECIPROCAL = (`-**73**)!!!~'

`-**DEATH/DAY** = (**2/23**) = (22 x 3) = (`-**66**) = "AGE of `-DEATH for AMERICAN RADIO & TELEVISION HOST ALAN COLMES (`-**66**)"!!!~'

11

`-**BIRTH/YEAR** = (`-**1950**) = "FLIP EVERY (`-**9**) OVER to a (`-**6**)" = (`-**1650**) = (6 + 0) (1 + 5) = (`-**66**) = "**AGE of `-DEATH for AMERICAN RADIO & TELEVISION HOST ALAN COLMES (`-66)**"!!!~'

JUDGE WAPNER (JOSEPH ALBERT WAPNER) `-DIED on FEBRUARY **26**th within `-2017!!!~' `-HE was `-BORN on *NOVEMBER 15th* in `-*1919*!!!~' `-HE `-DIED at the `-AGE of (`-**97**)!!!~'

`-DIED on a (`-**26**th) = RECIPROCAL = (`-**62**) = "FLIP EVERY (`-**2**) OVER to a (`-**7**)" & "FLIP EVERY (`-**6**) OVER to a (`-**9**)" = (`-**97**) = "**AGE of `-DEATH for JUDGE WAPNER (JOSEPH ALBERT WAPNER) (`-97)**"!!!~'

`-**BIRTH** = (**11/15**) = (11 + 15) = (`-**26**) = RECIPROCAL = (`-**62**) = "FLIP EVERY (`-**2**) OVER to a (`-**7**)" & "FLIP EVERY (`-**6**) OVER to a (`-**9**)" = (`-**97**) = "**AGE of `-DEATH for JUDGE WAPNER (JOSEPH ALBERT WAPNER) (`-97)**"!!!~'

JUDGE WAPNER (JOSEPH ALBERT WAPNER) had `-DIED (`-**103**) `-DAYS after `-HIS `-LAST `-BIRTHDAY!!!!!~'

(365 (-) 103) = `-**262** = "FLIP EVERY (`-**2**) OVER to a (`-**7**)" & "FLIP EVERY (`-**6**) OVER to a (`-**9**)" = (`-**797**) from `-BIRTH to `-DEATH; and, `-DIED at the `-AGE of (`-**97**)!!!~'

ACTOR ROBERT OSBORNE `-DIED on *MARCH 6th* within `-2017!!!~' `-HE was `-BORN on *MAY 3rd* in `-19**32**!!!~' `-HE `-DIED at the `-AGE of (`-**84**)!!!~'

`-**BIRTH** = (**5/3**) = RECIPROCAL = (**3/5**) = "**DIED** the `-VERY `-NEXT `-DAY on (**3/6**)"!!!~'

`-**BIRTH** = (**5/3**) = "FLIP EVERY (`-**3**) to an (`-**8**)" = (**5/8**)!!!~'

ROBERT OSBORNE had `-DIED (`-**58**) `-DAYS before `-HIS `-NEXT `-BIRTHDAY!!!!!~'

MUSIC ARTIST JONI SLEDGE from "SISTER SLEDGE" `-DIED on **MARCH 10**th within `-2017!!!~' `-SHE was `-BORN on **SEPTEMBER 13**th in `-19**56**!!!~' `-SHE `-DIED at the `-AGE of (`-**60**)!!!~'

`-**DEATH** = (**3/10**) = RECIPROCAL = `-**BIRTH** (SEPTEMBER 13) = (**9/13**) = RECIPROCAL = (**31/9**) = (3) (1 + 9) = (**3/10**)!!!~'

JOURNALIST & AUTHOR JIMMY BRESLIN `-DIED on **MARCH 19**th within `-20**17**!!!~' `-HE was `-BORN on OCTOBER **17**th in `-1930!!!~' `-HE `-DIED at the `-AGE of (`-**86**)!!!~'

`-**DEATH** = (**3/19**) = "FLIP EVERY (`-**3**) to an (`-**8**)" & "FLIP EVERY (`-**9**) to a (`-**6**)" = (**8/16**) = (86 x 1) = (`-**86**) = **"AGE of `-DEATH for JOURNALIST & AUTHOR JIMMY BRESLIN (`-86)"!!!~'**

JOURNALIST & AUTHOR JIMMY BRESLIN had `-DIED (`-**153**) `-DAYS after `-HIS `-LAST `-BIRTHDAY!!!!!~'

(`-**153**) = RECIPROCAL = (`-**351**) = "FLIP EVERY (`-**3**) to an (`-**8**)" = (`-**851**) = (8) (5 + 1) = (`-**86**) = **"AGE of `-DEATH for JOURNALIST & AUTHOR JIMMY BRESLIN (`-86)"!!!~'**

`-**BORN** on a (`-**17**th); and, `-**DIED** in a (`-**17**)!!!~'

(17 + 17) = (`-**34**) x (`-**2**) = (`-**68**) = RECIPROCAL = (`-**86**) = **"AGE of `-DEATH for JOURNALIST & AUTHOR JIMMY BRESLIN (`-86)"!!!~'**

AMERICAN GAME SHOW CREATOR CHUCK BARRIS (CHARLES HIRSCH "CHUCK" BARRIS) `-DIED on *MARCH 21*[st] within `-2017!!!~' `-HE was `-BORN on *JUNE 3rd* in `-*1929*!!!~' `-HE `-DIED at the `-AGE of (`-**87**)!!!~'

`-**DEATH** = (**3/21**) = "FLIP EVERY (`-**3**) OVER to an (`-**8**)" & "FLIP EVERY (`-**2**) OVER to a (`-**7**)" = (**8/71**) = (87 x 1) = (`-**87**) = "AGE of `DEATH for AMERICAN GAME SHOW CREATOR CHUCK BARRIS (CHARLES HIRSCH "CHUCK" BARRIS) (`-**87**)"!!!~'

`-**BORN** = (**6/3**) = RECIPROCAL = (**3/6**) = "FLIP EVERY (`-**3**) to an (`-**8**)" = (**8/6**) = "ONE `-YEAR `-AWAY (`-**86**) from `-AGE of `-DEATH (`-**87**)"!!!~'

`-**BIRTH/YEAR** = (`-**1929**) = (1 (-) 9) (2 (-) 9) = = (`-**87**) = "AGE of `DEATH for AMERICAN GAME SHOW CREATOR CHUCK BARRIS (CHARLES HIRSCH "CHUCK" BARRIS) (`-**87**)"!!!~'

COMEDIAN CHARLIE MURPHY (CHARLES QUINTON MURPHY) `-DIED on *APRIL 12*[th] within `-2017!!!~' `-HE was `-BORN on JULY 12th in `-1959!!!~' `-HE `-DIED at the `-AGE of (`-**57**)!!!~'

`-**DEATH** = (**4/12**) = "FLIP EVERY (`-**2**) OVER to a (`-**7**)" = (**4/17**) = (4 + 1) (7) = (`-**57**) = "AGE of `-DEATH for COMEDIAN CHARLIE MURPHY (CHARLES QUINTON MURPHY) (`-**57**)"!!!~'

JONATHAN DEMME (ROBERT JONATHAN DEMME) AMERICAN FILM DIRECTOR, PRODUCER; and, SCREENWRITER `-DIED on APRIL 26[th] within `-*2017*!!!~' `-HE was `-BORN on FEBRUARY 22nd in `-*1944*!!!~' `-HE `-DIED at the `-AGE of (`-**73**)!!!~'

`-**BIRTH** = (`-**1944**) = (19 + 44) = (`-**63**)!!!~'

JONATHAN DEMME had `-DIED (`-**63**) `-DAYS after `-HIS `-LAST `-BIRTHDAY!!!!!~'

(365 (-) 63) = (`-**302**) = RECIPROCAL = (`-**203**) = "FLIP EVERY (`-**2**) OVER to a (`-**7**)" = (`-**703**) = (73 + 0) = (`-**73**) = "AGE of `-DEATH for JONATHAN DEMME (ROBERT JONATHAN DEMME) AMERICAN FILM DIRECTOR, PRODUCER; and, SCREENWRITER (`-**73**)"!!!~'

`-**DEATH** = (`-**2017**) = RECIPROCAL = (`-**7102**) = (7) (1 + 0 + 2) = (`-**73**) = "AGE of `-DEATH for JONATHAN DEMME (ROBERT JONATHAN DEMME) AMERICAN FILM DIRECTOR, PRODUCER; and, SCREENWRITER (`-**73**)"!!!~'

PRINCESS DIANA SPENCER (PRINCESS OF WALES) `-**DIED** on *AUGUST 31ˢᵗ* within `-19**97**!!!~' `-SHE was `-**BORN** on *JULY 1ˢᵗ* in `-19**61**!!!~' `-SHE `-DIED at the `-AGE of (`-**36**)!!!~'

`-**DEATH/DAY** = (**8/31**) = (8 + 31) = (`-**39**) = "FLIP EVERY (`-**9**) OVER to a (`-**6**)" = (`-**36**) = "AGE of `-DEATH for PRINCESS DIANA SPENCER (PRINCESS OF WALES) (`-**36**)"!!!~'

`-**DEATH/YEAR** = (`-**97**) = (9 x 7) = (`-**63**) = RECIPROCAL = (`-**36**) = "AGE of `-DEATH for PRINCESS DIANA SPENCER (PRINCESS OF WALES) (`-**36**)"!!!~'

`-**DEATH/YEAR** = (`-**1997**) = (19 + 97) = (`-**116**) = (16 x 1) = (`-**16**) = RECIPROCAL = (`-**61**) = `-**BORN** in (`-**61**)!!!~'

PRINCESS DIANA SPENCER had `-DIED (`-**61**) `-DAYS after `-HER `-LAST `-BIRTHDAY!!!!!~'

(365 (-) 61) = (`-**304**) = (3 + 0 + 4) = (`-**7**) = (`-**BIRTH/MONTH**)!!!~'

15

SINGER/MUSICIAN CHRIS CORNELL `-DIED on **MAY _17_<sup>th</sup>** within `-20**17**!!!~' `-HE was `-BORN on **JULY 20th** in `-19**64**!!!~' `-HE `-DIED at the `-AGE of (`-**52**)!!!~'

`-**DEATH/DAY** = (**5/17**) = "FLIP EVERY (`-**7**) OVER to a (`-**2**)" = (**5/12**) = (52 x 1) = (`-**52**) = **"AGE of `-DEATH for SINGER/MUSICIAN CHRIS CORNELL (`-52)"**!!!~'

CHRIS CORNELL had `-DIED (`-**64**) `-DAYS before `-HIS `-NEXT `-BIRTHDAY!!!!!~'

SINGER/MUSICIAN CHRIS CORNELL was `-**BORN** in (`-**64**)!!!~'

CHRIS CORNELL `-**DIED** on a (`-**17**th) in the `-**YEAR** of (`-**17**) = RECIPROCAL = (`-**71**)!!!~'

`-**BORN** (**7/20**) = (72 + 0) = (`-**72**)!!!~'

ACTOR SIR ROGER MOORE `-DIED on **MAY _23_<sup>rd</sup>** within `-2**017**!!!~' `-HE was `-BORN on OCTOBER 14th in `-19**27**!!!~' `-HE `-DIED at the `-AGE of (`-**89**)!!!~'

`-**DEATH/DAY** = (**5/23**) = **"DAY of `-DEATH"** = (`-**23**) = RECIPROCAL = (`-**32**)!!!~'

(32 (-) **5**) = (`-**27**) = "WAS `-**BORN** in (`-**27**); and, **"AGE of `-DEATH"** = (`-**89**) = (8 x 9) = (`-**72**) = RECIPROCAL = (`-**27**)!!!~' `-**DIED** in (`-**2017**)!!!~'

ACTRESS DINA MERRILL `-DIED on **MAY _22_<sup>nd</sup>** within `-2**017**!!!~' `-SHE was `-BORN on DECEMBER 29th in `-19**23**!!!~' `-SHE `-DIED at the `-AGE of (`-**93**)!!!~'

"DAY of `-DEATH"** = (`-22**) = "FLIP EVERY (`-**2**) OVER to a (`-**7**)"
= (`-**27**) = (9 x 3) = (`-**93**) = **"AGE of `-DEATH for ACTRESS DINA
MERRILL (`-93)"!!!~'**

`-**DEATH/DAY** = (**5/22**) = (`-**22**) = "FLIP EVERY (`-**2**) OVER to a (`-
7)" = (`-**77**) = (77 (-) 5) = (`-**72**) = RECIPROCAL = (`-**27**) = `-**DIED** in
(`-**2017**)!!!~'

`-**DEATH/DAY** = (**5/22**) = (5 + 22) = (`-**27**) = (9 x 3) = (`-**93**) = **"AGE
of `-DEATH for ACTRESS DINA MERRILL (`-93)"!!!~'**

ACTRESS DINA MERRILL had `-DIED (`-**144**) `-DAYS after `-HER
`-BIRTHDAY!!!~'

(365 (-) 144) = `-**221** = "FLIP EVERY (`-**2**) OVER to a (`-**7**)" = (`-**771**)
= (77 x 1) = (`-**77**) = **2**(**7's**) = (`-**27**) = `-**DEATH/DAY** = (**5/22**) = (5 +
22) = (`-**27**)!!!~'

SINGER GREGG ALLMAN (GREGG LeNOIR ALLMAN) from the
ALLMAN BROTHERS BAND `-DIED on MAY **27**th within `-**2017**!!!~'
`-HE was `-BORN on DECEMBER 8th in `-**1947**!!!~' `-HE `-DIED at
the `-AGE of (`-**69**)!!!~'

SINGER GREGG ALLMAN `-BIRTHDAY # = `-EQUALS = (12 + 8 +
19 + 47) = (`-**86**) = RECIPROCAL = (`-**68**)!!!~'

SINGER GREGG ALLMAN `-DEATH/DAY # = `-EQUALS = (5 + 27
+ 20 + 17) = (`-**69**)

SINGER GREGG ALLMAN'S `-**DEATH/DAY** # = (`-**69**) = **"AGE
of `-DEATH for SINGER GREGG ALLMAN (GREGG LeNOIR
ALLMAN) from the ALLMAN BROTHERS BAND (`-69)"!!!~'**

SINGER GREGG ALLMAN had `-DIED (`-**170**) `-DAYS after `-HIS
`-LAST `-BIRTHDAY!!!!!~' (70 (-) 1) = (`-**69**) = **"AGE of `-DEATH for**

17

SINGER GREGG ALLMAN (GREGG LeNOIR ALLMAN) from the ALLMAN BROTHERS BAND (`-69`)"!!!~'

(365 (-) 170) = `-195` = `-DEATH in `-DAYS before `-HIS `-NEXT `-BIRTHDAY!!!~'

(`-195`) = (1 + 5) (9) = (`-69`) = "AGE of `-DEATH for SINGER GREGG ALLMAN (GREGG LeNOIR ALLMAN) from the ALLMAN BROTHERS BAND (`-69`)"!!!~'

`-BIRTH/YEAR = (`-1947`) = (19 + 47) = (`-66`) = "FLIP EVERY (`-6`) OVER to a (`-9`)" = (`-69`) = "AGE of `-DEATH for SINGER GREGG ALLMAN (GREGG LeNOIR ALLMAN) from the ALLMAN BROTHERS BAND (`-69`)"!!!~'

"DAY of `-DEATH" = (`-27`th) = `-DIED in (`-2017`)!!!~'

ACTOR ADAM WEST (**BATMAN**) `-DIED on *JUNE 9th* within `-2017!!!~' `-HE was `-BORN on *SEPTEMBER 19th* in `-1928!!!~' `-HE `-DIED at the `-AGE of (`-88`)!!!~'

ACTOR ADAM WEST (BATMAN) `-BIRTHDAY # = `-EQUALS = (9 + 19 + 19 + 28) = (`-75`) = RECIPROCAL = (`-57`)!!!~'

ACTOR ADAM WEST (BATMAN) `-DEATH/DAY # = `-EQUALS = (6 + 9 + 20 + 17) = (`-52`) = "FLIP EVERY (`-2`) OVER to a (`-7`)" = (`-57`)!!!~'

ACTOR ADAM WEST (BATMAN) had `-DIED (`-102`) `-DAYS before `-HIS `-NEXT `-BIRTHDAY!!!!!~'

(365 (-) 102) = `-263` = "FLIP EVERY (`-3`) OVER to an (`-8`) = (`-268`) = (2 + 6) (8) = (`-88`) = "AGE of `-DEATH for ACTOR ADAM WEST (BATMAN) (`-88`)"!!!~'

`-DEATH CIPHERS/CYPHERS FOR LIFE & DEATH!!!~'

`-**BORN** = (**9/19**) = "FLIP EVERY (`-**9**) OVER to a (`-**6**)" = (**6/19**) = (69 x 1) = (`-**69**) = `-**DEATH/DAY** for ACTOR ADAM WEST (**BATMAN**) (`-**6/9**) / (JUNE 9th)!!!~'

`-**BORN** in (`-**28**) = **2**(**8's**) = (`-**88**) = "AGE of `-DEATH for ACTOR ADAM WEST (**BATMAN**) (`-**88**)"!!!~'

`-**BIRTH/DAY** = (**9/19**) = (9 + 19) = (`-**28**) = **2**(**8's**) = (`-**88**) = "AGE of `-DEATH for ACTOR ADAM WEST (**BATMAN**) (`-**88**)"!!!~'

EIKO ISHIOKA (ART DIRECTOR) was `-**BORN** on *JULY* `-*12th* in `-19**38**!!!~' SHE `-DIED at the `-AGE of (`-**73**) on *JANUARY 21st* in `-20**12**!!!~'

`-**BIRTH** = (**7/12**) = (7) (1 + 2) = (`-**73**) = "AGE of `-DEATH for EIKO ISHIOKA (ART DIRECTOR) (`-**73**)"!!!~'

`-**BIRTH** = (**7/12**) = "FLIP EVERY (`-**7**) OVER to a (`-**2**)" = (**2/12**) = "**DIED** in (**2**(0)**12**)"!!!~'

`-**DEATH/YEAR** = (`-**2012**) = "FLIP EVERY (`-**2**) OVER to a (`-**7**) = (`-**7012**) = (712) + (0) = (`-**712**) = `-**BIRTH** = (**7/12**)!!!~'

`-**BORN** on a (`-**12**th) = **RECIPROCAL** = `-**DIED** on a (`-**21**st) = **RECIPROCAL** = in the `-**YEAR** of (`-**12**)!!!~'

`-**AGE** of `-**DEATH** = (`-**73**) = (7 x 3) = (`-**21**)!!!~'

EIKO ISHIOKA (ART DIRECTOR) had `-DIED (`-**172**) `-DAYS before `-HER `-NEXT `-BIRTHDAY!!!!!~'

(`-**172**) = (72 + 1) = (`-**73**) = "AGE of `-DEATH for EIKO ISHIOKA (ART DIRECTOR) (`-**73**)"!!!~'

(365 (-) 172) = (`-**193**) = "FLIP EVERY (`-**9**) OVER to a (`-**6**)" = (`-**163**) = (1 + 6) (3) = (`-**73**) = "AGE of `-DEATH for EIKO ISHIOKA (ART DIRECTOR) (`-**73**)"!!!~'

ACTOR MARTIN LANDAU `-DIED on *JULY 15*[th] within `-**2017**!!!~' `-HE was `-BORN on *JUNE 20*[th] in `-**1928**!!!~' `-HE `-DIED at the `-AGE of (`-**89**)!!!~'

`-**DEATH** = (**7/15**) = (7) (1 + 5) = (`-**76**)!!!~'

`-**BIRTH** = (**6/20**) = "FLIP EVERY (`-**2**) OVER to a (`-**7**)" = (**6/70**) = (67 + 0) = (`-**67**) = RECIPROCAL = (`-**76**)!!!~'

`-**AGE of `-DEATH** = (`-**89**) = (8 x 9) = (`-**72**) = RECIPROCAL = (`-**27**) = "**DIED** in (`-**2017**)"!!!~'

`-**BIRTH/YEAR** = (`-**1928**) = (1 (-) 9) (2 (-) 8) = (`-**86**) = "FLIP EVERY (`-**6**) OVER to a (`-**9**)" = (`-**89**) = "AGE of `-DEATH for ACTOR MARTIN LANDAU (`-**89**)"!!!~'

FILMMAKER GEORGE A. ROMERO `-DIED on *JULY 16*[th] within `-**2017**!!!~' `-HE was `-BORN on *FEBRUARY 4*[th] in `-**1940**!!!~' `-HE `-DIED at the `-AGE of (`-**77**)!!!~'

`-**DEATH/DAY** = (7/16) = (7) (1 + 6) = (`-**77**) = "AGE of `-DEATH for FILMMAKER GEORGE A. ROMERO (`-**77**)"!!!~'

GEORGE A. ROMERO had `-DIED (`-**162**) `-DAYS after `-HIS `-LAST `-BIRTHDAY!!!!!~'

(`-**162**) = "FLIP EVERY (`-**2**) OVER to a (`-**7**)" = (`-**167**) = (1 + 6) (7) = (`-**77**) = "AGE of `-DEATH for FILMMAKER GEORGE A. ROMERO (`-**77**)"!!!~'

`-DEATH CIPHERS/CYPHERS FOR LIFE & DEATH!!!~'

(365 (-) 162) = (`-203) = (23 + 0) = `-23 = -a PROPHETIC NUMBER!!!~'

`-AGE of `-DEATH = (`-77) = 2(7's) = (`-27) = "DIED in (`-2017)"!!!~'

`-BIRTH = (2/4/1940) = "FLIP EVERY (`-9) OVER to a (`-6)" = (2/4/1640) = (2 + 4 + 16 + 40) = (`-62) = "FLIP EVERY (`-2) OVER to a (`-7)" = (`-67) = RECIPROCAL = (`-76) = `-DEATH/DAY = (`-7/16) = (76 x 1) = (`-76)!!!~'

`-DEATH/DAY = (7/16) = (7) (1 + 6) = (`-77) = 2(7's) = (`-27) = "DIED in (`-2017)"!!!~'

`-DEATH/DAY = (7/16) = "FLIP EVERY (`-7) OVER to a (`-2)" = (2/16) = (2) (1 + 6) = (`-27) = "DIED in (`-2017)"!!!~'

SINGER/SONGWRITER CHESTER BENNINGTON `-DIED on JULY 20th within `-2017!!!~' `-HE was `-BORN on MARCH 20th in `-1976!!!~' `-HE `-DIED at the `-AGE of (`-41)!!!~'

`-DEATH/DAY = (7/20) = (7 + 20) = (`-27) = "DIED in (`-2017)"!!!~'

`-DEATH/DAY = (7/20) = (72 + 0) = (`-72) = RECIPROCAL = (`-27) = "DIED in (`-2017)"!!!~'

`-BORN on a (`-20th); and, `-DIED on a (`-20th) = "FLIP EVERY (`-2) OVER to a (`-7)" = (`-70) / (`-70) = (70 + 70) = (`-140) = (14 + 0) = (`-14) = RECIPROCAL = (`-41) = "AGE of `-DEATH for SINGER/SONGWRITER CHESTER BENNINGTON (`-41)"!!!~'

SINGER/SONGWRITER CHESTER BENNINGTON had `-DIED (`-123) `-DAYS after `-HIS `-LAST `-BIRTHDAY!!!~'

(`-123) = (23 x 1) = (`-23) = RECIPROCAL = (`-32)!!!~'

`-__BIRTH/DAY__ = (__3/2__0) = (32 + 0) = `-__32__ = -a PROPHETIC NUMBER!!!~'

(365 (-) 123) = (`-__242__)!!!~'

`-__BORN__ in (`-__76__) = (7 x 6) = (`-__42__) = RECIPROCAL = (`-__24__)!!!~'

ACTOR JOHN HEARD `-DIED on *JULY 21ˢᵗ* within `-__201__7!!!~' `-HE was `-BORN on *MARCH 7ᵗʰ* in `-__1945__!!!~' `-HE `-DIED at the `-AGE of (`-__72__)!!!~'

`-__DEATH/DAY__ = (__7/21__) = (72 x 1) = (`-__72__) = RECIPROCAL = (`-__27__) = "DIED in (`-__201__7)"!!!~'

`-__DEATH/DAY__ = (__7/21__) = (72 x 1) = (`-__72__) = "AGE of `-DEATH for ACTOR JOHN HEARD (`-__72__)"!!!~'

ACTOR JOHN HEARD `-BIRTH/DAY # `-NUMBER = `-EQUALS = (3 + 7 + 19 + 45) = (`-__74__)!!!~'

`-__BIRTH/DAY__ = MARCH 7ᵗʰ = (__3/7__) = (37 x 2) = `-__74__ = `-BIRTH/DAY # `-NUMBER (`-__74__)!!!~'

`-__BIRTH/DAY__ = MARCH 7ᵗʰ = (__3/7__) = (`-__37__) = (20 + 17) = `-__DEATH/ YEAR__ (`-__20/17__)!!!~'

(`-__136__) = (13 x 6) = (`-__78__) = "FLIP EVERY (`-__8__) OVER to a (`-__3__)" = (`-__73__) = RECIPROCAL = (`-__37__)!!!~'

ACTOR JOHN HEARD had `-DIED (`-__136__) `-DAYS after `-HIS `-LAST `-BIRTHDAY!!!~'

(`-__136__) = (1 + 36) = (`-__37__) = (__3/7__) = `-__BIRTH/DAY__ = (MARCH 7ᵗʰ)!!!~'

(365 (-) 136) = (`-**229**) = (22 x 9) = (`-**198**) = "FLIP EVERY (`-**8**) OVER to a (`-**3**)" & "FLIP EVERY (`-**9**) OVER to a (`-**6**)" = (`-**163**) = (63 x 1) = (`-**63**) = RECIPROCAL = (`-**36**)!!!~'

(`-**36**) x (`-**2**) = (`-**72**) = "AGE of `-DEATH for ACTOR JOHN HEARD (`-**72**)"!!!~'

BARBARA SINATRA "LADY BLUE EYES" `-DIED on JULY **25**th within `-**2017**!!!~' `-SHE was `-BORN on *MARCH 10th* in `-19**27**!!!~' `-SHE `-DIED at the `-AGE of (`-**90**)!!!~'

`-**DEATH/DAY** = (**7/25**) = (7) (2 + 5) = (`-**77**) = 2(7's) = (`-**27**) = `-**DEATH/YEAR** (`-**2**0/1**7**)!!!~'

`-**BIRTH/DAY** = (**3/10**) = "FLIP EVERY (`-**3**) OVER to an (`-8)" = (**8/10**) = (8 + 1) (0) = (`-**90**) = "AGE of `-DEATH for BARBARA SINATRA "LADY BLUE EYES" (`-**90**)"!!!~'

`-**BIRTH/YEAR** = (`-**27**) = `-**DEATH/YEAR** (`-**2**0/1**7**)!!!~'

ACTRESS AVA LAVINIA GARDNER `-DIED on *JANUARY 25th* within `-1990!!!~' `-SHE was `-BORN on *DECEMBER 24th* in `-*1922*!!!~' `-SHE `-DIED at the `-AGE of (`-**67**)!!!~'

`-**DEATH/DAY** = (**1/25**) = "FLIP EVERY (`-**2**) OVER to a (`-**7**)" = (**1/75**) = (75 + 1) = (`-**76**) = RECIPROCAL = (`-**67**) = "AGE of `-DEATH for ACTRESS AVA LAVINIA GARDNER (`-**67**)"!!!~'

`-**BIRTH/YEAR** = (`-**1922**) = "FLIP EVERY (`-**2**) OVER to a (`-**7**)" = (`-**1977**) = (1 + 9) (77) = *(10) (77)* = (77 (-) 10) = (`-**67**) = "AGE of `-DEATH for ACTRESS AVA LAVINIA GARDNER (`-**67**)"!!!~'

`-**DEATH/DAY** = (**12/5**) = (75 + 1) = (`-**76**) = RECIPROCAL = (`-**67**) = "AGE of `-DEATH for ACTRESS AVA LAVINIA GARDNER (`-**67**)"!!!~'

`-**BIRTH/DAY** = (**12/24**) = (12) (2 + 4) = (**12/6**) = "FLIP EVERY (`-**2**) OVER to a (`-**7**)" = (**17/6**) = (76 x 1) = (`-**76**) = RECIPROCAL = (`-**67**) = "AGE of `-DEATH for ACTRESS AVA LAVINIA GARDNER (`-**67**)"!!!~'

AMERICAN VOICE ACTRESS JUNE LUCILLE FORAY `-DIED on *JULY 26th* within `-2017!!!~' `-SHE was `-BORN on *SEPTEMBER 18th* in `-19**17**!!!~' `-SHE `-DIED at the `-AGE of (`-**99**)!!!~'

`-**DEATH/DAY** = (**7/26**) = "FLIP EVERY (`-**6**) OVER to a (`-**9**)" = (7/29) = (7 + 2) (9) = (`-**99**) = "AGE of `-DEATH for AMERICAN VOICE ACTRESS JUNE LUCILLE FORAY (`-**99**)"!!!~'

`-**DEATH/DAY** = (**7/26**) = "FLIP EVERY (`-**6**) OVER to a (`-**9**)" = (7/29) = RECIPROCAL = (92/7) = (92 + 7) = (`-**99**) = "AGE of `-DEATH for AMERICAN VOICE ACTRESS JUNE LUCILLE FORAY (`-**99**)"!!!~'

`-**BIRTH/DAY** = (**9/18**) = (9) (1 + 8) = (`-**99**) = "AGE of `-DEATH for AMERICAN VOICE ACTRESS JUNE LUCILLE FORAY (`-**99**)"!!!~'

`-**BORN** in (`-**17**); and, `-**DIED** in (`-**17**)!!!~'

`-**BIRTH/YEAR** = (`-**1917**) = (9) (1 + 1 + 7) = (`-**99**) = "AGE of `-DEATH for AMERICAN VOICE ACTRESS JUNE LUCILLE FORAY (`-**99**)"!!!~'

AMERICAN VOICE ACTRESS JUNE LUCILLE FORAY had `-DIED (`-**54**) `-DAYS before `-HER `-NEXT `-BIRTHDAY!!!~'

(`-**54**) = RECIPROCAL = (`-**45**)!!!~'

(54 + 45) = (`-**99**) = "AGE of `-DEATH for AMERICAN VOICE ACTRESS JUNE LUCILLE FORAY (`-**99**)"!!!~'

(365 (-) 54) = (`-**311**) = (11 x 3) = (`-**33**) x (`-**3**) = (`-**99**) = "AGE of `-DEATH for AMERICAN VOICE ACTRESS JUNE LUCILLE FORAY (`-**99**)"!!!~'

AMERICAN PLAYWRIGHT SAM SHEPARD `-DIED on *JULY 30*th within `-*2017*!!!~' `-HE was `-BORN on *NOVEMBER 5*th in `-*1943*!!!~' `-HE `-DIED at the `-AGE of (`-**73**)!!!~'

`-**DEATH/DAY** = (**7/30**) = (73 + 0) = (`-**73**) = "AGE of `-DEATH for AMERICAN PLAYWRIGHT SAM SHEPARD (`-**73**)"!!!~'

`-**DEATH/YEAR** = (`-**2017**) = RECIPROCAL = (`-**7102**) = (7) (1 + 0 + 2) = (`-**73**) = "AGE of `-DEATH for AMERICAN PLAYWRIGHT SAM SHEPARD (`-**73**)"!!!~'

AMERICAN PLAYWRIGHT Sam Shepard `-**DIED** on (0**7**/**3**0) at the `-AGE of (**73**)!!!~' HIS DEATH/DAY # `-NUMBER was (**74**)!!!~' The *DAY before* HIS `-**DEATH/DAY** would be (`-**73**)!!!~' `-HE `-DIED the `-VERY `-NEXT `-DAY after the `-DEATH/DAY # `-NUMBER of (`-**73**) at the `-AGE of (`-**73**)!!!~'

AMERICAN PLAYWRIGHT SAM SHEPARD `-BIRTHDAY # `-NUMBER = `-EQUALS = (*11 + 5 + 19 + 43*) = (`-**78**) = "FLIP EVERY (`-**8**) OVER to a (`-**3**) = (`-**73**) = "AGE of `-DEATH for AMERICAN PLAYWRIGHT SAM SHEPARD (`-**73**)"!!!~'

AMERICAN PLAYWRIGHT SAM SHEPARD `-DEATH/DAY # `-NUMBER = `-EQUALS = (*7 + 30 + 20 + 17*) = (`-**74**)!!!~'

AMERICAN PLAYWRIGHT SAM SHEPARD had `-DIED (`-**98**) `-DAYS before `-HIS `-NEXT `-BIRTHDAY!!!~'

(`-**98**) = (9 x 8) = (`-**72**)!!!~'

25

(74 + 72) = (`-**146**) / `-DIVIDED by / (`-**2**) = (`-**73**) = **"AGE of `-DEATH for AMERICAN PLAYWRIGHT SAM SHEPARD (`-73)"**!!!~'

(365 (-) 98) = (`-**267**) = (2 + 6) (7) = (`-**87**) = "FLIP EVERY (`-**8**) OVER to a (`-**3**)" = (`-**37**) = RECIPROCAL = (`-**73**) = **"AGE of `-DEATH for AMERICAN PLAYWRIGHT SAM SHEPARD (`-73)"**!!!~'

AMERICAN ACTRESS LEE ANN REMICK `-DIED on *JULY 2^nd* within `-**1991**!!!!!~' `-SHE was `-BORN on *DECEMBER 14th* in `-19**35**!!!!!~' `-SHE `-DIED at the `-AGE of (`-**55**)!!!!!~'

`-**DEATH/YEAR** = (`-**1991**) = (91 (-) 19) = (`-**72**) = `-**DEATH/DAY** = (**7/2**) = (JULY 2nd)!!!~'

`-**DEATH/YEAR** = (`-**1991**) = (19 + 91) = (`-**110**) / `-DIVIDED by / (`-**2**) = (`-**55**) = **"AGE of `-DEATH for AMERICAN ACTRESS LEE ANN REMICK (`-55)"**!!!~'

(`-**14**) = RECIPROCAL = (`-**41**)!!!~'

`-**BIRTH/DAY** = (**12/14**) = (12 + 41) = (`-**53**) = RECIPROCAL = (`-**35**) = **"YEAR of `-BIRTH (`-35)"**!!!~'

`-**BIRTH/YEAR** = (`-**1935**) = (19 + 35) = (`-**54**) = *"ONE `-YEAR `-AWAY* from `-AGE of `-DEATH (`-**55**)"**!!!~'

`-**BIRTH/DAY # `-NUMBER** = (12 + 14 + 19 + 35) = (`-**80**)!!!~'

(`-**80**) (-) *MINUS* (-) `-AGE of `-DEATH (`-**55**) = (`-**25**) = 2(5's) = (`-**55**) = **"AGE of `-DEATH for AMERICAN ACTRESS LEE ANN REMICK (`-55)"**!!!~'

(`-**55**) = (5 x 5) = (`-**25**)!!!~'

AMERICAN ACTRESS LEE ANN REMICK had `-DIED (`-**200**) `-DAYS after `-HER `-BIRTHDAY!!!~'

(365 (-) 200) = (`-**165**) = RECIPROCAL = (`-**561**) = (5) (6 (-) 1) = (`-**55**) = "AGE of `-DEATH for AMERICAN ACTRESS LEE ANN REMICK (`-**55**)"!!!~'

CANADIAN ACTOR CHRISTOPHER PLUMMER (`-**91**) DIES on (**2/5/2021**) = (2 + 5 + 20 + 21) = (`-**48**) = `-**DEATH/DAY** # `-**NUMBER**!!!~' HE was `-BORN on (1**2**/1**3**/19**29**) = (12 + 13 + 19 + 29) = (`-**73**) = `-**BIRTH/DAY** # `-**NUMBER**!!!~'

`-**BIRTH/YEAR** = (`-**1929**) = (19 + 29) = (`-**48**) = `-**DEATH/DAY** # `-**NUMBER** (`-**48**)!!!~'

`-YEAR of `-BIRTH = (`-**29**) = RECIPROCAL = (`-**92**) = `-**DIED** in the `-**YEAR** that `-**HE** would have `-**TURNED** (`-**92**) **YEARS** of `-**AGE**!!!~'

`-**DEATH/DAY** = (**2/5**) = `-**BIRTH/DAY** = (**12/13**) = (12 + 13) = (`-**25**)!!!~'

`-**AGE of `-DEATH** (`-**91**) (-) MINUS (-) (`-**54**) = (`-**37**) = `-**BIRTH/DAY** = (**12/13**) = "FLIP EVERY (`-**2**) OVER to a (`-**7**)" = (**17/13**) = (73 x 1 x 1) = (`-**73**) = RECIPROCAL = (`-**37**)!!!~'

`-HE `-DIED (`-**54**) DAYS after `-HIS `-LAST `-BIRTH/DAY!!!~'

(365 (-) 54) = (`-**311**) = "FLIP EVERY (`-**3**) OVER to an (`-**8**)" = (`-**811**) = (8 + 1) (1) = (`-**91**) = "AGE of `-DEATH for CANADIAN ACTOR CHRISTOPHER PLUMMER (`-**91**)"!!!~'

`-**DEATH/YEAR** = (`-**2021**) = "FLIP EVERY (`-**2**) OVER to a (`-**7**)" = (`-**2071**) = (20 + 71) = (`-**91**) = "AGE of `-DEATH for CANADIAN ACTOR CHRISTOPHER PLUMMER (`-**91**)"!!!~'

COMEDIAN JERRY LEWIS `-DIED on **AUGUST 20**<sup>th</sup> within `-**2017**!!!~' `-HE was `-BORN on **MARCH 16**th in `-19**26**!!!~' `-HE `-DIED at the `-AGE of (`-**91**)!!!~'

(**MARCH 16**th) = (**3/16**) = (3 x 16) = (`-**48**) = (4 x 8) = (`-**32**) = -a PROPHETIC # `-NUMBER!!!~'

(`-**17**) = RECIPROCAL = (`-**71**)!!!~'

`-**DEATH/YEAR** = (`-**2017**) = (20 + 71) = (`-**91**) = "AGE of `-DEATH of `-COMEDIAN `-JERRY `-LEWIS (`-**91**)"!!!~'

`-**BIRTH/DAY** = (3/16) = (3 + 16) = (`-**19**) = RECIPROCAL = (`-**91**) = "AGE of `-DEATH of `-COMEDIAN `-JERRY `-LEWIS (`-**91**)"!!!~'

`-**DAY** of `-**BIRTH** = (`-**16**<sup>th</sup>) = "FLIP EVERY (`-**6**) OVER to a (`-**9**)" = (`-**19**) = RECIPROCAL = (`-**91**) = "AGE of `-DEATH of `-COMEDIAN `-JERRY `-LEWIS (`-**91**)"!!!~'

COMEDIAN JERRY LEWIS `-**DIED** the `-**VERY** `-**NEXT** `-**DAY AFTER THE** `-**DEATH/DAY # OF** = (`-**64**) = **WHICH WOULD HAVE EQUALED** `-**HIS** `-**BIRTHDAY #** `-**NUMBER = (**`-**64**)!!!~'

COMEDIAN JERRY LEWIS `-**BIRTHDAY #** `-**NUMBER** = `-EQUALS = (3 + 16 + 19 + 26) = (`-**64**)!!!~'

COMEDIAN JERRY LEWIS `-**DEATH/DAY #** `-**NUMBER** = `-EQUALS = (8 + 20 + 20 + 17) = (`-**65**)!!!~'

(65 + 64) = (`-**129**) = **RECIPROCAL** = (`-**921**) = 92(1) = (92 (-) 1) = (`-**91**) = "AGE of `-DEATH of `-COMEDIAN `-JERRY `-LEWIS (`-**91**)"!!!~'

COMEDIAN JERRY LEWIS had `-DIED (`-**157**) `-DAYS after `-HIS `-LAST `-BIRTHDAY!!!!!~'

(365 (-) 157) = `-**208** = "DAYS `-BEFORE `-HIS `-NEXT `-BIRTHDAY"!!!~'

(`-**208**) = 20(8) = RECIPROCAL = 8(20) = "AUGUST 20<sup>th</sup>" = "<u>DAY</u> of `-<u>DEATH</u>" of `-COMEDIAN `-JERRY `-LEWIS (**8/20**)!!!~'

AMERICAN SINGER CUBA GOODING, SR. `-DIED on <u>APRIL 20</u><sup>th</sup> within `-**2017**!!!~' `-HE was `-BORN on <u>APRIL 27</u>th in `-19**44**!!!~' `-HE `-DIED at the `-AGE of (`-**72**)!!!~'

`-**AGE** of `-DEATH = (`-**72**) = RECIPROCAL = (`-**27**) = `-<u>DIED</u> in the `-<u>DEATH/YEAR</u> of = (`-**2017**)!!!~'

`-**DAY** of `-BIRTH = (`-**27**) = RECIPROCAL = (`-**72**) = "AGE of `-DEATH for AMERICAN SINGER CUBA GOODING, SR. (`-**72**)!!!~'

`-**BIRTH/YEAR** = (`-**44**) = `-<u>BORN</u> in (`-**4**); and, `-<u>DIED</u> in (`-**4**) = (`-**44**)!!!~'

(44 + 44) = (`-**88**)!!!~'

`-**BIRTH/DAY** = (**4/27**) = (4 x 27) = (`-**108**) = RECIPROCAL = (`-**801**) = (80 x 1) = (`-**80**)!!!~'

`-**DEATH/DAY** = (**4/20**) = (4 x 20) = (`-**80**)!!!~'

(`-**80/80**) = (88 + 0 + 0) = (`-**88**)!!!~'

AMERICAN ACTOR/COMEDIAN BERNIE MAC `-<u>BIRTHDAY</u> = (**10/5**/19/**57**) = (**10** + **5** + 19 + **57**) = (`-**91**) = RECIPROCAL (INVERSE/ MIRROR) = (`-**19**)!!!~'

(91 (-) 19) = (`-**72**) = (8 x 9) = (**8/9**) = `-<u>DEATH/DAY</u> for AMERICAN ACTOR/COMEDIAN BERNIE MAC (`-<u>AUGUST 9</u>th)"!!!~'

`-**BIRTH/DAY** = (**10/5**) = (10 x 5) = (`-**50**) = "AGE of `-DEATH for AMERICAN ACTOR/COMEDIAN BERNIE MAC (`-**50**)"!!!~'

DWAYNE W. ANDERSON

AMERICAN ACTOR/COMEDIAN BERNIE MAC `-DEATH/DAY = (8/9/20/08) = (8 + 9 + 20 + 08) = (`-45)!!!~`

(`-89) / `-DIVIDED by / (`-2) = (`-44.5)!!!~`

AMERICAN ACTOR/COMEDIAN BERNIE MAC `-DIED (`-57) DAYS AWAY from `-HIS `-BIRTHDAY!!!~` (`-57) = AMERICAN ACTOR/ COMEDIAN BERNIE MAC was `-BORN in (`-57)!!!~`

SINGER/SONGWRITER TAMMY WYNETTE `-BIRTHDAY = (5/5/19/42) = (5 + 5 + 19 + 42) = (`-71) = RECIPROCAL (INVERSE/ MIRROR) = (`-17)!!!~`

(71 (-) 17) = (`-54) = "ONE `-YEAR `-AWAY from `-AGE of `-DEATH (`-55)"!!!~'

`-DEATH/DAY # `-NUMBER in `-REVERSE = (98 (-) 19 (-) 6 (-) 4) = (`-69) = (6 x 9) = (`-54) = "ONE `-YEAR `-AWAY from `-AGE of `-DEATH (`-55)"!!!~'

`-BIRTH/DAY = (`-5/5) = (`-55) = "AGE of `-DEATH for SINGER/ SONGWRITER TAMMY WYNETTE (`-55)"!!!~`

SINGER/SONGWRITER TAMMY WYNETTE `-DEATH/DAY = (4/6/19/98) = (4 + 6 + 19 + 98) = (`-127) = "FLIP EVERY (`-2) OVER to a (`-7)" = (`-177) = (77 (-) 1) = (`-76) = (7 x 6) = (`-42) = `-BIRTH/ YEAR for SINGER/SONGWRITER TAMMY WYNETTE (`-42)!!!~`

`-BIRTH/YEAR = (`-1942) = (42 (-) 19) = (`-23) x (`-2) = (`-46) = `-DEATH/DAY = (`-46) = (APRIL 6th)!!!~`

FILM DIRECTOR WILLIAM TOBY HOOPER `-DIED on AUGUST 26th within `-2017!!!~` `-HE was `-BORN on JANUARY 25th in `-1943!!!~` `-HE `-DIED at the `-AGE of (`-74)!!!~`

30

`-**BIRTH/DAY** = (**1/25**) = "FLIP EVERY (`-**2**) OVER to a (`-**7**)" = (**1/75**) = (75 (-) 1) = (`-**74**) = "**AGE of `-DEATH of FILM DIRECTOR WILLIAM TOBY HOOPER (`-74)**"!!!~'

FILM DIRECTOR WILLIAM TOBY HOOPER `-**BIRTHDAY # `-NUMBER** = `-EQUALS = (1 + 25 + 19 + 43) = (`-**88**)!!!~'

`-**DEATH/DAY** = (**8/26**) = (8) (2 + 6) = (`-**88**)!!!~'

FILM DIRECTOR WILLIAM TOBY HOOPER `-**DEATH/DAY # `-NUMBER** = `-EQUALS = (8 + 26 + 20 + 17) = (`-**71**) = RECIPROCAL = (`-**17**) = `-**DIED in the `-YEAR of (`-17)**!!!~'

FILM DIRECTOR WILLIAM TOBY HOOPER had `-DIED (`-**213**) `-DAYS after `-HIS `-LAST `-BIRTHDAY!!!~'

(`-**213**) = "FLIP EVERY (`-**2**) OVER to an (`-**7**)" = (`-**713**) = (7) (1 + 3) = (`-**74**) = "**AGE of `-DEATH of FILM DIRECTOR WILLIAM TOBY HOOPER (`-74)**"!!!~'

(365 (-) 213) = `-**152** = "**DAYS `-BEFORE `-HIS `-NEXT `-BIRTHDAY**"!!!~'

(`-**152**) = "FLIP EVERY (`-**2**) OVER to an (`-**7**)" = (`-**157**) = RECIPROCAL = (`-**751**) = (7) (5 (-) 1) = (`-**74**) = "**AGE of `-DEATH of FILM DIRECTOR WILLIAM TOBY HOOPER (`-74)**"!!!~'

`-**BIRTH/YEAR** = (`-**1943**) = (9 (-) 3 + 1) (4) = (`-**74**) = "**AGE of `-DEATH of FILM DIRECTOR WILLIAM TOBY HOOPER (`-74)**"!!!~'

`-**BIRTH/YEAR** = (`-**1943**) = (1 + 9) (43) = "FLIP EVERY (`-**3**) OVER to an (`-**8**)" = (10) (84) = (84 (-) 10) = (`-**74**) = "**AGE of `-DEATH of FILM DIRECTOR WILLIAM TOBY HOOPER (`-74)**"!!!~'

ACTOR BOB CRANE from "HOGAN'S HEROES" `-DIED on **JUNE 29**th within `-19**78**!!!!!~' `-HE was `-BORN on *JULY 13*th in `-19**28**!!!!!~' `-HE `-DIED at the `-AGE of (`-**49**)!!!!!~'

`-**BIRTH/DAY** = (**7/13**) = (7) (1 + 3) = (`-**74**)!!!~'

`-**BIRTH/YEAR** = (`-**1928**) = (`-**47**) = RECIPROCAL = (`-**74**)!!!~'

(74 + 74) = (`-**148**) = (48 + 1) = (`-**49**) = **"AGE of `-DEATH for ACTOR BOB CRANE from "HOGAN'S HEROES" (`-49)"**!!!~'

`-**DEATH/DAY** = (**6/29**) = RECIPROCAL = (**92/6**) = "FLIP EVERY (`-**6**) OVER to a (`-**9**)" = (**92/9**) = (9 (-) 2) (9) = (`-**79**)!!!~'

`-**BIRTH/DAY** = (**7/13**) = "FLIP EVERY (`-**3**) OVER to an (`-**8**)" = (**7/18**) = (7) (1 + 8) = (`-**79**)!!!~'

`-**BORN** in (`-**28**) = "FLIP EVERY (`-**2**) OVER to a (`-**7**) = (`-**78**) = `-**DEATH/YEAR** = (`-**78**)!!!~'

`-**DEATH/DAY** = (**6/29**) = (6 (-) 2) (9) = (`-**49**) = **"AGE of `-DEATH for ACTOR BOB CRANE from "HOGAN'S HEROES" (`-49)"**!!!~'

ACTOR BOB CRANE from "HOGAN'S HEROES" `-**BIRTHDAY # `-NUMBER** = `-EQUALS = (**7** + 1**3** + 19 + 28) = `-**67**

ACTOR BOB CRANE from "HOGAN'S HEROES" `-**DEATH/DAY # `-NUMBER** = `-EQUALS = (6 + 29 + 19 + 78) = `-**132** = (13 x 2) = (`-**26**) = "FLIP EVERY (`-**2**) OVER to a (`-**7**) = (`-**76**) = RECIPROCAL = (`-**67**)!!!~'

ACTOR BOB CRANE from "HOGAN'S HEROES" had `-DIED (`-**14**) `-DAYS before `-HIS `-NEXT `-BIRTHDAY!!!!!~'

(365 (-) 14) = (`-**351**) = **"DAYS `-AFTER `-HIS `-LAST `-BIRTHDAY"**!!!!!~'

`-DEATH CIPHERS/CYPHERS FOR LIFE & DEATH!!!~'

(`-351) = RECIPROCAL = (`-153) = (1 + 5) (3) = (`-63) = RECIPROCAL = (`-36) = (4 x 9) = (`-49) = "AGE of `-DEATH for ACTOR BOB CRANE from "HOGAN'S HEROES" (`-49)"!!!~'

AMERICAN ACTOR PETER HANSEN `-DIED on *APRIL 9th* within `-2017!!!~' `-HE was `-BORN on *DECEMBER 5th* in `-*1921*!!!~' `-HE `-DIED at the `-AGE of (`-95)!!!~'

`-DEATH/DAY = (`-4/9) = RECIPROCAL = (`-9/4) = (`-94) = "ONE `-YEAR `-AWAY from `-AGE of `-DEATH (`-95)"!!!~'

AMERICAN ACTOR PETER HANSEN had `-DIED (`-125) `-DAYS after `-HIS `-LAST `-BIRTHDAY!!!!!~'

(365 (-) 125) = (`-240) = "DAYS `-BEFORE `-HIS `-NEXT `-BIRTHDAY"!!!~'

(`-240) = (24 + 0) = (`-24) = "FLIP EVERY (`-2) OVER to a (`-7)" = (`-74)!!!~'

`-BIRTH/DAY = (12/5) = "FLIP EVERY (`-2) OVER to a (`-7)" = (17/5) = (75 (-) 1) = (`-74)!!!~'

SOAP OPERA STAR / AMERICAN ACTOR / PETER HANSEN `-DIED (`-125) DAYS AFTER HIS LAST BIRTHDAY & WAS BORN ON (`-125) = DECEMBER (5th)!!!~' HE DIED ON a `-9 (APRIL (9th)) and WAS BORN on a (5th)!!!~' (`-95) was `-HIS `-AGE of `-DEATH!!!~'

`-BIRTH/YEAR = (`-1921) = (9) (1 + 2 + 1) = (`-94) = RECIPROCAL = (`-49) = `-DEATH/DAY for SOAP OPERA STAR / AMERICAN ACTOR / PETER HANSEN (`-4/9)!!!~'

`-BIRTH/DAY = (12/5) = (12 x 5) = (`-60)!!!~'

`-DEATH/DAY = (4/9) = (4 x 9) = (`-36)!!!~'

33

(60 + 36) = (`-**96**) = "ONE `-YEAR `-AWAY from `-AGE of `-DEATH (`-**95**)"!!!~'

AMERICAN ACTOR HARRY DEAN STANTON `-DIED on *SEPTEMBER 15*^th within `-*2017*!!!!!~' `-HE was `-BORN on *JULY 14*^th in `-*1926*!!!!!~' `-HE `-DIED at the `-AGE of (`-**91**)!!!!!~'

`-**BIRTH/DAY** = (**7/14**) = (7 + 14) = (`-**21**) = "FLIP EVERY (`-**2**) OVER to a (`-**7**)" = (`-**71**) = RECIPROCAL = (`-**17**) = `-**DEATH/YEAR** = (`-**17**)!!!~'

(`-**17**) = RECIPROCAL = (`-**71**)!!!~'

`-**DEATH/YEAR** = (`-**2017**) = (71 + 20) = (`-**91**) = "AGE of `-DEATH for AMERICAN ACTOR HARRY DEAN STANTON (`-**91**)"!!!~'

AMERICAN ACTOR HARRY DEAN STANTON `-**BIRTHDAY # `-NUMBER** = `-EQUALS = (**7** + **14** + 19 + 26) = (`-**66**) = "FLIP EVERY (`-**6**) OVER to a (`-**9**)" = (`-**96**) = `-**DEATH/DAY** = (**9/15**) = (9) (1 + 5) = (`-**96**)!!!~'

`-**BIRTH/YEAR** = (`-**1926**) = (9) (1 + 2 + 6) = (`-**99**) = "FLIP EVERY (`-**9**) OVER to a (`-**6**)" = (`-**66**) = AMERICAN ACTOR HARRY DEAN STANTON `-BIRTHDAY # = `-EQUALS = (**7** + **14** + 19 + 26) = (`-**66**)!!!~'

AMERICAN ACTOR HARRY DEAN STANTON `-**DEATH/DAY # `-NUMBER** = `-EQUALS = (9 + 15 + 20 + 17) = (`-**61**) = "FLIP EVERY (`-**6**) OVER to a (`-**9**)" = (`-**91**) = "AGE of `-DEATH for AMERICAN ACTOR HARRY DEAN STANTON (`-**91**)"!!!~'

AMERICAN ACTOR DENNIS LEE HOPPER `-DIED on *MAY 29*^th within `-2010!!!~' `-HE was `-BORN on *MAY 17*^th in `-*1936*!!!~' `-HE `-DIED at the `-AGE of (`-**74**)!!!~'

`-**DAY** of `-**BIRTH** = (`-**17**th)!!!~'

`-**BIRTH/YEAR** = (`-**1936**) = (36 (-) 19) = (`-**17**)!!!~'

(17 + 17) = (`-**34**)!!!~'

`-**DEATH/DAY** = (**5/29**) = (5 + 29) = (`-**34**)!!!~'

`-**DEATH/DAY** = (**5/29**) = (29 (-) 5) = (`-**24**) = "FLIP EVERY (`-**2**) OVER to a (`-**7**)" = (`-**74**) = "AGE of `-DEATH for AMERICAN ACTOR DENNIS LEE HOPPER (`-**74**)"!!!~'

`-**BIRTH/DAY** = (**5/17**) = RECIPROCAL = (**71/5**) = (7) (1 (-) 5) = (`-**74**) = "AGE of `-DEATH for AMERICAN ACTOR DENNIS LEE HOPPER (`-**74**)"!!!~'

`-**DEATH/DAY** = (**5/29**) = RECIPROCAL = (**92/5**) = (9 (-) 2) (5) = (`-**75**) = "ONE `-YEAR `-AWAY from `-AGE of `-DEATH (`-**74**)"!!!~'

`-**DEATH/DAY** = (**5/29**) = (5) (2 (-) 9) = (`-**57**) = `-**BIRTH/DAY** = (**5/1/7**) = (57 x 1) = (`-**57**)!!!~'

`-**DAY** of `-**BIRTH** = (`-**17**<sup>th</sup>) = "FLIP EVERY (`-**7**) OVER to a (`-**2**)" = (`-**12**)!!!~'

AMERICAN ACTOR DENNIS LEE HOPPER had `-DIED (`-**12**) `-DAYS after `-HIS `-LAST `-BIRTHDAY!!!!!~'

(365 (-) 12) = `-**353** = **R**ECIPROCAL-**S**EQUENCING-**N**UMEROLOGY-**RSN**!!!~'

AMERICAN ACTOR MIGUEL FERRER `-DIED on *JANUARY 19<sup>th</sup>* within `-**2017**!!!~' `-HE was `-BORN on *FEBRUARY 7th* in `-19**55**!!!~' `-HE `-DIED at the `-AGE of (`-**61**)!!!~'

`-**BIRTH/DAY** = (**2/7**) = `-**DIES** in (`-**2**01**7**)!!!~'

`-**DAY** of `-**DEATH** = (`-**19**[th]) = "FLIP EVERY (`-**9**) OVER to a (`-**6**)" = (`-**16**) = RECIPROCAL = (`-**61**) = "AGE of `-DEATH for AMERICAN ACTOR MIGUEL FERRER (`-**61**)"!!!~'

AMERICAN ACTOR MIGUEL FERRER had `-DIED (`-**19**) `-DAYS before `-HIS `-NEXT `-BIRTHDAY!!!!!~'

(365 (-) 19) = (`-**346**) = RECIPROCAL = (`-**643**) = (6) (4 (-) 3) = (`-**61**) = "AGE of `-DEATH for AMERICAN ACTOR MIGUEL FERRER (`-**61**)"!!!~'

AMERICAN ACTOR MIGUEL FERRER `-BIRTHDAY # `-NUMBER = `-EQUALS = (2 + 7 + 19 + 55) = (`-**83**)!!!~'

AMERICAN ACTOR MIGUEL FERRER `-DEATH/DAY # `-NUMBER = `-EQUALS = (1 + 19 + 20 + 17) = (`-**57**)!!!~'

ACTOR MIGUEL FERRER `-**DIED** ON JANUARY (`-**19**[th]) /||\ (`-**19**) DAYS BEFORE HIS `-**NEXT** `-**BIRTHDAY**!!!~' (19 + 19) = (`-**38**) = RECIPROCAL = (`-**83**) = `-HIS `-BIRTHDAY `# `-NUMBER = (2+7+19+55) = FEBRUARY 7th, 1955!!!~'

AMERICAN JOURNALIST GWEN IFILL`-DIED on **NOVEMBER 14**[th] within `-**2016**!!!~' `-SHE was `-BORN on **SEPTEMBER 29**[th] in `-19**55**!!!~' `-SHE `-DIED at the `-AGE of (`-**61**)!!!~'

`-**BIRTH/YEAR** = (`-**1955**) = (55 (-) 19) = (`-**36**) = `-**DEATH/YEAR** = (`-**2016**) = (20 + 16) = (`-**36**)!!!~'

`-**BIRTH/YEAR** = (`-**55**) = 2(5's) = (`-**25**) = `-**DEATH/DAY** = (**11/14**) = (11 + 14) = (`-**25**)!!!~'

`-**DEATH/YEAR** = (`-**16**) = RECIPROCAL = (`-**61**) = "AGE of `-DEATH for AMERICAN JOURNALIST GWEN IFILL (`-**61**)"!!!~'

`-**DEATH/DAY** = (**11/14**) = (11 x 14) = (`-**154**) = RECIPROCAL = (`-**451**) = (4 + 5) (1) = (`-**91**) = "FLIP EVERY (`-**9**) OVER to a (`-**6**)" = (`-**61**) = "AGE of `-DEATH for AMERICAN JOURNALIST GWEN IFILL (`-**61**)"!!!~'

`-**BIRTH/DAY** = (**9/29**) = (9 x 29) = (`-**(2)61**)!!!~'

AMERICAN JOURNALIST GWEN IFILL `-**BIRTHDAY #** `-**NUMBER** = `-EQUALS = (9 + 29 + 19 + 55) = (`-**112**)!!!~'

AMERICAN JOURNALIST GWEN IFILL `-**DEATH/DAY #** `-**NUMBER** = `-EQUALS = (11 + 14 + 20 + 16) = (`-**61**) = "AGE of `-DEATH for AMERICAN JOURNALIST GWEN IFILL (`-**61**)"!!!~'

AMERICAN ACTOR ROBERT VAUGHN `-DIED on **NOVEMBER 11**th within `-**2016**!!!!!~' `-HE was `-BORN on *NOVEMBER 22*nd in `-19**32**!!!!!~' `-HE `-DIED at the `-AGE of (`-**83**)!!!!!~'

`-**BIRTH/YEAR** = (`-**32**) = "FLIP EVERY (`-**3**) OVER to an (`-**8**)" = (`-**82**) = "ONE `-YEAR `-AWAY from `-AGE of `-DEATH (`-**83**)"!!!~'

`-**BIRTH/DAY** = (**11/22**) = (11 + 22) = (`-**33**) = "FLIP EVERY (`-**3**) OVER to an (`-**8**)" = (`-**83**) = "AGE of `-DEATH for AMERICAN ACTOR ROBERT VAUGHN (`-**83**)"!!!~'

AMERICAN ACTOR ROBERT VAUGHN `-**BIRTHDAY #** `-**NUMBER** = `-EQUALS = (11 + 22 + 19 + 32) = (`-**84**)!!!~'

AMERICAN ACTOR ROBERT VAUGHN `-**DEATH/DAY #** `-**NUMBER** = `-EQUALS = (11 + 11 + 20 + 16) = (`-**58**) = RECIPROCAL = (`-**85**)!!!~'

AMERICAN ACTOR ROBERT VAUGHN had `-DIED (`-**11**) `-DAYS before `-HIS `-NEXT `-BIRTHDAY!!!~'

`-**BORN** & `-**DIED** in the `-**MONTH** of (`-**11**) (`-**ELEVEN**)!!!~'

(365 (-) 11) = (`-**354**) = (3 + 5) (4) = (`-**84**) = `-**BIRTH/DAY #** `-**NUMBER** (`-**84**) of AMERICAN ACTOR ROBERT VAUGHN!!!~'

AMERICAN ACTOR JAY THOMAS `-DIED on **AUGUST 24**th within `-**2017**!!!~' `-HE was `-BORN on **JULY 12**th in `-19**48**!!!~' `-HE `-DIED at the `-AGE of (`-**69**)!!!~'

(`-**17**) = RECIPROCAL = (`-**71**)!!!~'

`-**DEATH/YEAR** = (`-**2017**) = RECIPROCAL = (`-**7102**) = (71 + 0 (-) 2) = (`-**69**) = "AGE of `-DEATH for AMERICAN ACTOR JAY THOMAS (`-**69**)"!!!~'

`-**BIRTH/DAY** = (**7/12**) = (71 (-) 2) = (`-**69**) = "AGE of `-DEATH for AMERICAN ACTOR JAY THOMAS (`-**69**)"!!!~'

`-**BIRTH/YEAR** = (`-**1948**) = (19 + 48) = (`-**67**) = "TWO `-YEARS `-AWAY from `-AGE of `-DEATH (`-**69**)"!!!~'

AMERICAN ACTOR JAY THOMAS `-**BIRTHDAY #** `-**NUMBER** = `-EQUALS = (7 + 12 + 19 + 48) = (`-**86**) = RECIPROCAL = (`-**68**) = "ONE `-YEAR `-AWAY from `-AGE of `-DEATH (`-**69**)"!!!~'

AMERICAN ACTOR JAY THOMAS `-**BIRTHDAY #** `-**NUMBER** = `-EQUALS = (7 + 12 + 19 + 48) = (`-**86**) = `-**DEATH/DAY** = (**8/24**) = (8) (2 + 4) = (`-**86**)!!!~'

AMERICAN ACTOR JAY THOMAS `-**DEATH/DAY #** `-**NUMBER** = `-EQUALS = (8 + 24 + 20 + 17) = (`-**69**) = "AGE of `-DEATH for AMERICAN ACTOR JAY THOMAS (`-**69**)"!!!~'

AMERICAN ACTOR JAY THOMAS had `-DIED (`-**43**) `-DAYS after `-HIS `-LAST `-BIRTHDAY!!!!!~'

(`-**43**) x (`-**2**) = (`-**86**) = AMERICAN ACTOR JAY THOMAS' `-BIRTHDAY # `-NUMBER = `-EQUALS = (7 + 12 + 19 + 48) = (`-**86**)!!!~'

(365 (-) 43) = (`-**322**) = RECIPROCAL = (`-**223**) = (2 + 2) (3) = (`-**43**)!!!~'

HUNGARIAN AMERICAN ACTRESS ZSA ZSA GABOR `-DIED on *DECEMBER 18th* within `-**2016**!!!~' `-SHE was `-BORN on *FEBRUARY 6th* in `-**1917**!!!~' `-SHE `-DIED at the `-AGE of (`-**99**)!!!~'

`-**DEATH/DAY** = (**12/18**) = (1 + 1) (2 (-) 8) = (2)(6) = (`-**26**) = `-**BIRTH/ DAY** (`-**2/6**) = (FEBRUARY 6th)!!!~'

`-**BIRTH/DAY** = (**2/6**) = (`-**26**) = 2(6's) = (`-**66**) = "FLIP EVERY (`-**6**) OVER to a (`-**9**)" = (`-**99**) = "AGE of `-DEATH for HUNGARIAN AMERICAN ACTRESS ZSA ZSA GABOR (`-**99**)"!!!~'

`-**BIRTH/YEAR** = (`-**1917**) = (19 + 17) = (`-**36**) = `-**DEATH/YEAR** = (`-**2016**) = (20 + 16) = (`-**36**)!!!~'

HUNGARIAN AMERICAN ACTRESS ZSA ZSA GABOR `-BIRTHDAY # `-NUMBER = `-EQUALS = (2 + 6 + 19 + 17) = (`-**44**)!!!~'

HUNGARIAN AMERICAN ACTRESS ZSA ZSA GABOR `-DEATH/ DAY # `-NUMBER = `-EQUALS = (12 + 18 + 20 + 16) = (`-**66**) = "FLIP EVERY (`-**6**) OVER to a (`-**9**)" = (`-**99**) = "AGE of `-DEATH for HUNGARIAN AMERICAN ACTRESS ZSA ZSA GABOR (`-**99**)"!!!~'

HUNGARIAN AMERICAN ACTRESS ZSA ZSA GABOR `-DEATH/ DAY # `-NUMBER = `-EQUALS = (12 + 18 + 20 + 16) = (`-**66**) = "SISTER /|\ MAGDA GABOR /|\ `-DIED on (`-**6/6**) with a `-BIRTH/ DAY of (**6/11**) = (6 x 11) = (`-**66**)"!!!~'

39

HUNGARIAN AMERICAN ACTRESS MAGDA GABOR `-DIED on *JUNE 6<sup>th</sup>* within `-**1997**!!!~' `-SHE was `-BORN on *JUNE 11th* in `-**1915**!!!~' `-SHE `-DIED at the `-AGE of (`-**81**) = (9 x 9) = (`-**99**) = "AGE of `-DEATH for (SISTER) HUNGARIAN AMERICAN ACTRESS ZSA ZSA GABOR (`-**99**)"!!!~'

`-**DEATH/YEAR** = (`-**1997**) = (19 + 97) = (`-**116**) = *RECIPROCAL* = (`-**611**) = `-**BIRTH/DAY** = (**6/11**) = (**JUNE 11**th)!!!~'

`-**BIRTH/YEAR** = (`-**1915**) = (9) (1 + 1 + 5) = (`-**97**) = "YEAR of `-DEATH for HUNGARIAN AMERICAN ACTRESS MAGDA GABOR"!!!~'

HUNGARIAN AMERICAN ACTRESS EVA GABOR `-DIED on *JULY 4<sup>th</sup>* within `-**1995**!!!~' `-SHE was `-BORN on *FEBRUARY 11th* in `-**1919**!!!~' `-SHE `-DIED at the `-AGE of (`-**76**)!!!~'

`-**BIRTH/DAY** = (**2/11**) = (2 x 11) = (`-**22**) = "FLIP EVERY (`-**2**) OVER to a (`-**7**)" = (`-**77**) = "ONE `-YEAR `-AWAY from `-AGE of `-DEATH (`-**76**)"!!!~'

`-**BIRTH/DAY** = (**2/11**) = "FLIP EVERY (`-**2**) OVER to a (`-**7**)" = (**7/11**) = (7) (1 + 1) = (**7/2**) = `-**DIED** (`-**TWO**) `-**DAYS** `-**LATER** on (`-**7/4**) = `-**DEATH/DAY** = (**JULY 4**th)!!!~'

`-**AGE** of `-**DEATH** = (`-**76**) = (7 x 6) = (`-**42**) = "FLIP EVERY (`-**2**) OVER to a (`-**7**)" = (`-**47**) = RECIPROCAL = (`-**74**) = (**7/4**) = `-**DEATH/DAY** = (**JULY 4**th)!!!~'

HUNGARIAN AMERICAN ACTRESS EVA GABOR `-**BIRTHDAY** # `-**NUMBER** = `-**EQUALS** = (2 + 11 + 19 + 19) = (`-**51**) = "SAME `-BIRTH/DAY # `-NUMBER as `-SISTER `-MAGDA `-GABOR (`-**51**)"!!!~'

HUNGARIAN AMERICAN ACTRESS EVA GABOR `-DEATH/DAY #
`-NUMBER = `-EQUALS = (7 + 4 + 19 + 95) = (`-125) = RECIPROCAL
= (`-521) = (52 (-) 1) = (`-51)!!!~'

(125 (-) 51) = (`-74) = (7/4) = `-DEATH/DAY = (JULY 4th)!!!~'

(125 + 51) = (`-176) = (76 x 1) = (`-76) = "AGE of `-DEATH for
HUNGARIAN AMERICAN ACTRESS EVA GABOR (`-76)!!!~'

HUNGARIAN AMERICAN ACTRESS EVA GABOR had `-DIED (`-
143) `-DAYS after `-HER `-LAST `-BIRTHDAY!!!~'

(`-143) = (43 + 1) = (`-44) = `-BIRTH/DAY # `-NUMBER for (SISTER)
HUNGARIAN AMERICAN ACTRESS ZSA ZSA GABOR (`-44)!!!~'

(365 (-) 143) = (`-222) = (2 x 22) = (`-44) = `-BIRTH/DAY # `-NUMBER
for (SISTER) HUNGARIAN AMERICAN ACTRESS ZSA ZSA
GABOR (`-44)!!!~'

`-DEATH/YEAR = (`-1995) = (95 (-) 19) = (`-76) = "AGE of `-DEATH
for HUNGARIAN AMERICAN ACTRESS EVA GABOR (`-76)!!!~'

HUNGARIAN AMERICAN ACTRESS EVA GABOR was `-BORN
in (`-1919) = 99(11) = (99 x 1 x 1) = (`-99) = `-AGE of `-DEATH for
`-SISTER HUNGARIAN AMERICAN ACTRESS ZSA ZSA GABOR
= (`-99)!!!~'

THE "RAGING BULL" BOXER JAKE LAMOTTA `-DIES at (`-96)!!!~'
(BIRTH: JULY 10, 1921) (DEATH: SEPTEMBER 19, 2017)!!!~'

`-DEATH/DAY = (9/19) = "FLIP EVERY (`-9) OVER to (`-6)" = (9/16)
= (96 x 1) = (`-96) = "AGE of `-DEATH for THE "RAGING BULL"
BOXER JAKE LAMOTTA (`-96)"!!!~'

`-BIRTH/YEAR = (`-21) = "FLIP EVERY (`-2) OVER to a (`-7)" = (`-71)
= RECIPROCAL = (`-17) = `-DEATH/YEAR!!!~'

`-**BIRTH/DAY** = (`-**7/10**) = (7 + 10) = (`-**17**) = RECIPROCAL = (`-**71**)!!!~'

SINGER/SONGWRITER/MUSICIAN TOM PETTY `-DIES at (`-**66**)!!!~' (BIRTH: *OCTOBER 20, 1950*) (DEATH: *OCTOBER 2, 2017*)!!!~'

FROM `-**BIRTH** to `-**DEATH** just `-**DELETE** a (`-**0**)/(`-**ZERO**) `-**BETWEEN** `-**THEM** = (`-**20**) / (`-**2**); and, `-**YOU have the** `-**SAME** # `-**NUMBER** (**10/2**)!!!~'

`-**BIRTH/DAY** # `-**NUMBER** = (10 + 20 + 19 + 50) = (`-**99**) = "FLIP EVERY (`-**9**) OVER to a (`-**6**)" = (`-**66**) = "**AGE of** `-**DEATH for SINGER/SONGWRITER/MUSICIAN TOM PETTY** (`-**66**)"!!!~'

(10 + 20 + 19) = (`-**49**)!!!~'

`-**DEATH/DAY** # `-**NUMBER** = (10 + 2 + 20 + 17) = (`-**49**) = (4 x 9) = (`-**36**) = 3(6's) = (`-**666**) = (6 x 6 x 6) = (`-**216**) = (26 x 1) = (`-**26**) = 2(6's) = (`-**66**) = "**AGE of** `-**DEATH for SINGER/SONGWRITER/ MUSICIAN TOM PETTY** (`-**66**)"!!!~'

`-**AGE of** `-**DEATH** = (`-**66**) = (6 x 6) = (`-**36**) = (4 x 9) = (`-**49**) = `-**DEATH/DAY** # `-**NUMBER** (`-**49**)!!!~'

`-**BIRTH/YEAR** = (`-**1950**) = (19 + 50) = (`-**69**) = "FLIP EVERY (`-**9**) OVER to a (`-**6**)" = (`-**66**) = "**AGE of** `-**DEATH for SINGER/ SONGWRITER/MUSICIAN TOM PETTY** (`-**66**)"!!!~'

`-**DEATH/YEAR** = (`-**2017**) = (27 + 0 (-) 1) = (`-**26**) = 2(6's) = (`-**66**) = "**AGE of** `-**DEATH for SINGER/SONGWRITER/MUSICIAN TOM PETTY** (`-**66**)"!!!~'

`-**DEATH/DAY** = (**10/2**) = (10 + 2) = (`-**12**) = (2 x 6) = (`-**26**) = 2(6's) = (`-**66**) = "**AGE of** `-**DEATH for SINGER/SONGWRITER/MUSICIAN TOM PETTY** (`-**66**)"!!!~'

`-BIRTH/DAY # `-NUMBER = (`-**99**) = (9 x 9) = (`-**81**) = RECIPROCAL = (`-**18**)!!!~'

SINGER/SONGWRITER/MUSICIAN TOM PETTY `-DIED (`-**18**) `-DAYS BEFORE HIS NEXT BIRTHDAY!!!~'

(`-**18**) = (3 x 6) = (`-**36**) = 3(6's) = (`-**666**) = (6 x 6 x 6) = (`-**216**) = (26 x 1) = (`-**26**) = 2(6's) = (`-**66**) = "AGE of `-DEATH for SINGER/ SONGWRITER/MUSICIAN TOM PETTY (`-**66**)"!!!~'

(365 (-) 18) = (`-**347**) = "FLIP EVERY (`-**7**) OVER to a (`-**2**)" = (`-**342**) = (3 x 42) = (`-**126**) = (26 x 1) = (`-**26**) = 2(6's) = (`-**66**) = "AGE of `-DEATH for SINGER/SONGWRITER/MUSICIAN TOM PETTY (`-**66**)"!!!~'

ACTOR ROBERT GUILLAUME (PHANTOM of the `-OPERA) `-DIED on *OCTOBER 24th* within `-**2017**!!!!!~' `-HE was `-BORN on *NOVEMBER 30th* in `-19**27**!!!!!~' `-HE `-DIED at the `-AGE of (`-**89**)!!!!!~'

`-**DEATH/DAY** = (**10/24**) = (24 (-) 10) = (`-**14**) = RECIPROCAL = (`-**41**) = `-**BIRTH/DAY** = (**11/30**) = (11 + 30) = (`-**41**)!!!~'

`-**AGE of `-DEATH** = (`-**89**) = (8 x 9) = (`-**72**) = RECIPROCAL = (`-**27**) = `-**BIRTH/YEAR** (`-**27**) = "DIED within (`-**2017**)"!!!~'

ACTOR ROBERT GUILLAUME (PHANTOM of the `-OPERA) `-BIRTHDAY # = `-EQUALS = (11 + 30 + 19 + 27) = (`-**87**) = "TWO `-YEARS `-AWAY (`-**87**) from `-AGE of `-DEATH (`-**89**)"!!!~'

ACTOR ROBERT GUILLAUME (PHANTOM of the `-OPERA) `-DEATH/DAY # = `-EQUALS = (10 + 24 + 20 + 17) = (`-**71**) = RECIPROCAL = (`-**17**) = `-**DIED** within the `-**YEAR** of (`-**17**)!!!~'

ACTOR ROBERT GUILLAUME (PHANTOM of the `-OPERA) had `-DIED (`-**37**) `-DAYS before `-HIS `-NEXT `-BIRTHDAY!!!~'

(`-**37**) = "FLIP EVERY (`-**3**) OVER to an (`-**8**)" = (`-**87**) = **"TWO `-YEARS `-AWAY (`-87) from `-AGE of `-DEATH (`-89)"**!!!~`

(365 (-) 37) = (`-**328**) = (3 x 2) (8) = (`-**68**) = RECIPROCAL = (`-**86**) = "FLIP EVERY (`-**6**) OVER to a (`-**9**)" = (`-**89**) = **"AGE of `-DEATH for ACTOR ROBERT GUILLAUME (PHANTOM of the `-OPERA) (`-89)"**!!!~`

BASEBALL PLAYER HARRY LEROY "DOC" HALLADAY `-DIED on **NOVEMBER 7**$^{th}$ within `-**2017**!!!~` `-HE was `-BORN on **MAY 14**$^{th}$ in `-19**77**!!!~` `-HE `-DIED at the `-AGE of (`-**40**)!!!~`

`-**DEATH/DAY** = (**11/7**) = (11 x 7) = (`-**77**) = `-**BIRTH/YEAR** = (`-**77**) = 2(7's) = (`-**27**) = `-**DIED within (`-2017)**!!!~`

`-**DAY of `-BIRTH** = (`-**14**$^{th}$) = RECIPROCAL = (`-**41**) = **"ONE `-YEAR `-AWAY (`-41) from `-AGE of `-DEATH (`-40)"**!!!~`

`-**BIRTH/YEAR** = (`-**1977**) = (1 + 9) (7 + 7) = (10) (14) = (14 (-) 10) = (`-**4**) = `-**DIED at the `-AGE of (`-4) (0)** !!!~`

BASEBALL PLAYER HARRY LEROY "DOC" HALLADAY had `-DIED (`-**188**) `-DAYS before `-HIS `-NEXT `-BIRTHDAY!!!~`

(`-**188**) = (18 x 8) = (`-**144**) = (1 + 4) (4) = (`-**54**) = `-**BIRTH/DAY = (5/14)**!!!~`

(365 (-) 188) = (`-1**77**) = (77 x 1) = (`-**77**) = `-**DEATH/DAY** = (**11/7**) = (11 x 7) = (`-**77**) = `-**BIRTH/YEAR** = (`-**77**) = 2(7's) = (`-**27**) = `-**DIED within (`-2017)**!!!~`

MUSICIAN ANTOINE "FAT'S" DOMINO JR. `-DIED on *OCTOBER 24th* within `-*2017*!!!~' `-HE was `-BORN on *FEBRUARY 26th* in `-*1928*!!!~' `-HE `-DIED at the `-AGE of (`-**89**)!!!~

`-**BIRTH/DAY** = (**2/26**) = "FLIP EVERY (`-**6**) OVER to a (`-**9**)" = (**2/29**) = RECIPROCAL = (**92/2**) = (92 (-) 2) = (`-**90**) = "ONE `-YEAR `-AWAY (`-**90**) from `-AGE of `-DEATH (`-**89**)"!!!~'

`-**DEATH/DAY** = (**10/24**) = (10 + 24) = (`-**34**) = "FLIP EVERY (`-**3**) OVER to an (`-**8**)" = (`-**84**)!!!~'

`-**AGE of `-DEATH** = (`-**89**) = (8 x 9) = (`-**72**) = RECIPROCAL = (`-**27**) = "**DIED** within (`-**2017**)"!!!~'

`-**BIRTH/YEAR** = (`-**1928**) = (1 (-) 9) (2 (-) 8) = (8) (6) = (`-**86**) = "FLIP EVERY (`-**6**) OVER to a (`-**9**)" = (`-**89**) = "AGE of `-DEATH for MUSICIAN ANTOINE "FAT'S" DOMINO JR. (`-**89**)"!!!~'

COLUMNIST MARY ELIZABETH SMITH `-DIED on *NOVEMBER 12th* within `-2017!!!~' `-SHE was `-BORN on *FEBRUARY 2nd* in `-19**23**!!!~' `-SHE `-DIED at the `-AGE of (`-**94**)!!!~'

`-**DEATH/DAY** = (**11/12**) = (11 + 12) = (`-**23**) = `-**BIRTH/YEAR** = (`-**23**)!!!~'

`-**DEATH/DAY** = (**11/12**) = RECIPROCAL = (**21/11**) = (2 x 1) (1 + 1) = (`-**2/2**) = `-**BIRTH/DAY** = (**FEBRUARY 2nd**)!!!~'

COLUMNIST MARY ELIZABETH SMITH `-**BIRTHDAY # `-NUMBER** = `-EQUALS = (2 + 2 + 19 + 23) = (`-**46**) = "FLIP EVERY (`-**6**) OVER to a (`-**9**)" = (`-**49**) = RECIPROCAL = (`-**94**) = "AGE of `-DEATH for COLUMNIST MARY ELIZABETH SMITH (`-**94**)"!!!~'

COLUMNIST MARY ELIZABETH SMITH `-**DEATH/DAY # `-NUMBER** = `-EQUALS = (11 + 12 + 20 + 17) = (`-**60**) = "FLIP EVERY (`-**6**) OVER to a (`-**9**)" = (`-**90**)!!!~'

`-**BIRTH/DAY** = (**2/2**) = "FLIP EVERY (`-**2**) OVER to a (`-**7**)" = (`-**27**) = `-**DIED** within (`-**2017**)!!!~'

AMERICAN CRIMINAL CHARLES MANSON `-DIED on **NOVEMBER 19**[th] within `-**2017**!!!!!~' `-HE was `-BORN on **NOVEMBER 12**[th] in `-19**34**!!!!!~' `-HE `-DIED at the `-AGE of (`-**83**)!!!!!~'

`-**DEATH/DAY** = (**11/19**) (+) `-**BIRTH/DAY** = (**11/12**) = (11 + 19 + 11 + 12) = (`-**53**)!!!~'

`-**BIRTH/YEAR** = (`-**1934**) = (19 + 34) = (`-**53**)!!!~'

`-**BIRTH/YEAR** = (`-**34**) = "FLIP EVERY (`-**3**) OVER to an (`-**8**)" = (`-**84**) = "ONE `-YEAR `-AWAY (`-**84**) from `-AGE of `-DEATH (`-**83**)"!!!~'

`-**BIRTH/DAY** = (**11/12**) = "FLIP EVERY (`-**2**) OVER to a (`-**7**)" = (**11/17**) = (1 + 1) (1 x 7) = (2) (7) = (`-**27**) = `-**DIED** within (`-**2017**)!!!~'

`-**BIRTH/DAY** = (**11/12**) = "FLIP EVERY (`-**2**) OVER to a (`-**7**)" = (**11/17**) = RECIPROCAL = (**71/11**) = (71 + 11) = (`-**82**) = "ONE `-YEAR `-AWAY (`-**82**) from `-AGE of `-DEATH (`-**83**)"!!!~'

`-**DEATH/YEAR** = (`-**2017**) = RECIPROCAL = (`-**7102**) = (7 + 1) (0 + 2) = (`-**82**) = "ONE `-YEAR `-AWAY (`-**82**) from `-AGE of `-DEATH (`-**83**)"!!!~'

`-**DEATH/DAY** = (**11/19**) = RECIPROCAL = (**91/11**) = (91 (-) 11) = (`-**80**)!!!~'

AMERICAN CRIMINAL CHARLES MANSON `-**BIRTHDAY # `-NUMBER** = `-EQUALS = (11 + 12 + 19 + 34) = (`-**76**) = RECIPROCAL = (`-**67**) = `-**DEATH/DAY # `-NUMBER**!!!~'

AMERICAN CRIMINAL CHARLES MANSON `-**DEATH/DAY #**
`-**NUMBER** = `-EQUALS = (11 + 19 + 20 + 17) = (`-**67**) = RECIPROCAL
= (`-**76**) = `-**BIRTH/DAY # `-NUMBER!!!~'**

AMERICAN CRIMINAL CHARLES MANSON had `-DIED (`-**7**)
`-DAYS after `-HIS `-LAST `-BIRTHDAY!!!~'

(365 (-) 7) = (`-**358**) = (35 + 8) = (`-**43**) = RECIPROCAL = (`-**34**) =
`-**BIRTH/YEAR** (`-**34**)!!!~'

(`-**358**) = (3 + 5) (8) = (`-**88**) = "FLIP EVERY (`-**8**) OVER to a (`-**3**)" =
(`-**83**) = **"AGE of `-DEATH for AMERICAN CRIMINAL CHARLES
MANSON (`-83)"!!!~'**

AMERICAN GOSPEL SINGER & ACTRESS DELLA REESE `-DIED
on *NOVEMBER 19th* within `-*2017*!!!~' `-SHE was `-BORN on *JULY
6th* in `-19**31**!!!~' `-SHE `-DIED at the `-AGE of (`-**86**)!!!~'

AMERICAN GOSPEL SINGER & ACTRESS DELLA REESE
`-**BIRTHDAY # `-NUMBER** = `-EQUALS = (7 + 6 + 19 + 31) = (`-**63**)
= RECIPROCAL = (`-**36**) = "FLIP EVERY (`-**3**) OVER to an (`-**8**)" =
(`-**86**) = **"AGE of `-DEATH for AMERICAN GOSPEL SINGER &
ACTRESS DELLA REESE (`-86)"!!!~'**

AMERICAN GOSPEL SINGER & ACTRESS DELLA REESE
`-**DEATH/DAY # `-NUMBER** = `-EQUALS = (11 + 19 + 20 + 17) =
(`-**67**) = RECIPROCAL = (`-**76**) = `-**BIRTHDAY (7/6)** = (**JULY 6th**)!!!~'

AMERICAN GOSPEL SINGER & ACTRESS DELLA REESE had
`-DIED (`-**229**) `-DAYS before `-HER `-NEXT `-BIRTHDAY!!!~'

(`-**229**) = "FLIP EVERY (`-**2**) OVER to a (`-**7**)" = (`-**779**) = (77 + 9) =
(`-**86**) = **"AGE of `-DEATH for AMERICAN GOSPEL SINGER &
ACTRESS DELLA REESE (`-86)"!!!~'**

(365 (-) 229 = (`-**136**) = (36 x 1) = (`-**36**) = "FLIP EVERY (`-**3**) OVER to an (`-**8**)" = (`-**86**) = "**AGE of `-DEATH for AMERICAN GOSPEL SINGER & ACTRESS DELLA REESE (`-86)**"!!!~'

`-**DEATH/YEAR** = (`-**2017**) = RECIPROCAL = (`-**7102**) = (7 + 1) (0 + 2) = (`-**82**) = "FLIP EVERY (`-**2**) OVER to a (-**7**)" = (`-**87**) = "**ONE `-YEAR `-AWAY (`-87) from `-AGE of `-DEATH (`-86)**"!!!~'

AMERICAN ACTOR & SINGER DAVID CASSIDY `-DIED on **NOVEMBER 21**ˢᵗ within `-**2017**!!!!!~' `-HE was `-BORN on **APRIL 12**ᵗʰ in `-**1950**!!!!!~' `-HE `-DIED at the `-AGE of (`-**67**)!!!!!~'

`-**BIRTH/DAY** = (**4/12**) = "FLIP EVERY (`-**2**) OVER to a (`-**7**)" = (**4/17**) = RECIPROCAL = (**71/4**) = (71 (-) 4) = (`-**67**) = "**AGE of `-DEATH for AMERICAN ACTOR & SINGER DAVID CASSIDY (`-67)**"!!!~'

`-**BORN** in (`-**4**); and, `-**DIED** in (`-**11**) = (`-**411**) = (**4/11**) = "**BORN the `-VERY `-NEXT `-DAY**"!!!~'

`-**DAY** of `-**BIRTH** = (`-**12**ᵗʰ) = RECIPROCAL = (`-**21**ˢᵗ) = "**DAY of `-DEATH**"!!!~'

`-**DEATH/DAY** = (**11/21**) = "FLIP EVERY (`-**2**) OVER to a (`-**7**)" = (**11/71**) = (71 (-) (1 + 1)) = (`-**69**) = `-**DEATH/DAY # `-NUMBER (`-69)**!!!~'

`-**BIRTH/YEAR** = (`-**1950**) = (19 + 50) = (`-**69**) = `-**DEATH/DAY # `-NUMBER (`-69)**!!!~'

`-**DEATH/YEAR** = (`-**2017**) = "FLIP EVERY (`-**2**) OVER to a (`-**7**)" = (`-**7017**) = (7 (-) 1) (0 + 7) = (`-**67**) = "**AGE of `-DEATH for AMERICAN ACTOR & SINGER DAVID CASSIDY (`-67)**"!!!~'

AMERICAN ACTOR & SINGER DAVID CASSIDY `-**BIRTHDAY # `-NUMBER** = `-**EQUALS** = (4 + 12 + 19 + 50) = (`-**85**)!!!~'

AMERICAN ACTOR & SINGER DAVID CASSIDY `-**DEATH/DAY #**
`-**NUMBER** = `-EQUALS = (11 + 21 + 20 + 17) = (`-**69**) = (19 + 50) =
`-**BIRTH/YEAR** (**19/50**)!!!~'

AMERICAN ACTOR & SINGER DAVID CASSIDY had `-DIED (`-**142**)
`-DAYS before `-HIS `-NEXT `-BIRTHDAY!!!~'

(`-**142**) = "**SWIPE** `-**ONE** to the `-**LEFT**" = (`-**4/12**) = `-**BIRTH/DAY**
= (**APRIL 12**ᵗʰ)!!!~'

(365 (-) 142) = (`-**223**) = "FLIP EVERY (`-**3**) OVER to an (`-**8**)" =
(`-**228**) = (2 + 2) (8) = (`-**48**) = (4 x 12) = `-**BIRTH/DAY** = (**APRIL
12**ᵗʰ)!!!~'

AMERICAN ACTOR RANCE HOWARD (FATHER of RON & CLINT
HOWARD) `-DIED on **NOVEMBER 25**ᵗʰ within `-**2017**!!!~' `-HE was
`-BORN on **NOVEMBER 17**ᵗʰ in `-19**28**!!!~' `-HE `-DIED at the `-AGE
of (`-**89**)!!!~'

`-**DEATH/YEAR** = (`-**2017**) = (2 + 7) (0) (1) = (90 (-) 1) = (`-**89**) = "**AGE**
of `-**DEATH for AMERICAN ACTOR RANCE HOWARD (FATHER**
of RON & CLINT HOWARD) (`-89)"!!!~'

`-**AGE of** `-**DEATH** = (`-**89**) = (8 x 9) = (`-**72**) = RECIPROCAL = (`-**27**)
= `-DIED within (`-**2017**)!!!~'

`-**DEATH/DAY** = (**11/25**) = (11 + 25) = (`-**36**) = "FLIP EVERY (`-**3**)
OVER to an (`-**8**)" = (`-**86**) = & "FLIP EVERY (`-**6**) OVER to a (`-
9)" = (`-**89**) = "**AGE of** `-**DEATH for AMERICAN ACTOR RANCE**
HOWARD (FATHER of RON & CLINT HOWARD) (`-89)"!!!~'

`-**BIRTH/DAY** = (**11/17**) = (11 + 17) = (`-**28**) = `-**BIRTH/YEAR** =
(`-**28**)!!!~'

`-**BIRTH/YEAR** = (`-**28**) = RECIPROCAL = (`-**82**) = "FLIP EVERY (`-**2**) OVER to a (`-**7**)" = (`-**87**) = **"TWO `-YEARS `-AWAY (`-87) from `-AGE of `-DEATH (`-89)"**!!!~'

AMERICAN ACTOR RANCE HOWARD (FATHER of RON & CLINT HOWARD) `-BIRTHDAY # = `-EQUALS = (11 + 17 + 19 + 28) = (`-**75**) = "FLIP EVERY (`-**7**) OVER to a (`-**2**)" = (`-**25**) = **"DAY of `-DEATH"**!!!~'

AMERICAN ACTOR RANCE HOWARD (FATHER of RON & CLINT HOWARD) `-DEATH/DAY # = `-EQUALS = (11 + 25 + 20 + 17) = (`-**73**) = **"AGE of `-DEATH of `-WIFE JEAN SPEEGLE HOWARD (`-73)"**!!!~'

AMERICAN ACTRESS JEAN SPEEGLE HOWARD (MOTHER of RON & CLINT HOWARD) `-DIED on *SEPTEMBER 2ⁿᵈ* within `-2**000**!!!~' `-SHE was `-BORN on *JANUARY 31ˢᵗ* in `-19**27**!!!~' `-SHE `-DIED at the `-AGE of (`-**73**)!!!~'

`-**DEATH/DAY** = (**9/2**) = "FLIP EVERY (`-**9**) OVER to a (`-**6**)" & "FLIP EVERY (`-**2**) OVER to a (`-**7**)" = (`-**67**) = RECIPROCAL = (`-**76**)!!!~'

`-**BIRTH/YEAR** = (`-**1927**) = (9 (-) 2) (1 (-) 7) = (`-**76**)!!!~'

RANCE HOWARD'S DEATHDAY # `-NUMBER (`-**73**) = "AGE of `-DEATH of `-**WIFE JEAN SPEEGLE HOWARD (`-73)**"!!!~'

AMERICAN ACTRESS JEAN SPEEGLE HOWARD'S (`-**31**) **DEATHDAY # `-NUMBER** = (`-**31**) = **"DAY of `-BIRTH (`-31ˢᵗ)"**!!!~'

`-**BIRTH/DAY** = (**1/31**) = (1 + 31) = (`-**32**) = RECIPROCAL = (`-**23**) = "FLIP EVERY (`-**2**) OVER to a (`-**7**)" = (`-**73**) = **"AGE of `-DEATH for AMERICAN ACTRESS JEAN SPEEGLE HOWARD (MOTHER of RON & CLINT HOWARD) (`-73)"**!!!~'

`-**BIRTH/YEAR** = (`-**27**) = RECIPROCAL = (`-**72**) = **"ONE `-YEAR `-AWAY (`-72) from `-AGE of `-DEATH (`-73)"**!!!~'

AMERICAN ACTRESS JEAN SPEEGLE HOWARD (MOTHER of RON & CLINT HOWARD) `-BIRTHDAY # = `-EQUALS = (1 + 31 + 19 + 27) = (`-**78**) = "FLIP EVERY (`-**8**) OVER to a (`-**3**)" = (`-**73**) = **"AGE of `-DEATH for AMERICAN ACTRESS JEAN SPEEGLE HOWARD (MOTHER of RON & CLINT HOWARD) (`-73)"**!!!~'

AMERICAN ACTRESS JEAN SPEEGLE HOWARD (MOTHER of RON & CLINT HOWARD) `-DEATH/DAY # = `-EQUALS = (9 + 2 + 20 + 00) = (`-**31**) = **"DAY of `-BIRTH (`-31st)"**!!!~'

AMERICAN ACTRESS JEAN SPEEGLE HOWARD (MOTHER of RON & CLINT HOWARD) had `-DIED (`-**151**) `-DAYS before `-HER `-NEXT `-BIRTHDAY!!!~'

(`-**151**)= (51 x 1) = `-**51** = **"YEARS of `-MARRIAGE"**!!!~'

(365 (-) 151 = (`-**214**) = "FLIP EVERY (`-**2**) OVER to a (`-**7**)" = (`-**714**) = (7) (1 (-) 4) = (`-**73**) = **"AGE of `-DEATH for AMERICAN ACTRESS JEAN SPEEGLE HOWARD (MOTHER of RON & CLINT HOWARD) (`-73)"**!!!~'

AMERICAN POLITICIAN MARCH FONG EU `-DIED on DECEMBER 21$^{st}$ within `-2017!!!~' `-SHE was `-BORN on *MARCH 29th* in `-*1922*!!!~' `-SHE `-DIED at the `-AGE of (`-**95**)!!!~'

`-**BIRTH/DAY # `-NUMBER** = (3/29/19/22) = (3 + 29 + 19 + 22) = (`-**73**)!!!~'

`-**BIRTH/DAY** = (**3/29**) = RECIPROCAL = (**92/3**) = (92 + 3) = (`-**95**) = **"AGE of `-DEATH for AMERICAN POLITICIAN MARCH FONG EU (`-95)"**!!!~'

`-**BIRTH/YEAR** = (`-**1922**) = (9) (1 + 2 + 2) = (`-**95**) = "**AGE of** `-**DEATH for AMERICAN POLITICIAN MARCH FONG EU** (`-**95**)"!!!~'

AMERICAN POLITICIAN MARCH FONG EU had `-DIED (`-**98**) `-DAYS before `-HER `-NEXT `-BIRTHDAY!!!~'

(`-**98**) = "FLIP EVERY (`-**8**) OVER to a (`-**3**)" = (`-**93**)!!!~'

(8 (-) 3) = (`-**5**) = (`-**95**) = "**AGE of** `-**DEATH for AMERICAN POLITICIAN MARCH FONG EU** (`-**95**)"!!!~'

(365 (-) 98) = (`-**267**) = (67 x 2) = (`-**134**)) = "FLIP EVERY (`-**3**) OVER to an (`-**8**)" = (`-**184**) = (1 + 8) (4) = (`-**94**) = "**ONE** `-**YEAR** `-**AWAY** (`-**94**) from `-**AGE of** `-**DEATH** (`-**95**)"!!!~'

ACTRESS/AMERICAN-CANADIAN MODEL HEATHER MENZIES URICH (The SOUND of MUSIC) `-DIED on *DECEMBER 24*[th] within `-**2017**!!!!!~' `-SHE was `-BORN on **DECEMBER 3**[rd] in `-**1949**!!!!!~' `-SHE `-DIED at the `-AGE of (`-**68**)!!!!!~'

`-**DEATH/DAY** = (**12/24**) = RECIPROCAL = (**42/21**) = (4 + 2) (2 + 1) = (`-**63**) = "FLIP EVERY (`-**3**) OVER to an (`-**8**)" = (`-**68**) = "**AGE of** `-**DEATH for ACTRESS/AMERICAN-CANADIAN MODEL HEATHER MENZIES URICH (The SOUND of MUSIC)** (`-**68**)"!!!~'

`-**BIRTH/DAY** = (**12/3**) = RECIPROCAL = (**3/21**) = "FLIP EVERY (`-**3**) OVER to an (`-**8**)" = (**8/21**) = "FLIP EVERY (`-**2**) OVER to a (`-**7**)" = (**8/71**) = (8) (7 (-) 1) = (`-**86**) = RECIPROCAL = (`-**68**) = "**AGE of** `-**DEATH for ACTRESS/AMERICAN-CANADIAN MODEL HEATHER MENZIES URICH (The SOUND of MUSIC)** (`-**68**)"!!!~'

`-**BIRTH/YEAR** = (`-**1949**) = (19 + 49) = (`-**68**) = "**AGE of** `-**DEATH for ACTRESS/AMERICAN-CANADIAN MODEL HEATHER MENZIES URICH (The SOUND of MUSIC)** (`-**68**)"!!!~'

`-**DEATH/YEAR** = (`-**2017**) = RECIPROCAL = (`-**7102**) = (71 (-) 02) = (`-**69**) = "ONE `-YEAR `-AWAY (`-**69**) from `-AGE of `-DEATH (`-**68**)"!!!~'

ACTRESS/AMERICAN-CANADIAN MODEL HEATHER MENZIES URICH `-**BIRTHDAY # **`-**NUMBER** = `-EQUALS = (12 + 3 + 19 + 49) = (`-**83**) = "FLIP EVERY (`-**3**) OVER to an (`-**8**)" = (`-**88**)!!!~'

ACTRESS/AMERICAN-CANADIAN MODEL HEATHER MENZIES URICH `-**DEATH/DAY # **`-**NUMBER** = `-EQUALS = (12 + 24 + 20 + 17) = (`-**73**)!!!~'

ACTRESS/AMERICAN-CANADIAN MODEL HEATHER MENZIES URICH had `-DIED (`-**21**) `-DAYS after `-HER `-LAST `-BIRTHDAY!!!~'

(`-**21**) = "FLIP EVERY (`-**2**) OVER to a (`-**7**)" = (`-**71**) = RECIPROCAL = (`-**17**) = "**DIED** within (`-**2017**)"!!!~'

(365 (-) 21) = (`-**344**) = "FLIP EVERY (`-**3**) OVER to an (`-**8**)" = (`-**844**) = (8) (4 + 4) = (`-**88**)!!!~'

PUERTO RICAN ACTRESS MIRIAM COLON `-DIED on MARCH 3rd within `-2017!!!~' `-SHE was `-BORN on AUGUST 20th in `-1936!!!~' `-SHE `-DIED at the `-AGE of (`-**80**)!!!~'

(`-**170**) = (17 + 0) = (`-**17**) = `-**DIED** within the `-**YEAR** of (`-**2017**)!!!~'

PUERTO RICAN ACTRESS MIRIAM COLON had `-DIED (`-**170**) `-DAYS before `-HER `-NEXT `-BIRTHDAY!!!~'

(`-**170**) = (1 + 7) (0) = (`-**80**) = "**AGE of `-DEATH for PUERTO RICAN ACTRESS MIRIAM COLON (`-80)**"!!!~'

AMERICAN ECONOMIST, STATESMAN; AND, BUSINESSMAN GEORGE PRATT SHULTZ `-**DIES** at the `-**AGE** of (`-**100**) on (**2/6/2021**)!!!~' `-**BORN** on (**12/13/1920**)!!!~'

`-**BIRTH/DAY** = (**12/13**) = (12 + 13) = (`-**25**) = `-**DIES** the `-**VERY** `-**NEXT** `-**DAY** on (`-**2/6**) = (**FEBRUARY 6**th)!!!~'

`-**BIRTH/DAY** = (**12/13**) = (1 + 1) (2 x 3) = (2) (6) = (`-**26**) = `-**HIS** `-**VERY** `-**OWN** `-**DEATH/DAY** = (`-**2/6**) = (**FEBRUARY 6**th)!!!~'

AMERICAN ECONOMIST, STATESMAN; AND, BUSINESSMAN GEORGE PRATT SHULTZ `-**DIES** (`-**55**) DAYS after `-**HIS** `-**LAST** `-**BIRTH/DAY**!!!~'

`-**BIRTH/DAY** = (`-**12/13**) = (12 x 13) = (`-**156**) = (56 (-) 1) = (`-**55**)!!!~'

`-**DEATH/YEAR** = (`-**2021**) = RECIPROCAL = (`-1**202**) = (10) (2 (-) 2) = (`-**100**) = "AGE of `-**DEATH** for AMERICAN ECONOMIST, STATESMAN; AND, BUSINESSMAN GEORGE PRATT SHULTZ (`-**100**)"!!!~'

AMERICAN ACTRESS ROSE MARIE (DICK VAN DYKE SHOW) `-DIED on **DECEMBER 28**th within `-2017!!!~' `-SHE was `-BORN on **AUGUST 15**th in `-**1923**!!!~' `-SHE `-DIED at the `-AGE of (`-**94**)!!!~'

`-**BIRTH/DAY** = (**8/15**) = (8 + 1) (5) = (`-**95**) = "ONE `-YEAR `-AWAY (`-**95**) from `-AGE of `-DEATH (`-**94**)"!!!~'

(`-**12**) = RECIPROCAL = (`-**21**)!!!~'

`-**DEATH/DAY** = (**12**/28) = RECIPROCAL = (**82**/21) = (82 + 12) = (`-**94**) = "AGE of `-DEATH for AMERICAN ACTRESS ROSE MARIE (DICK VAN DYKE SHOW) (`-**94**)"!!!~'

`-**BIRTH/YEAR** = (`-**1923**) = (9) (2 + 3 (-) 1) = (`-**94**) = "AGE of `-DEATH for AMERICAN ACTRESS ROSE MARIE (DICK VAN DYKE SHOW) (`-**94**)"!!!~'

AMERICAN ASTRONAUT JOHN WATTS YOUNG `-DIED on *JANUARY 5$^{th}$* within `-**2018**!!!!!~' `-HE was `-BORN on *SEPTEMBER 24th* in `-**1930**!!!!!~' `-HE `-DIED at the `-AGE of (`-**87**)!!!!!~'

`-**BIRTH/DAY** = (**9/24**) = (24 (-) 9) = (`-**15**) = `-**DEATH/DAY** = (**1/5**) = (**JANUARY 5**th)!!!~'

AMERICAN ASTRONAUT JOHN WATTS YOUNG `-**BIRTHDAY #** `-**NUMBER** = `-EQUALS = (9 + 24 + 19 + 30) = (`-**82**) = "FLIP EVERY (`-**2**) OVER to a (`-**7**)" = (`-**87**) = "AGE of `-DEATH for AMERICAN ASTRONAUT JOHN WATTS YOUNG (`-**87**)"!!!~'

AMERICAN ASTRONAUT JOHN WATTS YOUNG `-**DEATH/DAY #** `-**NUMBER** = `-EQUALS = (1 + 5 + 20 + 18) = (`-**44**) = `-TIMES "**X**" (`-**2**) = (`-**88**) = "ONE `-YEAR `-AWAY (`-**88**) from `-AGE of `-DEATH (`-**87**)"!!!~'

`-**BIRTH/YEAR** = (`-**1930**) = RECIPROCAL = (`-**0391**) = (91 (-) (3 + 0)) = (`-**88**) = "ONE `-YEAR `-AWAY (`-**88**) from `-AGE of `-DEATH (`-**87**)"!!!~'

`-**DEATH/YEAR** = (`-**2018**) = RECIPROCAL = (`-**8102**) = "FLIP EVERY (`-**2**) OVER to a (`-**7**)" = (`-**8107**) = (8 + 0) (1 x 7) = (`-**87**) = "AGE of `-DEATH for AMERICAN ASTRONAUT JOHN WATTS YOUNG (`-**87**)"!!!~'

AMERICAN ASTRONAUT JOHN WATTS YOUNG had `-**DIED** (`-**103**) `-DAYS after `-HIS `-LAST `-BIRTHDAY!!!~'

(365 (-) 103) = (`-**262**) = (2 + 6) (2) = (`-**82**) = "FLIP EVERY (`-**2**) OVER to a (`-**7**)" = (`-**87**) = "**AGE of** `-DEATH for **AMERICAN ASTRONAUT JOHN WATTS YOUNG** (`-**87**)"!!!~'

IRISH SINGER/SONGWRITER DOLORES O'RIORDAN (THE CRANBERRIES) `-DIED on *JANUARY 15<sup>th</sup>* within `-**2018**!!!~' `-SHE was `-BORN on *SEPTEMBER 6th* in `-*1971*!!!~' `-SHE `-DIED at the `-AGE of (`-**46**) = `-TIMES "**X**" (`-**2**) = (`-**92**)!!!~'

`-**DEATH/YEAR** = (`-**2018**) = RECIPROCAL = (`-**8102**) = (8 + 1) (0 + 2) = (`-**92**) / `-**DIVIDED** `-by (`-**2**) = (`-**46**) = "**AGE of** `-**DEATH** for IRISH SINGER/SONGWRITER DOLORES O'RIORDAN (THE CRANBERRIES)** (`-**46**)"!!!~'

`-**DEATH/DAY** = (**1/15**) = RECIPROCAL = (**51/1**) = (51 + 1) = (`-**52**) = `-**BIRTH/YEAR** = (`-**1971**) = (71 (-) 19) = (`-**52**)!!!~'

`-**BIRTH/DAY** = (**9/6**) = (9 + 6) = (`-**15**) = "**DAY of** `-**DEATH**" = (**1/15**) = (15 x 1) = (`-**15**)!!!~'

IRISH SINGER/SONGWRITER DOLORES O'RIORDAN (THE CRANBERRIES) `-**BIRTHDAY # **`-NUMBER** = `-EQUALS = (9 + 6 + 19 + 71) = (`-**105**) = (10 + 5) = (`-**15**) = "**DAY of** `-**DEATH**" = (**1/15**) = (15 x 1) = (`-**15**)!!!~'

IRISH SINGER/SONGWRITER DOLORES O'RIORDAN (THE CRANBERRIES) `-**DEATH/DAY # **`-NUMBER** = `-EQUALS = (1 + 15 + 20 + 18) = (`-**54**) = (9 x 6) = `-**BIRTH/DAY** = (**9/6**) = (**SEPTEMBER** `-**6**th)!!!~'

IRISH SINGER/SONGWRITER DOLORES O'RIORDAN (THE CRANBERRIES) had `-DIED (`-**131**) `-**DAYS after** `-**HER** `-**LAST** `-**BIRTHDAY**!!!~'

(365 (-) 131) = `-**234** = RECIPROCAL = (`-**432**) = (4) (3 x 2) = (`-**46**) = "AGE of `-DEATH for IRISH SINGER/SONGWRITER DOLORES O'RIORDAN (THE CRANBERRIES) (`-**46**)"!!!~'

AMERICAN GOSPEL SINGER EDWIN HAWKINS (OH HAPPY DAY) `-DIED on *JANUARY 15th* within `-**2018**!!!!!~' `-HE was `-BORN on *AUGUST 19th* in `-**1943**!!!!!~' `-HE `-DIED at the `-AGE of (`-**74**)!!!!!~'

`-**DEATH/DAY** = (**1/15**) = (1 + 1) (5) = (`-**25**) = "FLIP EVERY (`-**2**) OVER to a (`-**7**)" = (`-**75**) = "ONE `-YEAR `-AWAY (`-**75**) from `-AGE of `-DEATH (`-**74**)"!!!~'

`-**BIRTH/YEAR** = (`-**1943**) = (9 (-) 3 + 1) (4) = (`-**74**) = "AGE of `-DEATH for AMERICAN GOSPEL SINGER EDWIN HAWKINS (OH HAPPY DAY) (`-**74**)"!!!~'

`-**DEATH/YEAR** = (`-**2018**) = RECIPROCAL = (`-**8102**) = (8 (-) 1) (0 + 2) = (`-**72**) = "TWO `-YEARS `-AWAY (`-**72**) from `-AGE of `-DEATH (`-**74**)"!!!~'

AMERICAN GOSPEL SINGER EDWIN HAWKINS (OH HAPPY DAY) `-BIRTHDAY # = `-EQUALS = (8 + 19 + 19 + 43) = (`-**89**) = `-**BIRTH/DAY** = (**8/19**) = (89 x 1) = (`-**89**)!!!~'

AMERICAN GOSPEL SINGER EDWIN HAWKINS (OH HAPPY DAY) `-DEATH/DAY # = `-EQUALS = (1 + 15 + 20 + 18) = (`-**54**) = (6 x 9) = `-**BIRTH/DAY** = (**8/19**) = "FLIP EVERY (`-**9**) OVER to a (`-**6**)" = (**8/16**) = (8 + 1) (6) = (**9/6**) = RECIPROCAL = (**6/9**)!!!~'

AMERICAN GOSPEL SINGER EDWIN HAWKINS (OH HAPPY DAY) had `-DIED (`-**149**) `-DAYS after `-HIS `-LAST `-BIRTHDAY!!!~'

(`-**149**) = "FLIP EVERY (`-**9**) OVER to a (`-**6**)" = (`-**146**) = (1 + 6) (4) = (`-**74**) = "AGE of `-DEATH for AMERICAN GOSPEL SINGER EDWIN HAWKINS (OH HAPPY DAY) (`-**74**)"!!!~'

(365 (-) 149) = (`-**216**) = (2 x 16) = (`-**32**) = RECIPROCAL = (`-**23**) = "FLIP EVERY (`-**2**) OVER to a (`-**7**)" = (`-**73**) = "ONE `-YEAR `-AWAY (`-**73**) from `-AGE of `-DEATH (`-**74**)"!!!~'

AMERICAN SINGER VIC DAMONE `-DIED on *FEBRUARY 11th* within `-**2018**!!!~' `-HE was `-BORN on *JUNE 12th* in `-*1928*!!!~' `-HE `-DIED at the `-AGE of (`-**89**)!!!~'

`-**DEATH/YEAR** = (`-**2018**) = (2 + 0) (1 (-) 8) = (`-**27**) = RECIPROCAL = (`-**72**) = (8 x 9) = (`-**89**) = "AGE of `-DEATH for AMERICAN SINGER VIC DAMONE (`-**89**)"!!!~'

`-**DEATH/DAY** = (**2/11**) = (2 x 11) = (`-**22**) = "FLIP EVERY (`-**2**) OVER to a (`-**7**)" = (`-**77**) = 2(7's) = (`-**27**) = RECIPROCAL = (`-**72**) = (8 x 9) = (`-**89**) = "AGE of `-DEATH for AMERICAN SINGER VIC DAMONE (`-**89**)"!!!~'

`-**BIRTH/DAY** = (**6/12**) = (6 x 12) = (`-**72**) = (8 x 9) = (`-**89**) = "AGE of `-DEATH for AMERICAN SINGER VIC DAMONE (`-**89**)"!!!~'

`-**BIRTH/YEAR** = (`-**1928**) = (1 (-) 9) (2 (-) 8) = (`-**86**) = "FLIP EVERY (`-**6**) OVER to a (`-**9**)" = (`-**89**) = "AGE of `-DEATH for AMERICAN SINGER VIC DAMONE (`-**89**)"!!!~'

AMERICAN EVANGELIST BILLY GRAHAM `-DIED on *FEBRUARY 21st* within `-*2018*!!!~' `-HE was `-BORN on *NOVEMBER 7th* in `-*1918*!!!~' `-HE `-DIED at the `-AGE of (`-**99**)!!!~'

`-**BIRTH/DAY** = (**11/7**) = (11 x 7) = (`-**77**)!!!~'

`-**DEATH/DAY** = (**2/21**) = "FLIP EVERY (`-**2**) OVER to a (`-**7**)" = (`-**7/71**) = (77 x 1) = (`-**77**)!!!~'

`-BIRTH/YEAR** = (`-1918**) = (1 x 9) (1 + 8) = (`-**99**) = **"AGE of `-DEATH for AMERICAN EVANGELIST BILLY GRAHAM (`-99)"**!!!~'

`-DEATH/YEAR** = (`-2018**) = (2 + 0) (1 + 8) = (`-**29**) = 2(9's) = (`-**99**) = **"AGE of `-DEATH for AMERICAN EVANGELIST BILLY GRAHAM (`-99)"**!!!~'

TELEVISION PRODUCER STEVEN RONALD BOCHCO `-DIED on **APRIL 1ˢᵗ** within `-**2018**!!!~' `-HE was `-BORN on **DECEMBER 16ᵗʰ** in `-**1943**!!!~' `-HE `-DIED at the `-AGE of (`-**74**)!!!~'

`-BIRTH/YEAR** = (`-1943**) = (19 + 43) = (`-**62**) = RECIPROCAL = (`-**26**) = "FLIP EVERY (`-**2**) OVER to a (`-**7**)" = (`-**76**) = **"TWO `-YEARS `-AWAY (`-76) from `-AGE of `-DEATH (`-74)"**!!!~'

`-DEATH/YEAR** = (`-2018**) = (2 + 0) (1 (-) 8) = (`-**27**) = RECIPROCAL = (`-**72**) = **"TWO `-YEARS `-AWAY (`-72) from `-AGE of `-DEATH (`-74)"**!!!~'

`-DEATH/DAY** = (`-4/1**)!!!~'

`-AGE** of **`-DEATH = (`-**74**) = RECIPROCAL = (`-**47**) = "FLIP EVERY (`-**7**) OVER to a (`-**2**)" = (`-**42**) = (**4/2**) = **"DIED the `-VERY `-DAY `-BEFORE on (`-4/1)"**!!!~'

`-BIRTH/DAY** = (**12**/16) = RECIPROCAL = (**61**/21) = (61 + 12) = (`-73**) = **"ONE `-YEAR `-AWAY (`-73) from `-AGE of `-DEATH (`-74)"**!!!~'

TELEVISION PRODUCER STEVEN RONALD BOCHCO **`-BIRTHDAY # `-NUMBER** = `-EQUALS = (12 + 16 + 19 + 43) = (`-**90**)!!!~'

TELEVISION PRODUCER STEVEN RONALD BOCHCO **`-DEATH/ DAY # `-NUMBER** = `-EQUALS = (4 + 1 + 20 + 18) = (`-**43**) = **`-BIRTH/YEAR (`-43)**!!!~'

"**AGE** of `-**DEATH**" = (`-**74**) = (7 x 4) = (`-**28**) = `-**DIED** within (`-**2018**)!!!~'

ACTOR R. LEE ERMEY `-DIED on *APRIL 15ᵗʰ* within `-*2018*!!!~'
`-HE was `-BORN on *MARCH 24ᵗʰ* in `-*1944*!!!~' `-HE `-DIED at the
`-AGE of (`-**74**)!!!~'

`-**BIRTH/DAY** = (**3/24**) = RECIPROCAL = (**42/3**) = (4) (2 + 3) = (`-**45**)
= `-**DEATH/DAY** = (**4/15**) = (45 x 1) = (`-**45**)!!!~'

`-**DAY** of `-**BIRTH** = (`-**24**) = "FLIP EVERY (`-**2**) OVER to a (`-**7**)" =
(`-**74**) = "AGE of `-DEATH for ACTOR R. LEE ERMEY (`-**74**)"!!!~'

ACTOR R. LEE ERMEY `-**BIRTHDAY #** `-**NUMBER** = `-EQUALS =
(3 + 24 + 19 + 44) = (`-**90**) / `-**DIVIDED** `-by (`-**2**) = (`-**45**) = `-**DEATH/
DAY** = (**4/15**) = (45 x 1) = (`-**45**)!!!~'

ACTOR R. LEE ERMEY `-**BIRTHDAY #** `-**NUMBER** = `-EQUALS =
(3 + 24 + 19 + 44) = (`-**90**) / `-**DIVIDED** `-by (`-**2**) = (`-**45**) = `-**BIRTH/
DAY** = (**3/24**) = RECIPROCAL = (**42/3**) = (4) (2 + 3) = (`-**45**)!!!~'

ACTOR R. LEE ERMEY `-**DEATH/DAY #** `-**NUMBER** = `-EQUALS =
(4 + 15 + 20 + 18) = (`-**57**) = RECIPROCAL = (`-**75**) = "ONE `-YEAR
`-AWAY (`-**75**) from `-AGE of `-DEATH (`-**74**)"!!!~'

(90 + 57) = (`-**147**) = RECIPROCAL = (`-**741**) = (74 x 1) = (`-**74**) =
"AGE of `-DEATH for ACTOR R. LEE ERMEY (`-**74**)"!!!~'

`-**DEATH/YEAR** = (`-**2018**) = (2 + 0) (1 (-) 8) = (`-**27**) = RECIPROCAL
= (`-**72**) = "TWO `-YEARS `-AWAY (`-**72**) from `-AGE of `-DEATH
(`-**74**)"!!!~'

`-**BIRTH/DAY** = (**3/24**) = (3 x 24) = (`-**72**) = "TWO `-YEARS `-AWAY
(`-**72**) from `-AGE of `-DEATH (`-**74**)"!!!~'

`-DAY of `-BIRTH = (`-24) = 2(4's) = (`-44) = `-BIRTH/YEAR (`-44)!!!~'

"AGE of `-DEATH" = (`-74) = (7 x 4) = (`-28) = `-DIED within (`-2018)!!!~'

ACTOR HARRY ANDERSON `-DIED on *APRIL 16th* within `-*2018*!!!~' `-HE was `-BORN on *OCTOBER 14th* in `-*1952*!!!~' `-HE `-DIED at the `-AGE of (`-65)!!!~'

`-DEATH/DAY = (4/16) = RECIPROCAL = (61/4) = (61 + 4) = (`-65) = "AGE of `-DEATH for ACTOR HARRY ANDERSON (`-65)"!!!~'

ACTOR HARRY ANDERSON `-BIRTHDAY # `-NUMBER = `-EQUALS = (10 + 14 + 19 + 52) = (`-95) = "FLIP EVERY (`-9) OVER to a (`-6)" = (`-65) = "AGE of `-DEATH for ACTOR HARRY ANDERSON (`-65)"!!!~'

ACTOR HARRY ANDERSON `-DEATH/DAY # `-NUMBER = `-EQUALS = (4 + 16 + 20 + 18) = (`-58) = (5 x 8) = (`-40) = `-BIRTH/DAY = (10/14) = RECIPROCAL = (41/01) = (41 (-) 01) = (`-40)!!!~'

`-BIRTH/YEAR = (`-1952) = (52 (-) 19) = (`-33) = `-TIMES "X" (`-2) = (`-66) = "ONE `-YEAR `-AWAY (`-66) from `-AGE of `-DEATH (`-65)" = `-DIED within (`-66th) `-YEAR of `-EXISTING!!!~'

AMERICAN RADIO PERSONALITY CARL RAY KASELL `-DIED on *APRIL 17th* within `-*2018*!!!~' `-HE was `-BORN on *APRIL 2nd* in `-*1934*!!!~' `-HE `-DIED at the `-AGE of (`-84)!!!~'

`-DEATH/DAY = (4/17) = "FLIP EVERY (`-7) OVER to a (`-2)" = (4/12) = (42 x 1) = (`-42) = (4/2) = `-BIRTH/DAY = (APRIL 2nd)!!!~'

`-**BIRTH/YEAR** = (`-**34**) = "FLIP EVERY (`-**3**) OVER to an (`-**8**)" = (`-**84**) = "**AGE of** `-**DEATH for AMERICAN RADIO PERSONALITY CARL RAY KASELL (`-84)**"!!!~'

AMERICAN RADIO PERSONALITY CARL RAY KASELL `-BIRTHDAY # = `-EQUALS = (4 + 2 + 19 + 34) = (`-**59**) = `-**DEATH/ DAY #** `-**NUMBER** (`-**59**)!!!~'

AMERICAN RADIO PERSONALITY CARL RAY KASELL `-DEATH/ DAY # = `-EQUALS = (4 + 17 + 20 + 18) = (`-**59**) = `-**BIRTH/DAY #** `-**NUMBER** (`-**59**)!!!~'

AMERICAN AUTHOR & JOURNALIST TOM WOLFE `-DIED on *MAY 14*[th] within `-*2018*!!!~' `-HE was `-BORN on *MARCH 2*[nd] in `-*1930*!!!~' `-HE `-DIED at the `-AGE of (`-**88**)!!!~'

`-**BIRTH/DAY** = (**3/2**) = "FLIP EVERY (`-**3**) OVER to an (`-**8**)" = (`-**82**) = RECIPROCAL = (`-**28**) = 2(8's) = (`-**88**) = "**AGE of** `-**DEATH for AMERICAN AUTHOR & JOURNALIST TOM WOLFE (`-88)**!!!~'

`-**BIRTH/DAY** = (**3/2**) = "FLIP EVERY (`-**3**) OVER to an (`-**8**)" = (`-**82**) = RECIPROCAL = (`-**28**) = `-**DIED within** (`-**2018**)!!!~'

AMERICAN AUTHOR & JOURNALIST TOM WOLFE `-**BIRTHDAY #** `-**NUMBER** = `-EQUALS = (3 + 2 + 19 + 30) = (`-**54**) = `-**DEATH/ DAY** = (**5/14**) = (54 x 1) = (`-**54**)!!!~'

AMERICAN AUTHOR & JOURNALIST TOM WOLFE `-**DEATH/DAY #** `-**NUMBER** = `-EQUALS = (5 + 14 + 20 + 18) = (`-**57**)!!!~'

(54 + 57) = (`-**111**) = (-) **MINUS** (-) = "**AGE of** `-**DEATH**" (`-**88**) = (`-**23**) = RECIPROCAL = (`-**32**) = (**3/2**) = `-**BIRTH/DAY** = (**MARCH 2**[nd])!!!~'

`-**BIRTH/YEAR** = (`-**1930**) = (1 (-) 9) (3 + 0) = (`-**83**) = "FLIP EVERY (`-**3**) OVER to an (`-**8**)" = (`-**88**) = "**AGE of `-DEATH for AMERICAN AUTHOR & JOURNALIST TOM WOLFE (`-88)**!!!~'

AMERICAN CHEF ANTHONY BOURDAIN `-DIED on *JUNE 8th* within `-**2018**!!!~' `-HE was `-BORN on *JUNE 25th* in `-**1956**!!!~' `-HE `-DIED at the `-AGE of (`-**61**)!!!~'

`-**BIRTH/DAY** = (**6/25**) = (6) (2 + 5) = (`-**67**) = (**6/7**) = "**DIED** the `-**VERY** `-**NEXT** `-**DAY** on (`-**6/8**)" = (**JUNE** 8th)!!!~'

`-**DEATH/YEAR** = (`-**2018**) = (2 (-) 8) (0 + 1) = (`-**61**) = "**AGE of `-DEATH for AMERICAN CHEF ANTHONY BOURDAIN (`-61)**!!!~'

AMERICAN CHEF ANTHONY BOURDAIN `-**BIRTHDAY** # `-**NUMBER** = `-EQUALS = (6 + 25 + 19 + 56) = (`-**106**) = (16 + 0) = (`-**16**) = RECIPROCAL = (`-**61**) = "**AGE of `-DEATH for AMERICAN CHEF ANTHONY BOURDAIN (`-61)**!!!~'

AMERICAN CHEF ANTHONY BOURDAIN `-**DEATH/DAY** # `-**NUMBER** = `-EQUALS = (6 + 8 + 20 + 18) = (`-**52**) = RECIPROCAL = (`-**25**) = "**DAY** of `-**BIRTH**" = (`-**25th**)!!!~'

AMERICAN CHEF ANTHONY BOURDAIN `-**DEATH/DAY** # `-**NUMBER** = `-EQUALS = (6 + 8 + 20 + 18) = (`-**52**) = `-**BIRTH/ YEAR** = (`-**1956**) = (19 + 56) = (`-**75**) = "FLIP EVERY (`-**7**) OVER to a (`-**2**)" = (`-**25**) = RECIPROCAL = (`-**52**)!!!~'

CONSERVATIVE JOURNALIST IRVING CHARLES KRAUTHAMMER `-DIED on *JUNE 21st* within `-**2018**!!!~' `-HE was `-BORN on *MARCH 13th* in `-**1950**!!!~' `-HE `-DIED at the `-AGE of (`-**68**)!!!~'

DWAYNE W. ANDERSON

`-BIRTH/YEAR = (`-1950) = (19 + 50) = (`-69) = "ONE `-YEAR `-AWAY (`-69) from `-AGE of `-DEATH (`-68)"!!!~'

`-DEATH/DAY = (6/21) = "FLIP EVERY (`-2) OVER to a (`-7)" = (6/71) = (6) (7 + 1) = (`-68) = "AGE of `-DEATH for CONSERVATIVE JOURNALIST IRVING CHARLES KRAUTHAMMER (`-68)"!!!~'

`-DEATH/DAY = (6/21) = (6) (2 + 1) = (`-63) = "FLIP EVERY (`-3) OVER to an (`-8)" = (`-68) = "AGE of `-DEATH for CONSERVATIVE JOURNALIST IRVING CHARLES KRAUTHAMMER (`-68)"!!!~'

CONSERVATIVE JOURNALIST IRVING CHARLES KRAUTHAMMER `-BIRTHDAY # `-NUMBER = `-EQUALS = (3 + 13 + 19 + 50) = (`-85)!!!~'

CONSERVATIVE JOURNALIST IRVING CHARLES KRAUTHAMMER `-DEATH/DAY # `-NUMBER = `-EQUALS = (6 + 21 + 20 + 18) = (`-65)!!!~'

(85 + 65) = (`-150) = (50 x 1) = (`-50) = `-BIRTH/YEAR = (`-50)!!!~'

(85/65) = (`-86) (5 (-) 5) = (86 + 0) = (`-86) = RECIPROCAL = (`-68) = "AGE of `-DEATH for CONSERVATIVE JOURNALIST IRVING CHARLES KRAUTHAMMER (`-68)"!!!~'

CONSERVATIVE JOURNALIST IRVING CHARLES KRAUTHAMMER had `-DIED (`-100) `-DAYS after `-HIS `-LAST `-BIRTHDAY!!!~'

(365 (-) 100) = (`-265) = (65 + 2) = (`-67) = "ONE `-YEAR `-AWAY (`-67) from `-AGE of `-DEATH (`-68)"!!!~'

`-BIRTH/DAY = (3/13) = (3 x 13) = (`-39) = "FLIP EVERY (`-3) OVER to an (`-8)" = (`-89) = "FLIP EVERY (`-9) OVER to a (`-6)" = (`-86) = RECIPROCAL = (`-68) = "AGE of `-DEATH for CONSERVATIVE JOURNALIST IRVING CHARLES KRAUTHAMMER (`-68)"!!!~'

`-DEATH/YEAR** = (`-2018**) = RECIPROCAL = (`-**8102**) = (81) (-) (02) = (`-**79**) = (7 x 9) = (`-**63**) = "FLIP EVERY (`-**3**) OVER to an (`-**8**)" = (`-**68**) = "**AGE of `-DEATH for CONSERVATIVE JOURNALIST IRVING CHARLES KRAUTHAMMER (`-68)**"!!!~'

VINNIE PAUL DRUMMER of PANTERA `-DIED on *JUNE **22**nd* within `-*2018*!!!~' `-HE was `-BORN on *MARCH **11**th* in `-*1964*!!!~' `-HE `-DIED at the `-AGE of (`-**54**)!!!~'

`-BIRTH/YEAR** = (`-1964**) = (64 (-) 19) = (`-**45**) = RECIPROCAL = (`-**54**) = "**AGE of `-DEATH for VINNIE PAUL DRUMMER of PANTERA (`-54)**"!!!~'

VINNIE PAUL DRUMMER of PANTERA `-BIRTHDAY # = `-EQUALS = (3 + 11 + 19 + 64) = (`-**97**) = **`-DEATH/DAY** = (**6/22**) = "FLIP EVERY (`-**6**) OVER to a (`-**9**)" & "FLIP EVERY (`-**2**) OVER to a (`-**7**)" = (**9/77**)!!!~'

VINNIE PAUL DRUMMER of PANTERA `-DEATH/DAY # = `-EQUALS = (6 + 22 + 20 + 18) = (`-**66**) / **`-DIVIDED `-by** (`-**2**) = (`-**33**) = **`-BIRTH/DAY** = (**3/11**) = (3 x 11) = (`-**33**)!!!~'

RADIO DISC JOCKEY DAN INGRAM (DANIEL TROMBLEY INGRAM) `-DIED on *JUNE **24**th* within `-*2018*!!!~' `-HE was `-BORN on *SEPTEMBER **7**th* in `-*1934*!!!~' `-HE `-DIED at the `-AGE of (`-**83**)!!!~'

`-DEATH/DAY** = (**6/24**) = "FLIP EVERY (`-6**) OVER to a (`-**9**)" = (**9/24**) = (9) (2 + 4) = (`-**96**) = **`-BORN the `-VERY `-NEXT `-DAY** on (`-**9/7**) = (**SEPTEMBER 7**th)!!!~'

`-BIRTH/YEAR** = (`-34**) = **`-TIMES "X"** (`-**2**) = (`-**68**) = **`-DEATH/DAY # `-NUMBER** (`-**68**)!!!~'

`-**BIRTH/YEAR** = (`-**34**) = "FLIP EVERY (`-**3**) OVER to an (`-**8**)" = (`-**84**) = "ONE `-YEAR `-AWAY (`-**84**) from `-AGE of `-DEATH (`-**83**)"!!!~'

`-**DEATH/DAY** = (**6/24**) = (6) (2 + 4) = (`-**66**) = "FLIP EVERY (`-**6**) OVER to a (`-**9**)" = (`-**69**) = `-**BIRTH/DAY** # `-**NUMBER** (`-**69**)!!!~'

RADIO DISC JOCKEY DAN INGRAM `-**BIRTHDAY** # `-**NUMBER** = `-EQUALS = (9 + 7 + 19 + 34) = (`-**69**) = RECIPROCAL = (`-**96**) = `-**BORN** on (`-**97**)!!!~'

RADIO DISC JOCKEY DAN INGRAM `-**DEATH/DAY** # `-**NUMBER** = `-EQUALS = (6 + 24 + 20 + 18) = (`-**68**) = `-**DIED** on (**6/24**) = (6) (2 x 4) = (`-**68**)!!!~'

(69 + 68) = (`-**137**) = (1 + 7) (3) = (`-**83**) = "**AGE of `-DEATH for RADIO DISC JOCKEY DAN INGRAM (DANIEL TROMBLEY INGRAM) (`-83**)"!!!~'

`-DEATH/YEAR = (`-**2018**) = RECIPROCAL = (`-**8102**) = (81) + (02) = (`-**83**) = "**AGE of `-DEATH for RADIO DISC JOCKEY DAN INGRAM (DANIEL TROMBLEY INGRAM) (`-83**)"!!!~'

CHOREOGRAPHER GILLIAN BARBARA LYNNE "CATS" & "PHANTOM of the OPERA" `-DIED on *JULY 1ˢᵗ* within `-*2018*!!!~' `-SHE was `-BORN on *FEBRUARY 20ᵗʰ* in `-*1926*!!!~' `-SHE `-DIED at the `-AGE of (`-**92**)!!!~'

`-**AGE** of `-**DEATH** = (`-**92**) = (9 x 2) = (`-**18**) = `-**DIED within the `-YEAR of (`-18**)!!!~'

`-**DEATH/YEAR** = (`-**2018**) = RECIPROCAL = (`-**8102**) = (8 + 1) (0 + 2) = (`-**92**) = "**AGE of `-DEATH for CHOREOGRAPHER GILLIAN BARBARA LYNNE "CATS" & "PHANTOM of the OPERA" (`-92**)"!!!~'

`-**BIRTH/YEAR** = (`-**26**) = RECIPROCAL = (`-**62**) = "FLIP EVERY (`-**6**) OVER to a (`-**9**)" = (`-**92**) = "**AGE of `-DEATH for CHOREOGRAPHER GILLIAN BARBARA LYNNE "CATS" & "PHANTOM of the OPERA" (`-92**)"!!!~'

`-**BIRTHYEAR** = (`-**1926**) = (1 + 9 + 6) (2) = (16) (2) = (1 x 6) (2) = (`-**62**) = "FLIP EVERY (`-**6**) OVER to a (`-**9**)" = (`-**92**) = "**AGE of `-DEATH for CHOREOGRAPHER GILLIAN BARBARA LYNNE "CATS" & "PHANTOM of the OPERA" (`-92**)"!!!~'

`-**BIRTH/DAY** = (**2/20**) = "FLIP EVERY (`-**2**) OVER to a (`-**7**)" = (**7/70**) = (7 + 70) = (`-**77**) = (`-**7**) / `-**DIVIDED** `-**by** / (`-**7**) = (`-**1**) = `-**DEATH/ DAY** = (`-**7/1**) = (**JULY 1**ˢᵗ)!!!~'

CHOREOGRAPHER GILLIAN BARBARA LYNNE "CATS" & "PHANTOM of the OPERA" `-**BIRTHDAY # `-NUMBER** = `-EQUALS = (2 + 20 + 19 + 26) = (`-**67**) = "FLIP EVERY (`-**6**) OVER to a (`-**9**)" = (`-**97**) = "FLIP EVERY (`-**7**) OVER to a (`-**2**)" = (`-**92**) = "**AGE of `-DEATH for CHOREOGRAPHER GILLIAN BARBARA LYNNE "CATS" & "PHANTOM of the OPERA" (`-92**)"!!!~'

CHOREOGRAPHER GILLIAN BARBARA LYNNE "CATS" & "PHANTOM of the OPERA" `-**DEATH/DAY # `-NUMBER** = `-EQUALS = (7 + 1 + 20 + 18) = (`-**46**) = RECIPROCAL = (`-**64**) = "FLIP EVERY (`-**6**) OVER to a (`-**9**)" = (`-**94**) = "**TWO `-YEARS `-AWAY (`-94) from `-AGE of `-DEATH (`-92**)"!!!~'

(67 (-) 46) = (`-**21**) = "FLIP EVERY (`-**2**) OVER to a (`-**7**)" = (`-**71**) = `-**DEATH/DAY (`-7/1**) = (**JULY 1**ˢᵗ)!!!~'

ACTOR TAB HUNTER `-DIED on *JULY 8ᵗʰ* within `-**2018**!!!!!~' `-HE was `-BORN on *JULY 11ᵗʰ* in `-**1931**!!!!!~' `-HE `-DIED at the `-AGE of (`-**86**)!!!!!~'

`-**BIRTH/DAY** = (**7/11**) = (7 x 11) = (`-**77**) = `-**DIED** the `-**VERY `-NEXT `-DAY** on (`-**7/8**) = (**JULY 8**ᵗʰ)!!!~'

`-**DEATH/DAY** = (**7/8**) = RECIPROCAL = (**8/7**) = `-**DIED** (`-**3**) `-**DAYS** `-**SHY of** `-**TURNING** (`-**87**) `-**YEARS of** `-**AGE**!!!~`

ACTOR TAB HUNTER `-**BIRTHDAY #** `-**NUMBER** = `-EQUALS = (7 + 11 + 19 + 31) = `-**68**) = RECIPROCAL = (`-**86**) = "**AGE of** `-**DEATH for ACTOR TAB HUNTER (`-86)**"!!!~`

ACTOR TAB HUNTER `-**DEATH/DAY #** `-**NUMBER** = `-EQUALS = (7 + 8 + 20 + 18) = `-**53**) = RECIPROCAL = (`-**35**) = "FLIP EVERY (`-**3**) OVER to an (`-**8**)" = (`-**85**) = "**ONE `-YEAR `-AWAY (`-85) from** `-**AGE of** `-**DEATH (`-86)**"!!!~`

ACTOR **TAB HUNTER** had `-**DIED** (`-**3**) `-**DAYS before** `-**HIS** `-**NEXT** `-**BIRTHDAY**!!!~`

(365 (-) 3) = (`-**362**) = (3 x 62) = (`-**186**) = (86 x 1) = (`-**86**) = "**AGE of** `-**DEATH for ACTOR TAB HUNTER (`-86)**"!!!~`

`-**DEATH/YEAR** = (`-**2018**) = RECIPROCAL = (`-**8102**) = "FLIP EVERY (`-**2**) OVER to a (`-**7**)" = (`-**8107**) = (8 + 0) (1 (-) 7) = (`-**86**) = "**AGE of** `-**DEATH for ACTOR TAB HUNTER (`-86)**"!!!~`

`-**BIRTH/YEAR** = (`-**1931**) = "FLIP EVERY (`-**3**) OVER to an (`-**8**)" = (`-**1981**) = "FLIP EVERY (`-**9**) OVER to a (`-**6**)" = (`-**1681**) = RECIPROCAL = (`-**1861**) = (1 x 8) (6 x 1) = (`-**86**) = "**AGE of** `-**DEATH for ACTOR TAB HUNTER (`-86)**"!!!~`

ADRIAN CRONAUER "INSPIRATION FOR THE MOVIE "GOOD MORNING VIETNAM"" `-DIED on *JULY 18th* within `-*2018*!!!!!~` `-HE was `-BORN on *SEPTEMBER 8th* in `-*1938*!!!!!~` `-HE `-DIED at the `-AGE of (`-**79**)!!!!!~`

`-**DEATH/DAY** = (**7/18**) = RECIPROCAL = (**81/7**) = (8 + 1) (7) = (**9/7**) = `-**BORN the** `-**VERY** `-**NEXT** `-**DAY on** (`-**9/8**) = (**SEPTEMBER 8**th)!!!~`

`-**DEATH/DAY** = (**7/18**) = (7) (1 + 8) = (`-**79**) = "AGE of `-DEATH for ADRIAN CRONAUER "INSPIRATION FOR THE MOVIE "GOOD MORNING VIETNAM"" (`-**79**)"!!!~'

`-**DEATH/YEAR** = (`-**2018**) = "FLIP EVERY (`-**2**) OVER to a (`-**7**)" = (`-**7018**) = (7 + 0) (1 + 8) = (`-**79**) = "AGE of `-DEATH for ADRIAN CRONAUER "INSPIRATION FOR THE MOVIE "GOOD MORNING VIETNAM"" (`-**79**)"!!!~'

`-**BIRTH/YEAR** = (`-**1938**) = (9 + 3) (1 + 8) = (12) (9) = (1 x 2) (9) = (`-**29**) = "FLIP EVERY (`-**2**) OVER to a (`-**7**)" = (`-**79**) = "AGE of `-DEATH for ADRIAN CRONAUER "INSPIRATION FOR THE MOVIE "GOOD MORNING VIETNAM"" (`-**79**)"!!!~'

ADRIAN CRONAUER "INSPIRATION FOR THE MOVIE "GOOD MORNING VIETNAM"" `-BIRTHDAY # `-NUMBER = `-EQUALS = (9 + 8 + 19 + 38) = (`-**74**) = `-**DEATH/DAY** = (**7/18**) = "FLIP EVERY (`-**8**) OVER to a (`-**3**)" = (**7/13**) = (7) (1 + 3) = (`-**74**)!!!~'

ADRIAN CRONAUER "INSPIRATION FOR THE MOVIE "GOOD MORNING VIETNAM"" `-DEATH/DAY # `-NUMBER = `-EQUALS = (7 + 18 + 20 + 18) = (`-**63**) = (7 x 9) = (`-**79**) = "AGE of `-DEATH for ADRIAN CRONAUER "INSPIRATION FOR THE MOVIE "GOOD MORNING VIETNAM"" (`-**79**)"!!!~'

ADRIAN CRONAUER "INSPIRATION FOR THE MOVIE "GOOD MORNING VIETNAM"" `-DEATH/DAY # `-NUMBER = `-EQUALS = (7 + 18 + 20 + 18) = (`-**63**) = (7 x 9) = (`-**79**) = `-**DEATH/DAY** = (**7/18**) = (7) (1 + 8) = (`-**79**)!!!~'

(74 + 63) = (`-**137**) = RECIPROCAL = (`-**731**) = "FLIP EVERY (`-**3**) OVER to an (`-**8**)" = (`-**781**) = (7) (8 + 1) = (`-**79**) = "AGE of `-DEATH for ADRIAN CRONAUER "INSPIRATION FOR THE MOVIE "GOOD MORNING VIETNAM"" (`-**79**)"!!!~'

RICK GENEST "ZOMBIE BOY" `-DIED on **AUGUST 1**<sup>st</sup> within `-**2018**!!!~' `-HE was `-BORN on **AUGUST 7**th in `-**1985**!!!~' `-HE `-DIED at the `-AGE of (`-**32**)!!!~'

`-**AGE** of `-**DEATH** = (`-**32**) = "FLIP EVERY (`-**3**) OVER to an (`-**8**)" = (`-**82**) = "FLIP EVERY (`-**2**) OVER to a (`-**7**)" = (`-**87**) = `-**BIRTH/ DAY** = (**8/7**) = (**AUGUST 7**th)!!!~'

`-**AGE** of `-**DEATH** = (`-**32**) = "FLIP EVERY (`-**3**) OVER to an (`-**8**)" = (`-**82**) = RECIPROCAL = (`-**28**) = `-**DIED** within (`-**2018**)!!!~'

`-**AGE** of `-**DEATH** = (`-**32**) = "FLIP EVERY (`-**3**) OVER to an (`-**8**)" = (`-**82**) = RECIPROCAL = (`-**28**) = 2(8's) = (`-**88**) = `-**BORN; and,** `-**DIED** in the `-**MONTH** of (`-**8**)!!!~'

`-**DEATH/DAY** = (`-**8/1**) = RECIPROCAL = (`-**18**) = `-**DIED in the** `-**YEAR** of (`-**18**)!!!~'

`-**DEATH/YEAR** = (`-**2018**) = (20 + 18) = (`-**38**) = `-**BIRTH/YEAR** = (`-**1985**) = (1 (-) 9) (8 (-) 5) = (`-**83**) = RECIPROCAL = (`-**38**)!!!~'

STAN MIKITA "ICE HOCKEY PLAYER" `-DIED on **AUGUST 7**<sup>th</sup> within `-**2018**!!!~' `-HE was `-BORN on **MAY 20**th in `-**1940**!!!~' `-HE `-DIED at the `-AGE of (`-**78**)!!!~'

`-**DEATH/DAY** = (**8/7**) = RECIPROCAL = (**7/8**) = (`-**78**) = **"AGE of** `-**DEATH for STAN MIKITA "ICE HOCKEY PLAYER" (`-78)"**!!!~'

`-**DEATH/YEAR** = (`-**2018**) = "FLIP EVERY (`-**2**) OVER to a (`-**7**)" = (`-**7018**) = (7 x 1) (0 + 8) = (`-**78**) = **"AGE of `-DEATH for STAN MIKITA "ICE HOCKEY PLAYER" (`-78)"**!!!~'

STAN MIKITA "ICE HOCKEY PLAYER" `-**BIRTHDAY #** `-**NUMBER** = `-**EQUALS** = (5 + 20 + 19 + 40) = (`-**84**)!!!~'

STAN MIKITA "ICE HOCKEY PLAYER" `-DEATH/DAY # `-NUMBER
= `-EQUALS = (8 + 7 + 20 + 18) = (`-**53**)!!!~'

(84 + 53) = (`-**137**) = RECIPROCAL = (`-**731**) = "FLIP EVERY (`-**3**)
OVER to an (`-**8**)" = (`-**781**) = (78 x 1) = (`-**78**) = "AGE of `-DEATH
for STAN MIKITA "ICE HOCKEY PLAYER" (`-**78**)"!!!~'

STAN MIKITA "ICE HOCKEY PLAYER" had `-**DIED** (`-**79**) `-DAYS
after `-HIS `-LAST `-BIRTHDAY!!!~'

`-**DEATH/YEAR** = (`-**2018**) = (20 + 18) = (`-**38**)!!!~'

`-**BIRTH/YEAR** = (`-**1940**) = (19 + 40) = (`-**59**)!!!~'

(38 + 59) = (`-**97**) = RECIPROCAL = (`-**79**)!!!~'

(365 (-) 79) = (`-**286**) = RECIPROCAL = (`-**682**) = (82 (-) 6) = (`-**76**) =
"FLIP EVERY (`-**6**) OVER to a (`-**9**)" = (`-**79**)!!!~'

`-**AGE** of `-**DEATH** = (`-**78**) = DAYS (LIE-IN-BETWEEN) = `-HIS
`-**BIRTHDAY** & `-HIS `-**DEATH/DAY**!!!~'

WRESTLER BRIAN CHRISTOPHER LAWLER `-DIED on *JULY 29th*
within `-*2018*!!!~' `-HE was `-BORN on *JANUARY 10th* in `-*1972*!!!~'
`-HE `-DIED at the `-AGE of (`-**46**)!!!~'

`-**DEATH/DAY** = (`-**7/29**) = RECIPROCAL = (`-**92/7**) = "**SWIPE**
`-**ONE (`-1)**" = `-**BIRTH/YEAR** = (`-1**972**)!!!~'

`-**DAY** of `-**DEATH** = (`-**29**) = (2 + 9) = (`-**11**) = `-**BIRTH/DAY** = (**1/10**)
= (1 + 10) = (`-**11**)!!!~'

`-**DAY** of `-**DEATH** = (`-**29**) = RECIPROCAL = (`-**92**) / `-DIVIDED
`-by / (`-**2**) = (`-**46**) = "AGE of `-DEATH for WRESTLER BRIAN
CHRISTOPHER LAWLER (`-**46**)"!!!~'

`-**BIRTH/YEAR** = (`-**72**) = `-**DEATH/DAY** (**72**(9))**!!!~'**

`-**BIRTH/YEAR** = (`-**72**) = `-**DEATH/YEAR** = (`-**2018**) = RECIPROCAL = (`-**8102**) = (8 (-) 1) (0 + 2) = (`-**72**) = `-**BIRTH/YEAR** (`-**72**)**!!!~'**

`-**DEATH/YEAR** = (`-**2018**) = RECIPROCAL = (`-**8102**) = (8 + 1) (0 + 2) = (`-**92**) / `-**DIVIDED** `-**by** / (`-**2**) = (`-**46**) = "**AGE of** `-**DEATH for WRESTLER BRIAN CHRISTOPHER LAWLER (`-46)**"**!!!~'**

WRESTLER BRIAN CHRISTOPHER LAWLER `-**BIRTHDAY #** `-**NUMBER** = `-**EQUALS** = (1 + 10 + 19 + 72) = (`-**102**)**!!!~'**

WRESTLER BRIAN CHRISTOPHER LAWLER `-**DEATH/DAY #** `-**NUMBER** = `-**EQUALS** = (7 + 29 + 20 + 18) = (`-**74**)**!!!~'**

(102 + 74) = (`-**176**) = (76 + 1) = (`-**77**) = `-**DEATH/DAY** = (**7/29**) = (7) (2 (-) 9) = (`-**77**)**!!!~'**

(102 (-) 74) = (`-**28**) = `-**DIED** within the `-**YEAR** of (`-**2018**)**!!!~'**

WRESTLER BRIAN CHRISTOPHER LAWLER had `-DIED (`-**200**) `-DAYS after `-HIS `-LAST `-BIRTHDAY!!!~'

(365 (-) 200) = (`-**165**) = RECIPROCAL = (`-**561**) = (5 (-) 1) (6) = (`-**46**) = "**AGE of** `-**DEATH for WRESTLER BRIAN CHRISTOPHER LAWLER (`-46)**"**!!!~'**

WRESTLER NIKOLAI VOLKOFF `-DIED on *JULY 29th* within `-*2018*!!!~' `-HE was `-BORN on *OCTOBER 14th* in `-*1947*!!!~' `-HE `-DIED at the `-AGE of (`-**70**)!!!~'

`-**BIRTH/YEAR** = (`-**1947**) = (47 (-) 19) = (`-**28**) = `-**DIED** within the `-**YEAR** of (`-**2018**)**!!!~'**

`-**DEATH/DAY** = (**7/29**) (+) `-**BIRTH/DAY** = (**10/14**) = (7 + 29 + 10 + 14) = (`-**60**) = "FLIP EVERY (`-**6**) OVER to a (`-**9**)" = (`-**90**)**!!!~'**

WRESTLER NIKOLAI VOLKOFF `-**BIRTHDAY** # `-**NUMBER** =
`-**EQUALS** = (10 + 14 + 19 + 47) = (`-**90**)!!!~'

WRESTLER NIKOLAI VOLKOFF `-**DEATH/DAY** # `-**NUMBER** =
`-**EQUALS** = (7 + 29 + 20 + 18) = (`-**74**) = RECIPROCAL = (`-**47**) =
`-**BIRTH/YEAR** = (`-**47**)!!!~'

(90 + 74) = (`-**164**) = (1 + 6) (4) = (`-**74**) = RECIPROCAL = (`-**47**) =
`-**BIRTH/YEAR** = (`-**47**)!!!~'

"LIFESTYLES of the RICH & FAMOUS" HOST ROBIN LEACH
`-DIED on **AUGUST 24**th within `-**2018**!!!~' `-HE was `-BORN on
AUGUST 29th in `-**1941**!!!~' `-HE `-DIED at the `-AGE of (`-**76**)!!!~'

`-**BIRTH/DAY** = (**8/29**) = RECIPROCAL = (`-**92/8**) = (9 (-) 2) (8) =
(`-**78**) = "TWO `-YEARS `-AWAY (`-**78**) from `-AGE of `-DEATH
(`-**76**)"!!!~'

`-**BIRTH/YEAR** = (`-**1941**) = (9 (-) 1 (-) 1) (4) = (`-**74**) = "TWO `-YEARS
`-AWAY (`-**74**) from `-AGE of `-DEATH (`-**76**)"!!!~'

`-**DEATH/YEAR** = (`-**2018**) = "FLIP EVERY (`-**2**) OVER to a (`-**7**)"
= (`-**7018**) = (7 + 0) (1 (-) 8) = (`-**77**) = "ONE `-YEAR `-AWAY (`-**77**)
from `-AGE of `-DEATH (`-**76**)"!!!~'

`-**BIRTH/DAY** = (**8/29**) = RECIPROCAL = (**92/8**) = (92 (-) 8) = (`-**84**)
= `-**DEATH/DAY** = (`-**8**(2)**4**)!!!~'

`-**DEATH/DAY** = (**8/24**) = (8) (2 x 4) = (`-**88**) = `-**BIRTH/DAY** = (**8/29**)
= (8) (2 x 9) = (`-**8/18**) = (88 x 1) = (`-**88**)!!!~'

`-**DEATH/DAY** = (**8/24**) = (8) (2 x 4) = (`-**88**) = `-**BIRTH/DAY** = (**8/29**)
= (8) (2 + 9) = (`-**8/11**) = (8 x 11) = (`-**88**)!!!~'

`-**DAY** of `-**BIRTH** = (`-**29**th) = "FLIP EVERY (`-**2**) OVER to a (`-**7**)"
= (`-**79**) = "FLIP EVERY (`-**9**) OVER to a (`-**6**)" = (`-**76**) = "AGE

of `-DEATH for "LIFESTYLES of the RICH & FAMOUS" HOST ROBIN LEACH (`-**76**)"!!!~'

`-**DEATH/DAY** = (**8/24**) = (8 x 24) = (`-**192**) = RECIPROCAL = (`-**291**) = "FLIP EVERY (`-**2**) OVER to a (`-**7**)" = (`-**791**) = "FLIP EVERY (`-**9**) OVER to a (`-**6**)" = (`-**761**) = (76 x 1) = (`-**76**) = "AGE of `-DEATH for "LIFESTYLES of the RICH & FAMOUS" HOST ROBIN LEACH (`-**76**)"!!!~'

"LIFESTYLES of the RICH & FAMOUS" HOST ROBIN LEACH `-**BIRTHDAY # `-NUMBER** = `-EQUALS = (8 + 29 + 19 + 41) = (`-**97**) = RECIPROCAL = (`-**79**) = "FLIP EVERY (`-**9**) OVER to a (`-**6**)" = (`-**76**) = "AGE of `-DEATH for "LIFESTYLES of the RICH & FAMOUS" HOST ROBIN LEACH (`-**76**)"!!!~'

"LIFESTYLES of the RICH & FAMOUS" HOST ROBIN LEACH `-**DEATH/DAY # `-NUMBER** = `-EQUALS = (8 + 24 + 20 + 18) = (`-**70**)!!!~'

(97 + 70) = (`-**167**) = RECIPROCAL = (`-**761**) = (76 x 1) = (`-**76**) = "AGE of `-DEATH for "LIFESTYLES of the RICH & FAMOUS" HOST ROBIN LEACH (`-**76**)"!!!~'

SENATOR JOHN MCCAIN `-DIED on *AUGUST 25th* within `-*2018*!!!~' `-HE was `-BORN on *AUGUST 29th* in `-*1936*!!!~' `-HE `-DIED at the `-AGE of (`-**81**)!!!~'

`-**BIRTH/DAY** = (**8/29**) = (8) (2 (-) 9) = (`-**87**) = `-**DEATH/DAY** = (**8/25**) = (8) (2 + 5) = (`-**87**)!!!~'

`-**DEATH/YEAR** = (`-**18**) = RECIPROCAL = (`-**81**) = "AGE of `-DEATH for SENATOR JOHN MCCAIN (`-**81**)"!!!~'

`-**DEATH/YEAR** = (`-**2018**) = RECIPROCAL = (`-**8102**) = (82 (-) 01) = (`-**81**) = "AGE of `-DEATH for SENATOR JOHN MCCAIN (`-**81**)"!!!~'

"DAY of `-BIRTH"** = (`-29th) = (2 x 9) = (`-**18**) = RECIPROCAL = (`-81**) = **"AGE of `-DEATH for SENATOR JOHN MCCAIN (`-81)"**!!!~'

`-**BIRTH/YEAR** = (`-**36**) = (3 x 6) = (`-**18**) = RECIPROCAL = (`-**81**) = **"AGE of `-DEATH for SENATOR JOHN MCCAIN (`-81)"**!!!~'

SENATOR JOHN MCCAIN `-**BIRTHDAY # `-NUMBER** = `-EQUALS = (8 + 29 + 19 + 36) = (`-**92**) = RECIPROCAL = (`-**29**) = **"DAY of `-BIRTH"** = (`-**29**th)!!!~'

`-**BIRTH/DAY** = (**8/29**) (+) `-**DEATH/DAY** = (**8/25**) = (8 + 29 + 8 + 25) = (`-**70**)!!!~'

SENATOR JOHN MCCAIN `-**DEATH/DAY # `-NUMBER** = `-EQUALS = (8 + 25 + 20 + 18) = (`-**71**) = (7 + 1) = (`-**8**) = `-**BORN** & `-**DIED** in the `-**MONTH** of (`-**8**)!!!~'

(**8** / `-**DIVIDED** `-by / **8** = (`-**1**) = (`-**81**) = **"AGE of `-DEATH for SENATOR JOHN MCCAIN (`-81)"**!!!~'

SENATOR JOHN MCCAIN had `-DIED (`-**4**) `-DAYS before `-HIS `-NEXT `-BIRTHDAY!!!!!~'

(365 (-) 4) = (`-**361**) = (3 x 6 x 1) = (`-**18**) = RECIPROCAL = (`-**81**) = **"AGE of `-DEATH for SENATOR JOHN MCCAIN (`-81)"**!!!~'

AMERICAN PLAYWRIGHT NEIL SIMON `-DIED on *AUGUST 26<sup>th</sup>* within `-*2018*!!!~' `-HE was `-BORN on *JULY 4th* in `-*1927*!!!~' `-HE `-DIED at the `-AGE of (`-**91**)!!!~'

`-**BIRTH/DAY** = (**7/4**) = RECIPROCAL = (`-**4/7**)!!!~'

`-**DEATH/DAY** = (**8/26**) = RECIPROCAL = (**62/8**) = (6 (-) 2) (8) = (`-**4/8**)!!!~'

`-**DEATH/YEAR** = (`-**2018**) = (2 (-) 8) (0 + 1) = (`-**61**) = "FLIP EVERY (`-**6**) OVER to a (`-**9**)" = (`-**91**) = **"AGE of `-DEATH for AMERICAN PLAYWRIGHT NEIL SIMON (`-91)"!!!~**'

`-**BIRTH/YEAR** = (`-**1927**) = (1 + 9) (2 + 7) = (10) (9) = RECIPROCAL = (9) (10) = (91 + 0) = (`-**91**) = **"AGE of `-DEATH for AMERICAN PLAYWRIGHT NEIL SIMON (`-91)"!!!~**'

AMERICAN PLAYWRIGHT NEIL SIMON `-**BIRTHDAY # `-NUMBER** = `-EQUALS = (7 + 4 + 19 + 27) = (`-**57**)!!!~'

`-**AGE** of `-**DEATH** = (`-**91**) = (-) MINUS (-) = (`-**57**) = (`-**34**)!!!~'

`-**DEATH/DAY** = (**8/26**) = (8 + 26) = (`-**34**)!!!~'

AMERICAN PLAYWRIGHT NEIL SIMON `-**DEATH/DAY # `-NUMBER** = `-EQUALS = (8 + 26 + 20 + 18) = (`-**72**) = RECIPROCAL = (`-**27**) = `-**BIRTH/YEAR** = (`-**27**)!!!~'

`-**DEATH/DAY** = (**8/26**) = (8 x 26) = (`-**208**) = `-**DIED** in the `-**YEAR** of (`-**2018**)!!!~'

`-**DEATH/DAY** = (**8/26**) = (26 (-) 8) = (`-**18**) = `-**DIED** in the **YEAR** of (`-**18**)!!!~'

`-**BIRTH/DAY** = (**7/4**) = (7 x 4) = (`-**28**) = `-**DIED** in the `-**YEAR** of (`-**2018**)!!!~'

THE TELEVISION SHOW "ER" ACTRESS VANESSA MARQUEZ `-DIED on **AUGUST 30**[th] within `-**2018**!!!~' `-SHE was `-BORN on **DECEMBER 21**[st] in `-**1968**!!!~' `-SHE `-DIED at the `-AGE of (`-**49**)!!!~'

`-**BIRTH/DAY** = (**12/21**) = "FLIP EVERY (`-**2**) OVER to a (`-**7**)" = (**17/71**) = (1 x 7) (7 x 1) = (`-**77**) = (7 x 7) = (`-**49**) = **"AGE of**

`-DEATH for THE TELEVISION SHOW "ER" ACTRESS VANESSA MARQUEZ (`-**49**)"!!!~'

`-**DEATH/DAY** = (**8/30**) = (8 + 30) = (`-**38**) = `-**DEATH/YEAR** = (`-**20/18**) = (20 + 18) = (`-**38**)!!!~'

`-**BIRTH/YEAR** = (`-**1968**) = (68 (-) 19) = (`-**49**) = "AGE of `-DEATH for THE TELEVISION SHOW "ER" ACTRESS VANESSA MARQUEZ (`-**49**)"!!!~'

`-**BIRTH/YEAR** = (`-**68**) = "FLIP EVERY (`-**6**) OVER to a (`-**9**)" = (`-**98**) / `-DIVIDED `-by / (`-**2**) = (`-**49**) = "AGE of `-DEATH for THE TELEVISION SHOW "ER" ACTRESS VANESSA MARQUEZ (`-**49**)"!!!~'

AMERICAN RAPPER MAC MILLER `-DIED on *SEPTEMBER 7th* within `-**2018**!!!~' `-HE was `-BORN on *JANUARY 19th* in `-**1992**!!!~' `-HE `-DIED at the `-AGE of (`-**26**)!!!~'

`-**BIRTH/YEAR** = (`-**1992**) = (1 (-) 9 (-) 2) (9) = (`-**69**) = "FLIP EVERY (`-**9**) OVER to a (`-**6**)" = (`-**66**) = 2(6's) = (`-**26**) = "AGE of `-DEATH for AMERICAN RAPPER MAC MILLER (`-**26**)!!!~'

`-**BIRTH/DAY** = (**1/19**) = (1 + 1) (9) = (`-**29**) = "FLIP EVERY (`-**2**) OVER to a (`-**7**)" = (`-**79**) = RECIPROCAL = (`-**97**) = `-**DEATH/DAY** = (**9/7**) = (**SEPTEMBER 7**th)!!!~'

`-**BIRTH/DAY** = (**1/19**) = (1 + 1) (9) = (`-**29**) = "FLIP EVERY (`-**9**) OVER to a (`-**6**)" = (`-**26**) = "AGE of `-DEATH for AMERICAN RAPPER MAC MILLER (`-**26**)!!!~'

`-**BIRTH/YEAR** = (`-**92**) = RECIPROCAL = (`-**29**) = "FLIP EVERY (`-**9**) OVER to a (`-**6**) = (`-**26**) = "AGE of `-DEATH for AMERICAN RAPPER MAC MILLER (`-**26**)!!!~'

`-**BIRTH/YEAR** = (`-**92**) = "FLIP EVERY (`-**2**) OVER to a (`-**7**) = (`-**97**) = `-**DEATH/DAY** = (**9/7**) = (**SEPTEMBER 7**th)!!!~'=

AMERICAN RAPPER MAC MILLER `-**BIRTHDAY # **`-**NUMBER** = `-**EQUALS** = (1 + 19 + 19 + 92) = (`-**131**) = (1 + 1) (3) = (`-**23**) = "FLIP EVERY (`-**3**) OVER to an (`-**8**)" = (`-**28**) = "**TWO `-YEARS `-AWAY (`-28) from `-AGE of `-DEATH (`-26)**"!!!~'

AMERICAN RAPPER MAC MILLER `-**DEATH/DAY # **`-**NUMBER** = `-**EQUALS** = (9 + 7 + 20 + 18) = (`-**54**) / `-**DIVIDED** `-by / (`-**2**) = (`-**27**) = "**ONE `-YEAR `-AWAY (`-27) from `-AGE of `-DEATH (`-26)**"!!!~'

`-**DEATH/YEAR** = (`-**2018**) = (2 + 0) (1 (-) 8) = (`-**27**) = "**ONE `-YEAR `-AWAY (`-27) from `-AGE of `-DEATH (`-26)**"!!!~'

`-**DEATH/YEAR** = (`-**2018**) = RECIPROCAL = (`-**8102**) = (8 + 1) (0 + 2) = (`-**92**) = "FLIP EVERY (`-**2**) OVER to a (`-**7**) = (`-**97**) = (**9/7**) = `-**DEATH/DAY** = (**SEPTEMBER 7**th)!!!~'

STAR TREK ACTRESS & ELVIS CO-STAR CELESTE YARNALL `-DIED on *OCTOBER 7<sup>th</sup>* within `-**2018**!!!~' `-SHE was `-BORN on *JULY 26th* in `-**1944**!!!~' `-SHE `-DIED at the `-AGE of (`-**74**)!!!~'

`-**BIRTH/DAY** = (**7/26**) = (7) (2 (-) 6) = (`-**74**) = "**AGE of `-DEATH for STAR TREK ACTRESS & ELVIS CO-STAR CELESTE YARNALL (`-74)**!!!~'

`-**DAY** of `-**BIRTH** = (`-**26**<sup>th</sup>) = "FLIP EVERY (`-**2**) OVER to a (`-**7**)" = (`-**76**) = "**TWO `-YEARS `-AWAY (`-76) from `-AGE of `-DEATH (`-74)**"!!!~'

`-**DEATH/DAY** = (**10/7**) = RECIPROCAL = (**7/01**) = (71 + 0) = (`-**71**)!!!~'

`-**DEATH/DAY** = (**10/7**) = `-**DIED** in the `-**MONTH** of (`-**10**); and, was `-**BORN** in the `-**MONTH** of (`-**7**)!!!~'

`-DEATH CIPHERS/CYPHERS FOR LIFE & DEATH!!!~'

`-**BIRTH/YEAR** = (`-**1944**) = (44 (-) 19) = (`-**25**) = "FLIP EVERY (`-**2**) OVER to a (`-**7**)" = (`-**75**) = "**ONE** `-**YEAR** `-**AWAY** (`-**75**) **from** `-**AGE of** `-**DEATH** (`-**74**)"!!!~'

`-**DEATH/YEAR** = (`-**2018**) = RECIPROCAL = (`-**8102**) = (8 (-) 1) (0 + 2) = (`-**72**) = "**TWO** `-**YEARS** `-**AWAY** (`-**72**) **from** `-**AGE of** `-**DEATH** (`-**74**)"!!!~'

STAR TREK ACTRESS & ELVIS CO-STAR CELESTE YARNALL had `-DIED (`-**73**) `-**DAYS** after `-**HER** `-**LAST** `-**BIRTHDAY**!!!~'

(`-**73**) = `-**BIRTH/DAY** = (**JULY 26**th) = (**7/26**) = (7) (2 + 6) = (`-**78**) = "FLIP EVERY (`-**8**) OVER to a (`-**3**)" = (`-**73**)!!!~'

(365 (-) 73) = (`-**292**) = (2 (-) 9) (2) = (`-**72**) = "**TWO** `-**YEARS** `-**AWAY** (`-**72**) **from** `-**AGE of** `-**DEATH** (`-**74**)"!!!~'

(365 (-) 73) = (`-**292**) = **R**eciprocal-**S**equencing-**N**umerology-**RSN**!!!~'

AMERICAN SINGER MARY WILSON (FOUNDING MEMBER of "THE SUPREMES") `-DIED on *FEBRUARY 8th* within `-*2021*!!!~' `-SHE was `-BORN on *MARCH 6th* in `-*1944*!!!~' `-SHE `-DIED at the `-AGE of (`-**76**)!!!~'

`-**DEATH/YEAR** = (`-**2021**) = "FLIP EVERY (`-**2**) OVER to a (`-**7**)" = (`-**7071**) = (7 + 0) (7 (-) 1) = (`-**76**) = "**AGE of** `-**DEATH for AMERICAN SINGER MARY WILSON (FOUNDING MEMBER of "THE SUPREMES")** (`-**76**)"!!!~'

`-**DEATH/DAY** = (**2/8**) = "FLIP EVERY (`-**2**) OVER to a (`-**7**)" = (`-**78**) = "**TWO** `-**YEARS** `-**AWAY** (`-**78**) **from** `-**AGE of** `-**DEATH** (`-**76**)"!!!~'

`-**BIRTH/YEAR** = (`-**1944**) = (19 + 44) = (`-**63**) = RECIPROCAL = (`-**36**) = (**3/6**) = `-**BIRTH/DAY** = (**MARCH 6**th)!!!~'

79

DWAYNE W. ANDERSON

`-BIRTH/YEAR = (`-**1944**) = (44 (-) 19) = (`-**25**) = "FLIP EVERY (`-**2**) OVER to a (`-**7**)" = (`-**75**) = "ONE `-YEAR `-AWAY (`-**75**) from `-AGE of `-DEATH (`-**76**)"!!!~'

AMERICAN SINGER MARY WILSON (FOUNDING MEMBER of "THE SUPREMES") `-**BIRTHDAY #** `-**NUMBER** = `-EQUALS = (3 + 6 + 19 + 44) = (`-**72**) = "FLIP EVERY (`-**2**) OVER to a (`-**7**)" = (`-**77**) = "ONE `-YEAR `-AWAY (`-**77**) from `-AGE of `-DEATH (`-**76**)"!!!~'

(`-**72**) = RECIPROCAL = (`-**27**) = `-**DIED** the `-**VERY** `-**NEXT** `-**DAY** on (`-**2/8**) = (**FEBRUARY 8**th)!!!~'

AMERICAN SINGER MARY WILSON (FOUNDING MEMBER of "THE SUPREMES") `-**DEATH/DAY #** `-**NUMBER** = `-EQUALS = (2 + 8 + 20 + 21) = (`-**51**) = RECIPROCAL = (`-**15**)!!!~' (51 (-) 15) = (`-**36**) = (**3/6**) = `-**BIRTH/DAY** = (**MARCH 6**th)!!!~'

(72 + 51) = (`-**123**) = "**PROPHETIC-LINEAR-PROGRESSION-PLP**"!!!~'

`-**DIED** in the `-**MONTH** of (`-**2**); and, was `-**BORN** in the `-**MONTH** of (`-**3**)!!!~'

`-**DEATH/DAY** = (**2/8**) = "FLIP EVERY (`-**8**) OVER to a (`-**3**)" = (`-**23**)!!!~'

AMERICAN SINGER MARY WILSON (FOUNDING MEMBER of "THE SUPREMES") had `-DIED (`-**26**) `-**DAYS before** `-**HER** `-**NEXT** `-**BIRTHDAY**!!!~'

(`-**26**) = "FLIP EVERY (`-**2**) OVER to a (`-**7**)" = (`-**76**) = "AGE of `-**DEATH for** AMERICAN SINGER MARY WILSON (FOUNDING MEMBER of "THE SUPREMES") (`-**76**)"!!!~'

(365 (-) 26) = (`-**339**) = (39 (-) 3) = (`-**36**) = `-**BIRTH/DAY** = (`-**3/6**) = (**MARCH 6**th) for AMERICAN SINGER MARY WILSON (FOUNDING MEMBER of "THE SUPREMES")!!!~'

AMERICAN ACTRESS CONCHATA GALEN FERRELL `-DIED on *OCTOBER 12*th within `-*2020*!!!~' `-SHE was `-BORN on *MARCH 28*th in `-*1943*!!!~' `-SHE `-DIED at the `-AGE of (`-**77**)!!!~'

`-**DEATH/YEAR** = (`-**2020**) = "FLIP EVERY (`-**2**) OVER to a (`-**7**)" = (`-**7070**) = (7 + 0) (7 + 0) = (`-**77**) = "AGE of `-DEATH for AMERICAN ACTRESS CONCHATA GALEN FERRELL (`-**77**)"!!!~'

`-**DEATH/DAY** = (**10/12**) = (10 + 12) = (`-**22**) = "FLIP EVERY (`-**2**) OVER to a (`-**7**)" = (`-**77**) = "AGE of `-DEATH for AMERICAN ACTRESS CONCHATA GALEN FERRELL (`-**77**)"!!!~'

`-**BIRTH/YEAR** = (`-**1943**) = (19 + 43) = (`-**62**) = RECIPROCAL = (`-**26**) = "FLIP EVERY (`-**2**) OVER to a (`-**7**)" = (`-**76**) = "ONE `-YEAR `-AWAY (`-**76**) from `-AGE of `-DEATH (`-**77**)"!!!~'

`-**DEATH/DAY** = (**10/12**) = (10 + 12) = (`-**22**) = `-**DIED** in (`-**2020**)!!!~'

`-**BIRTH/DAY** = (**3/28**) = RECIPROCAL = (**82/3**) = (82 (-) 3) = (`-**79**) = "TWO `-YEARS `-AWAY (`-**79**) from `-AGE of `-DEATH (`-**77**)"!!!~'

AMERICAN ACTRESS CONCHATA GALEN FERRELL `-**BIRTHDAY** # `-**NUMBER** = `-EQUALS = (3 + 28 + 19 + 43) = (`-**93**) = (9 x 3) = (`-**27**) = 2(7's) = (`-**77**) = "AGE of `-DEATH for AMERICAN ACTRESS CONCHATA GALEN FERRELL (`-**77**)"!!!~'

AMERICAN ACTRESS CONCHATA GALEN FERRELL `-**BIRTHDAY** # `-**NUMBER** = `-EQUALS = (3 + 28 + 19 + 43) = (`-**93**) = "FLIP EVERY (`-**3**) OVER to an (`-**8**)" = (`-**98**) = `-**DIED** this `-**MANY** `-**DAYS** (`-**198**) `-**DAYS** `-**AWAY** from `-**HER** `-**BIRTH/DAY**!!!~'

AMERICAN ACTRESS CONCHATA GALEN FERRELL `-DEATH/ DAY # `-NUMBER = `-EQUALS = (10 + 12 + 20 + 20) = (`-62) = RECIPROCAL = (`-26) = "FLIP EVERY (`-2) OVER to a (`-7)" = (`-76) = "ONE `-YEAR `-AWAY (`-76) from `-AGE of `-DEATH (`-77)"!!!~'

(93 (-) 62) = (`-31) = `-BIRTH/DAY = (3/28) = (3 + 28) = (`-31)!!!~'

`-DIED in the `-MONTH of (`-10); and, was `-BORN in the `-MONTH of (`-3)!!!~'

`-DEATH/DAY = (10/12) = (10) (1 + 2) = (10/3) = (`-10 (DEATH) / `-3 (BIRTH))!!!~'

AMERICAN ACTRESS CONCHATA GALEN FERRELL had `-DIED (`-167) `-DAYS before `-HER `-NEXT `-BIRTHDAY!!!~'

(`-167) = RECIPROCAL = (`-761) = (76 + 1) = (`-77) = "AGE of `-DEATH for AMERICAN ACTRESS CONCHATA GALEN FERRELL (`-77)"!!!~'

(365 (-) 167) = (`-198) = (98 x 1) = (`-98) = "FLIP EVERY (`-8) OVER to a (`-3)" = (`-93) = `-BIRTH/DAY # `-NUMBER (`-93)!!!~'

Was `-MARRIED to ARNIE ANDERSON from (1986 -to- 2020) = (`-34) YEARS = RECIPROCAL = (`-43) = Was `-BORN in (`-43)!!!~'

MICROSOFT CO-FOUNDER BILLIONAIRE PAUL ALLEN `-DIED on OCTOBER 15th within `-2018!!!~' `-HE was `-BORN on JANUARY 21th in `-1953!!!~' `-HE `-DIED at the `-AGE of (`-65)!!!~'

`-DAY of `-DEATH = (`-15th) = (1 x 5) = (`-5) /||\ `-DAY of `-BIRTH = (`-21st) = (2 + 1) = (`-3) /||\ (`-53) = With a `-BIRTH/YEAR of (`-53)!!!~'

`-DAY of `-DEATH = (`-15th) (+) `-DAY of `-BIRTH = (`-21st) = (`-36) = RECIPROCAL = (`-63) = "TWO `-YEARS `-AWAY (`-63) from `-AGE of `-DEATH (`-65)"!!!~'

`-**DAY** of `-**DEATH** = (`-**15**<sup>th</sup>) (+) `-**DAY** of `-**BIRTH** = (`-**21**st) = (`-**36**)
= RECIPROCAL = (`-**63**) = `-**DEATH/DAY # `-NUMBER** (`-**63**)!!!~'

MICROSOFT CO-FOUNDER PAUL ALLEN `-**BIRTHDAY #
`-NUMBER** = `-EQUALS = (1 + 21 + 19 + 53) = (`-**94**) = "FLIP EVERY
(`-**9**) OVER to a (`-**6**)" = (`-**64**) = **"ONE `-YEAR `-AWAY** (`-**64**) from
`-**AGE** of `-**DEATH** (`-**65**)"!!!~'

MICROSOFT CO-FOUNDER PAUL ALLEN `-**DEATH/DAY #
`-NUMBER** = `-EQUALS = (10 + 15 + 20 + 18) = (`-**63**) = "FLIP
EVERY (`-**6**) OVER to a (`-**9**) = (`-**93**) = "FLIP EVERY (`-**3**) OVER to
an (`-**8**)" = (`-**98**)!!!~'

MICROSOFT CO-FOUNDER BILLIONAIRE PAUL ALLEN had
`-DIED (`-**98**) `-DAYS before `-HIS `-NEXT `-BIRTHDAY!!!~'

(365 (-) 98) = (`-**267**) = (67 (-) 2) = (`-**65**) = **"AGE of `-DEATH
for MICROSOFT CO-FOUNDER BILLIONAIRE PAUL ALLEN
(`-65**)"!!!~'

BASEBALL GREAT "SAN FRANCISCO GIANT'S" WILLIE
MCCOVEY `-DIED on *OCTOBER 31<sup>st</sup>* within `-*2018*!!!~' `-HE was
`-BORN on *JANUARY 10<sup>th</sup>* in `-*1938*!!!~' `-HE `-DIED at the `-AGE
of (`-**80**)!!!~'

`-**DEATH/DAY** = (**10/31**) = "FLIP EVERY (`-**3**) OVER to an (`-**8**)" =
(10/**81**) = RECIPROCAL = (18/**01**) = (81 (-) 01) = (`-**80**) = **"AGE of
`-DEATH for BASEBALL GREAT "SAN FRANCISCO GIANT'S"
WILLIE MCCOVEY (`-80**)!!!~'

`-**DEATH/YEAR** = (`-**2018**) = (20 + 18) = (`-**38**) = `-**BIRTH/YEAR** =
(`-**38**)!!!~'

`-**DAY** of `-**DEATH** = (`-**31**) (+) `-**DAY** of `-**BIRTH** = (`-**10**) = (`-**41**)!!!~'

`-**DEATH/DAY** = (**10/31**) = (10 + 31) = (`-**41**)!!!~`

(41 + 41) = (`-**82**) = "TWO `-YEARS `-AWAY (`-**82**) from `-AGE of `-**DEATH** (`-**80**)"!!!~`

`-**DEATH/YEAR** = (`-**2018**) = RECIPROCAL = (`-**8102**) = (82) (-) (01) = (`-**81**) = "ONE `-YEAR `-AWAY (`-**81**) from `-AGE of `-DEATH (`-**80**)"!!!~`

`-**BIRTH/YEAR** = (`-**1938**) = (38 (-) 19) = (`-**19**) = (**1/9**) = `-**BORN** the `-**VERY** `-**NEXT** `-**DAY** on (**1/10**)!!!~`

`-**DAY** of `-**DEATH** = (`-**31**) = "FLIP EVERY (`-**3**) OVER to an (`-**8**)" = (`-**81**) = "ONE `-YEAR `-AWAY (`-**81**) from `-AGE of `-DEATH (`-**80**)"!!!~`

`-**DEATH/DAY** = (**10/31**) (+) `-**BIRTH/DAY** = (**1/10**) = (10 + 31 + 1 + 10) = (`-**52**)!!!~`

`-**BIRTH/YEAR** = (`-**1938**) = (19 + 38) = (`-**57**) = "FLIP EVERY (`-**7**) OVER to a (`-**2**)" = (`-**52**)!!!~`

BASEBALL GREAT "SAN FRANCISCO GIANT'S" WILLIE MCCOVEY `-**BIRTHDAY # `-NUMBER** = `-**EQUALS** = (1 + 10 + 19 + 38) = (`-**68**) = "FLIP EVERY (`-**8**) OVER to a (`-**3**)" = (`-**63**) = (7 x 9) = `-**DEATH/DAY # `-NUMBER** (`-**79**)!!!~`

BASEBALL GREAT "SAN FRANCISCO GIANT'S" WILLIE MCCOVEY `-**DEATH/DAY # `-NUMBER** = `-**EQUALS** = (10 + 31 + 20 + 18) = (`-**79**) = (7 x 9) = (`-**63**) = "FLIP EVERY (`-**3**) OVER to an (`-**8**)" = (`-**68**) = `-**BIRTH/DAY # `-NUMBER** (`-**68**)!!!~`

BASEBALL GREAT "SAN FRANCISCO GIANT'S" WILLIE MCCOVEY had `-**DIED** (`-**71**) `-**DAYS** before `-**HIS** `-**NEXT** `-**BIRTHDAY**!!!~`

(365 (-) 71) = (`-**294**) = "FLIP EVERY (`-**2**) OVER to a (`-**7**)" = (`-**794**) = "FLIP EVERY (`-**9**) OVER to a (`-**6**)" = (`-**764**) = (76 + 4) = (`-**80**)

= "AGE of `-DEATH for BASEBALL GREAT "SAN FRANCISCO GIANT'S" WILLIE MCCOVEY (`-80)!!!~'

`-DIED in (`-10); and, was `-BORN; in RECIPROCAL = (`-01)!!!~'

COMIC BOOK LEGEND STAN LEE (STANLEY MARTIN LIEBER) `-DIED on *NOVEMBER 12th* within `-*2018*!!!~' `-HE was `-BORN on *DECEMBER 28th* in `-*1922*!!!~' `-HE `-DIED at the `-AGE of (`-95)!!!~'

`-BIRTH/YEAR = (`-1922) = (9) (1 + 2 + 2) = (`-95) = "AGE of `-DEATH for COMIC BOOK LEGEND STAN LEE (STANLEY MARTIN LIEBER) (`-95)"!!!~'

`-DAY of `-BIRTH = (`-28th) = `-DIED within the `-YEAR of (`-2018)!!!~'

`-BIRTH/DAY = (12/28) = RECIPROCAL = (`-82/21) = (82) + (12) = (`-94) = "ONE `-YEAR `-AWAY (`-94) from `-AGE of `-DEATH (`-95)"!!!~'

`-DEATH/DAY = (11/12) = (11 + 12) = (`-23) = "FLIP EVERY (`-3) OVER to an (`-8)" = (`-28) = "DAY of `-BIRTH"!!!~'

`-DEATH/DAY = (11/12) (+) `-BIRTH/DAY = (12/28) = (11 + 12 + 12 + 28) = (`-63) = FLIP EVERY (`-6) OVER to a (`-9)" = (`-93) = "TWO `-YEARS `-AWAY (`-93) from `-AGE of `-DEATH (`-95)"!!!~'

`-DEATH/YEAR = (`-2018) = RECIPROCAL = (`-8102) = (8 + 1) (0 + 2) = (`-92) = "FLIP EVERY (`-2) OVER to a (`-7)" = (`-97) = "TWO `-YEARS `-AWAY (`-97) from `-AGE of `-DEATH (`-95)"!!!~'

COMIC BOOK LEGEND STAN LEE (STANLEY MARTIN LIEBER) `-BIRTHDAY # `-NUMBER = `-EQUALS = (12 + 28 + 19 + 22) = (`-81)!!!~'

COMIC BOOK LEGEND STAN LEE (STANLEY MARTIN LIEBER) `-DEATH/DAY # `-NUMBER = `-EQUALS = (11 + 12 + 20 + 18) = (`-**61**) = (1 + 5) (1) = (`-**151**) = **FOR** `-**WIFE** `-**DAYS** in `-**DEATH** from `-**BIRTH**!!!~'

(81 + 61) = (`-**142**) = "**SWIPE ONE** to the `-**LEFT**" = "**WIFE'S** `-**BIRTH/DAY** = (`-**12/4**) = (**DECEMBER 4**th)" = "**SEE** `-**BELOW**"!!!~'

COMIC BOOK LEGEND STAN LEE (STANLEY MARTIN LIEBER) had `-**DIED** (`-**46**) `-**DAYS** before `-**HIS** `-**NEXT** `-**BIRTHDAY**!!!~'

(365 (-) 46) = (`-**319**) = RECIPROCAL = (`-**913**) = (91 + 3) = (`-**94**) = "**ONE** `-**YEAR** `-**AWAY** (`-**94**) from `-**AGE** of `-**DEATH** (`-**95**)"!!!~'

WIFE (JOAN B. LEE) = `-**BIRTHDAY** = (**DECEMBER 4**th, **1922**) /||\

`-**BIRTH/YEAR** = (`-**1922**) = (1 x 9) (2 x 2) = (`-**94**) = "**AGE of** `-**DEATH for WIFE (JOAN B. LEE)** (`-**94**)"!!!~'

WIFE (JOAN B. LEE) = `-**DEATHDAY** = (**JULY 6**th, **2017**) /||\

`-**DEATH/YEAR** = (`-**2017**) = (2 + 0) (1 x 7) = (`-**27**) = "FLIP EVERY (`-**7**) OVER to a (`-**2**)" = (`-**22**) = `-**BIRTH/YEAR** = (`-**22**)!!!~'

SHE `-**DIED** AT THE `-**AGE** of (`-**94**); & (`-**214**) `-**DAYS after** `-**HER** `-**LAST** `-**BIRTHDAY**!!!~'

`-**SHE was** (`-**24**) DAYS `-**OLDER than** `-**HER** `-**HUSBAND**!!!~'

`-**BIRTH/DAY** = (**12/4**) = (24 x 1) = (`-**24**)!!!~'

`-**DEATH/DAY** = (7 x 6) = (`-**42**) = RECIPROCAL = (`-**24**)!!!~'

(`-**214**) = (24 x 1) = (`-**24**)!!!~'

`-**BIRTH/DAY** = (**12/4**) = "**SWIPE ONE** to the `-**LEFT**" = (`-**214**) = `-**DAYS** in `-**BIRTH** from `-**DEATH**!!!~'

MARRIED to COMIC BOOK LEGEND STAN LEE (STANLEY MARTIN LIEBER) from (1947 -to- 2017) = `-**MARRIED** for (`-**69**) **YEARS!!!~'**

(`-**69**) = RECIPROCAL = (`-**96**) = "ONE `-YEAR `-AWAY (`-**96**) from `-AGE of `-DEATH (`-**95**)"!!!~'

CREATOR OF "SQUAREBOB SQUAREPANTS" STEPHEN HILLENBURG `-DIED on NOVEMBER 26th within `-2018!!!~' `-HE was `-BORN on AUGUST 21st in `-19**61**!!!~' `-HE `-DIED at the `-AGE of (`-**57**)!!!~'

CREATOR OF "SQUAREBOB SQUAREPANTS" STEPHEN HILLENBURG `-DEATH/DAY # = `-EQUALS = (11 + 26 + 20 + 18) = (`-**75**) = RECIPROCAL = (`-**57**) = "AGE of `-DEATH for CREATOR OF "SQUAREBOB SQUAREPANTS" STEPHEN HILLENBURG (`-**57**)"!!!~'

41st PRESIDENT of the (UNITED STATES of AMERICA) GEORGE HERBERT WALKER BUSH `-DIED on **NOVEMBER 30th** within `-2018!!!~' `-HE was `-BORN on JUNE 12th in `-1924!!!~' `-HE `-DIED at the `-AGE of (`-**94**)!!!~'

41st PRESIDENT of the (UNITED STATES of AMERICA) GEORGE HERBERT WALKER BUSH had `-DIED (`-**194**) `-DAYS before `-HIS `-NEXT `-BIRTHDAY!!!~'

(`-**194**) = (94 x 1) = (`-**94**) = "AGE of `-DEATH of (41st) PRESIDENT of the (UNITED STATES of AMERICA) GEORGE HERBERT WALKER BUSH"!!!~'

`-**DEATH/DAY** = (NOVEMBER 30<sup>th</sup>) = (11 + 30) = (`-**41**) = "**41st** PRESIDENT of the (UNITED STATES of AMERICA) GEORGE HERBERT WALKER BUSH"!!!~'

SINGER/SONGWRITER FLOYD PARTON `-DIED on *DECEMBER 6<sup>th</sup>* within `-*2018*!!!~' `-HE was `-BORN on *JUNE 1st* in `-*1957*!!!~' `-HE `-DIED at the `-AGE of (`-**61**)!!!~'

`-**BIRTH/DAY** = (**6/1**) = (`-**61**) = "AGE of `-DEATH for SINGER/ SONGWRITER FLOYD PARTON (`-**61**)"!!!~'

`-**DEATH/YEAR** = (`-**2018**) = (2 (-) 8) (0 + 1) = (`-**61**) = "AGE of `-DEATH for SINGER/SONGWRITER FLOYD PARTON (`-**61**)"!!!~'

`-**BIRTH/YEAR** = (`-**1957**) = (57 (-) 19) = (`-**38**) = `-**DEATH/YEAR** = (`-**2018**) = (20 + 18) = (`-**38**)!!!~'

`-**DEATH/DAY** = (**12/6**) = RECIPROCAL = (**6/21**) = (62 (-) 1) = (`-**61**) = "AGE of `-DEATH for SINGER/SONGWRITER FLOYD PARTON (`-**61**)"!!!~'

`-**BIRTH/DAY** = (**6/1**) = RECIPROCAL = `-**DEATH/DAY** = (**12/6**) = RECIPROCAL = (**6/2/1**)!!!~'

COMPUTER PIONEER EVELYN BEREZIN `-DIED on *DECEMBER 8<sup>th</sup>* within `-*2018*!!!~' `-SHE was `-BORN on *APRIL 12th* in `-*1925*!!!~' `-SHE `-DIED at the `-AGE of (`-**93**)!!!~'

`-**BIRTH/YEAR** = (`-**1925**) = (1 x 9) (2 (-) 5) = (-**93**) = "AGE of `-DEATH for COMPUTER PIONEER EVELYN BEREZIN (`-**93**)"!!!~'

`-**BIRTH/DAY** = (**4/12**) = (4 x 12) = (`-**48**)!!!~'

`-**DEATH/DAY** = (**12/8**) = (12 x 8) = (`-**96**) / `-**DIVIDED** `-by / (`-**2**) = (`-**48**)!!!~'

(12/**8**) /||\ (**4**/12) = (`-**84**) = RECIPROCAL = (`-**48**)!!!~'

COMPUTER PIONEER EVELYN BEREZIN had `-**DIED** (`-**125**) `-**DAYS** before `-**HER** `-**NEXT** `-**BIRTHDAY**!!!~'

(`-**125**) = (25 x 1) = (`-**25**) = `-**BIRTH/YEAR** = (`-**25**)!!!~'

`-**DEATH/DAY** = (**12/8**) (+) `-**BIRTH/DAY** = (**4/12**) = (12 + 8 + 4 + 12) = (`-**36**) = RECIPROCAL = (`-**63**) = FLIP EVERY (`-**6**) OVER to a (`-**9**)" = (`-**93**) = "**AGE of** `-**DEATH for COMPUTER PIONEER EVELYN BEREZIN (`-93)**"!!!~'

JUDGE WILLIAM ALFRED NEWSOM III `-DIED on *DECEMBER 12th* within `-*2018*!!!~' `-HE was `-BORN on *FEBRUARY 15th* in `-19**34**!!!~' `-HE `-DIED at the `-AGE of (`-**84**)!!!~'

`-**BIRTH/YEAR** = (`-**34**) = "FLIP EVERY (`-**3**) OVER to an (`-**8**) = (`-**84**) = "**AGE of** `-**DEATH for JUDGE WILLIAM ALFRED NEWSOM III (`-84)**!!!~'

JUDGE WILLIAM ALFRED NEWSOM III `-**DEATH/DAY #** `-**NUMBER** = `-**EQUALS** = (12 + 12 + 20 + 18) = (`-**62**) = `-**BIRTH/DAY** = (**2/15**) = RECIPROCAL = (**51/2**) = (5 + 1) (2) = (`-**62**)!!!~'

AMERICAN SINGER NANCY WILSON `-DIED on *DECEMBER 13th* within `-*2018*!!!~' `-SHE was `-BORN on *FEBRUARY 20th* in `-*1937*!!!~' `-SHE `-DIED at the `-AGE of (`-**81**)!!!~'

`-**DEATH/YEAR** = (`-**18**) = RECIPROCAL = (`-**81**) = "**AGE of** `-**DEATH for AMERICAN SINGER NANCY WILSON (`-81)**"!!!~'

DWAYNE W. ANDERSON

`-**DAY** of `-**DEATH** = (`-**13**th) = RECIPROCAL = (`-**31**) = "FLIP EVERY (`-**3**) OVER to an (`-**8**)" = (`-**81**) = "**AGE of `-DEATH for AMERICAN SINGER NANCY WILSON (`-81)**"!!!~'

`-**DEATH/YEAR** = (`-**2018**) = RECIPROCAL = (`-**8102**) = (82) (-) (01) = (`-**81**) = "**AGE of `-DEATH for AMERICAN SINGER NANCY WILSON (`-81)**"!!!~'

AMERICAN SINGER NANCY WILSON `-**BIRTHDAY # `-NUMBER** = `-EQUALS = (2 + 20 + 19 + 37) = (`-**78**) = (7 x 8) = (`-**56**) = `-**BIRTH/ YEAR** = (`-**1937**) = (19 + 37) = (`-**56**) = (7 x 8) = (`-**78**)!!!~'

`-**DEATH/DAY** = (**12/13**) = (12 x 13) = (`-**156**) = (56 x 1) = (`-**56**)!!!~'

AMERICAN SINGER NANCY WILSON `-**DEATH/DAY # `-NUMBER** = `-EQUALS = (12 + 13 + 20 + 18) = (`-**63**) = (6 x 3) = (`-**18**) = RECIPROCAL = (`-**81**) = "**AGE of `-DEATH for AMERICAN SINGER NANCY WILSON (`-81)**"!!!~'

AMERICAN SINGER NANCY WILSON had `-**DIED** (`-**69**) `-**DAYS** before `-HER `-NEXT `-BIRTHDAY!!!~'

(`-**69**) = "FLIP EVERY (`-**6**) OVER to a (`-**9**)" = (`-**99**) = (9 x 9) = (`-**81**) = "**AGE of `-DEATH for AMERICAN SINGER NANCY WILSON (`-81)**"!!!~'

(365 (-) 69) = (`-**296**) = (96 x 2) = (`-**192**) = (1 (-) 9) (2) = (`-**82**) = "**ONE `-YEAR `-AWAY (`-82) from `-AGE of `-DEATH (`-81)**"!!!~'

AMERICAN COUNTRY MUSIC SONGWRITER JERRY CHESNUT `-DIED on **DECEMBER 15**th within `-**2018**!!!!!~' `-HE was `-BORN on **MAY 7**th in `-**1931**!!!!!~' `-HE `-DIED at the `-AGE of (`-**87**)!!!!!~'

`-**DEATH/YEAR** = (`-**2018**) = RECIPROCAL = (`-**8102**) = "FLIP EVERY (`-**2**) OVER to a (`-**7**)" = (`-**8107**) = (8 x 1) (0 + 7) = (`-**87**) = "**AGE**

90

of `-DEATH for AMERICAN COUNTRY MUSIC SONGWRITER JERRY CHESNUT (`-87)"!!!~'

`-**BIRTH/YEAR** = (`-**1931**) = "FLIP EVERY (`-**3**) OVER to an (`-**8**)" = (`-**1981**) = (1 (-) 9) (8 (-) 1) = (`-**87**) = **"AGE of `-DEATH for AMERICAN COUNTRY MUSIC SONGWRITER JERRY CHESNUT (`-87)"!!!~'**

AMERICAN COUNTRY MUSIC SONGWRITER JERRY CHESNUT `-BIRTHDAY # `-NUMBER = `-EQUALS = (5 + 7 + 19 + 31) = (`-**62**) = `-**DEATH/DAY** = (**12/15**) = RECIPROCAL = (**51/21**) = (5 + 1) (2 x 1) = (`-**62**)!!!~'

AMERICAN COUNTRY MUSIC SONGWRITER JERRY CHESNUT `-DEATH/DAY # `-NUMBER = `-EQUALS = (12 + 15 + 20 + 18) = (`-**65**) = RECIPROCAL = (`-**56**) = **Was `-BORN the `-VERY `-NEXT `-DAY on (5/7) = (MAY 7**th**)!!!~'**

(62 + 65) = (`-**127**) = (1 + 2) (7) = (`-**37**) = "FLIP EVERY (`-**3**) OVER to an (`-**8**)" = (`-**87**) = **"AGE of `-DEATH for AMERICAN COUNTRY MUSIC SONGWRITER JERRY CHESNUT (`-87)"!!!~'**

AMERICAN COUNTRY MUSIC SONGWRITER JERRY CHESNUT had `-**DIED** (`-**143**) `-**DAYS before `-HIS `-NEXT `-BIRTHDAY!!!~'**

(`-**143**) = (43 x 1) = (`-**43**) = `-**DEATH/DAY** = (**12/15**) = RECIPROCAL = (**51/21**) = (5 (-) 1) (2 + 1) = (`-**43**)!!!~'

(43 + 43) = (`-**86**) = **"ONE `-YEAR `-AWAY (`-86) from `-AGE of `-DEATH (`-87)"!!!~'**

(365 (-) 143) = (`-**222**) = "FLIP EVERY (`-**2**) OVER to a (`-**7**)" = (`-**777**) = (7 x 7 x 7) = (`-**343**) = "FLIP EVERY (`-**3**) OVER to an (`-**8**)" = (`-**843**) = (8) (4 + 3) = (`-**87**) = **"AGE of `-DEATH for AMERICAN COUNTRY MUSIC SONGWRITER JERRY CHESNUT (`-87)"!!!~'**

DWAYNE W. ANDERSON

ROMANIAN/CANADIAN POP SINGER ANCA POP `-DIED on *DECEMBER 17th* within `-*2018*!!!~' `-SHE was `-BORN on *OCTOBER 22nd* in `-*1984*!!!~' `-SHE `-DIED at the `-AGE of (`-**34**)!!!~'

`-**BIRTH/YEAR** = (`-**84**) = "FLIP EVERY (`-**8**) OVER to a (`-**3**)" = (`-**34**) = "AGE of `-DEATH for ROMANIAN/CANADIAN POP SINGER ANCA POP (`-**34**)"!!!~'

`-**BIRTH/DAY** = (**10/22**) = (10 + 22) = (`-**32**) = "TWO `-YEARS `-AWAY (`-**32**) from `-AGE of `-DEATH (`-**34**)"!!!~'

ROMANIAN/CANADIAN POP SINGER ANCA POP `-**BIRTHDAY** # `-**NUMBER** = `-EQUALS = (10 + 22 + 19 + 84) = (`-**135**) = (35 (-) 1) = (`-**34**) = "AGE of `-DEATH for ROMANIAN/CANADIAN POP SINGER ANCA POP (`-**34**)"!!!~'

ROMANIAN/CANADIAN POP SINGER ANCA POP `-**DEATH/ DAY #** `-**NUMBER** = `-EQUALS = (12 + 17 + 20 + 18) = (`-**67**) = RECIPROCAL = (`-**76**) = "FLIP EVERY (`-**7**) OVER to a (`-**2**)" = (`-**26**) = "FLIP EVERY (`-**6**) OVER to a (`-**9**)" = (`-**29**) = `-**DEATH/DAY** = (**12/17**) = (12 + 17) = (`-**29**)!!!~'

(135 (-) 67) = (`-**68**) / `-DIVIDED `-by / (`-**2**) = (`-**34**) = "AGE of `-DEATH for ROMANIAN/CANADIAN POP SINGER ANCA POP (`-**34**)"!!!~'

ROMANIAN/CANADIAN POP SINGER ANCA POP had `-**DIED** (`-**56**) `-DAYS after `-HER `-LAST `-BIRTHDAY!!!~'

(`-**56**) = RECIPROCAL = (`-**65**) = `-**BIRTH/YEAR** = (`-**1984**) = (84 (-) 19) = (`-**65**) = RECIPROCAL = (`-**56**)!!!~'

(365 (-) 56) = (`-**309**) = "FLIP EVERY (`-**3**) OVER to an (`-**8**)" = (`-**809**) = "FLIP EVERY (`-**9**) OVER to a (`-**6**)" = (`-**806**) = (86 + 0) = (`-**86**) / `-DIVIDED `-by / (`-**2**) = (`-**43**) = RECIPROCAL = (`-**34**) = "AGE of

`-DEATH for ROMANIAN/CANADIAN POP SINGER ANCA POP (`-**34**)"!!!~'

AMERICAN ACTRESS, DIRECTOR; & PRODUCER PENNY MARSHALL `-DIED on *DECEMBER 17<sup>th</sup>* within `-**2018**!!!~' `-SHE was `-BORN on *OCTOBER 15th* in `-**1943**!!!~' `-SHE `-DIED at the `-AGE of (`-**75**)!!!~'

`-**BIRTH/DAY** = (**10/15**) = (10 + 15) = (`-**25**) = "FLIP EVERY (`-**2**) OVER to a (`-**7**)" = (`-**75**) = "AGE of `-DEATH for AMERICAN ACTRESS, DIRECTOR; & PRODUCER PENNY MARSHALL (`-**75**)"!!!~'

`-**DEATH/YEAR** = (`-**2018**) = "FLIP EVERY (`-**2**) OVER to a (`-**7**)" = (`-**7018**) = (7 + 0) (1 (-) 8) = (`-**77**) = "TWO `-YEARS `-AWAY (`-**77**) from `-AGE of `-DEATH (`-**75**)"!!!~'

`-**BIRTH/YEAR** = (`-**1943**) = "FLIP EVERY (`-**3**) OVER to a (`-**8**)" = (`-**1948**) = RECIPROCAL = (`-**8491**) = (8 (-) 1) (4 (-) 9) = (`-**75**) = "AGE of `-DEATH for AMERICAN ACTRESS, DIRECTOR; & PRODUCER PENNY MARSHALL (`-**75**)"!!!~'

`-**BIRTH/YEAR** = (`-**1943**) = (19 + 43) = (`-**62**) = RECIPROCAL = (`-**26**) = "FLIP EVERY (`-**2**) OVER to a (`-**7**)" = (`-**76**) = "ONE `-YEAR `-AWAY (`-**76**) from `-AGE of `-DEATH (`-**75**)"!!!~'

`-**BIRTH/YEAR** = (`-**1943**) = (43 (-) 19) = (`-**24**) = "FLIP EVERY (`-**2**) OVER to a (`-**7**)" = (`-**74**) = "ONE `-YEAR `-AWAY (`-**74**) from `-AGE of `-DEATH (`-**75**)"!!!~'

`-**DEATH/DAY** = (**12/17**) = RECIPROCAL = (**71/21**) = (71) (2 + 1) = (`-**74**) = "ONE `-YEAR `-AWAY (`-**74**) from `-AGE of `-DEATH (`-**75**)"!!!~'

AMERICAN ACTRESS, DIRECTOR; & PRODUCER PENNY MARSHALL `-**BIRTHDAY #** `-**NUMBER** = `-EQUALS = (10 + 15

+ 19 + 43) = (`-**87**) = `-TIMES "**X**" (`-**2**) = (`-**174**) = (74 + 1) = (`-**75**) = "AGE of `-DEATH for AMERICAN ACTRESS, DIRECTOR; & PRODUCER PENNY MARSHALL (`-**75**)"!!!~`

AMERICAN ACTRESS, DIRECTOR; & PRODUCER PENNY MARSHALL `-**DEATH/DAY # `-NUMBER** = `-EQUALS = (12 + 17 + 20 + 18) = (`-**67**) = RECIPROCAL = (`-**76**) = "ONE `-YEAR `-AWAY (`-**76**) from `-AGE of `-DEATH (`-**75**)"!!!~`

`-**BIRTH/YEAR** = (`-**1943**) = (19 + 43) = (`-**62**) = "FLIP EVERY (`-**2**) OVER to a (`-**7**)" = (`-**67**) = `-**DEATH/DAY # `-NUMBER** (`-**67**)!!!~`

AMERICAN ACTRESS, DIRECTOR; & PRODUCER PENNY MARSHALL had `-**DIED** (`-**63**) `-**DAYS** after `-HER `-LAST `-BIRTHDAY!!!~`

(365 (-) 63) = (`-**302**) = (32 + 0) = (`-**32**) = -a PROPHETIC NUMBER!!!~`

AUSTRALIAN MODEL & ACTRESS ANNALISE BRAAKENSIEK `-DIED on *JANUARY 6th* within `-*2019*!!!~` `-SHE was `-BORN on *DECEMBER 9th* in `-*1972*!!!~` `-SHE `-DIED at the `-AGE of (`-**46**)!!!~`

`-**BIRTH/YEAR** = (`-**1972**) = (19 + 72) = (`-**91**) = RECIPROCAL = (`-**19**) = "FLIP EVERY (`-**9**) OVER to a (`-**6**)" = (`-**16**) = (**1/6**) = `-**DEATH/DAY** = (**JANUARY 6**th)!!!~`

`-**BIRTH/YEAR** = (`-**1972**) = (19 + 72) = (`-**91**) = RECIPROCAL = (`-**19**) = `-**DIED** within the `-**YEAR** of (`-**19**)!!!~`

`-**DEATH/DAY** = (**1/6**) = "FLIP EVERY (`-**6**) OVER to a (`-**9**)" = (**1/9**) = `-**DIED** within the `-**YEAR** of (`-**19**)!!!~`

`-**DEATH/DAY** = (**1/6**)!!!~`

`-DEATH CIPHERS/CYPHERS FOR LIFE & DEATH!!!~'

`-BIRTH/DAY = (12/9) = "FLIP EVERY (`-9) OVER to a (`-6)" = (12/6) = (1/2/6)!!!~'

`-BIRTH/DAY = (12/9) = (1) (2 (-) 9) = (1/7) = `-DIED the `-PRIOR `-DAY on (1/6) = (JANUARY 6th)!!!~'

`-BIRTH/DAY = (12/9) = RECIPROCAL = (9/21) = (92 x 1) = (`-92) / `-DIVIDED `-by / (`-2) = (`-46) = "AGE of `-DEATH for AUSTRALIAN MODEL & ACTRESS ANNALISE BRAAKENSIEK (`-46)"!!!~'

`-DEATH/YEAR = (`-2019) = RECIPROCAL = (`-9102) = (92) (1 + 0) = (92 x 1) = (`-92) / `-DIVIDED `-by / (`-2) = (`-46) = "AGE of `-DEATH for AUSTRALIAN MODEL & ACTRESS ANNALISE BRAAKENSIEK (`-46)"!!!~'

AUSTRALIAN MODEL & ACTRESS ANNALISE BRAAKENSIEK `-DEATH/DAY # `-NUMBER = `-EQUALS = (1 + 6 + 20 + 19) = (`-46) = "AGE of `-DEATH for AUSTRALIAN MODEL & ACTRESS ANNALISE BRAAKENSIEK (`-46)"!!!~'

SHIRLEY BOONE; WIFE OF SINGER PAT BOONE & MOTHER OF SINGER DEBBY BOONE `-DIED on *JANUARY 11th* within `-*2019*!!!~' `-SHE was `-BORN on *APRIL 24th* in `-*1934*!!!~' `-SHE `-DIED at the `-AGE of (`-84)!!!~'

`-BIRTH/YEAR = (`-34) = "FLIP EVERY (`-3) OVER to an (`-8)" = (`-84) = "AGE of `-DEATH for SHIRLEY BOONE; WIFE OF SINGER PAT BOONE & MOTHER OF SINGER DEBBY BOONE (`-84)"!!!~'

`-BIRTH/DAY = (4/24) = RECIPROCAL = (42/4) = (4 x 2) (4) = (`-84) = "AGE of `-DEATH for SHIRLEY BOONE; WIFE OF SINGER PAT BOONE & MOTHER OF SINGER DEBBY BOONE (`-84)"!!!~'

`-BIRTH/DAY = (4/24) = (4 + 24) = (`-28) = RECIPROCAL = (`-82) = "TWO `-YEARS `-AWAY (`-82) from `-AGE of `-DEATH (`-84)"!!!~'

`-**DEATH/YEAR** = (`-**2019**) = RECIPROCAL = (`-**9102**) = (9 (-) 1) (0 + 2) = (`-**82**) = **"TWO `-YEARS `-AWAY (`-82) from `-AGE of `-DEATH (`-84)"**!!!~'

`-**BIRTH/YEAR** = (`-**1934**) = (19 + 34) = (`-**53**) = RECIPROCAL = (`-**35**) = **"FLIP EVERY (`-3) OVER to an (`-8)"** = (`-**85**) = **"ONE `-YEAR `-AWAY (`-85) from `-AGE of `-DEATH (`-84)"**!!!~'

SHIRLEY BOONE; WIFE OF SINGER PAT BOONE & MOTHER OF SINGER DEBBY BOONE `-**BIRTHDAY # `-NUMBER** = `-EQUALS = (4 + 24 + 19 + 34) = (`-**81**)!!!~'

SHIRLEY BOONE; WIFE OF SINGER PAT BOONE & MOTHER OF SINGER DEBBY BOONE `-**DEATH/DAY # `-NUMBER** = `-EQUALS = (1 + 11 + 20 + 19) = (`-**51**)!!!~'

(81 + 51) = (`-**132**) = (32 x 1) = (`-**32**) = (8 x 4) = (`-**84**) = **"AGE of `-DEATH for SHIRLEY BOONE; WIFE OF SINGER PAT BOONE & MOTHER OF SINGER DEBBY BOONE (`-84)"**!!!~'

(**81**) (**51**) = (8 x 1) (5 (-) 1) = (`-**84**) = **"AGE of `-DEATH for SHIRLEY BOONE; WIFE OF SINGER PAT BOONE & MOTHER OF SINGER DEBBY BOONE (`-84)"**!!!~'

(81 + 51) = (`-**132**) = **"FLIP EVERY (`-3) OVER to an (`-8)"** = (`-**182**) = (82 x 1) = (`-**82**) = **"TWO `-YEARS `-AWAY (`-82) from `-AGE of `-DEATH (`-84)"**!!!~'

`-**BIRTH/DAY** = (**4/24**) = RECIPROCAL = (**42**) (**4**)!!!~'

(**81**) = (8 x 1) = (**8**) = (**4** x **2**)!!!~'

(**51**) = (5 (-) 1) = (**4**)!!!~'

SHIRLEY BOONE; WIFE OF SINGER PAT BOONE & MOTHER OF SINGER DEBBY BOONE had `-**DIED** (`-**103**) `-DAYS before `-HER `-NEXT `-BIRTHDAY!!!~'

(365 (-) 103) = (`-262) = (2 + 6) (2) = (`-82) = "TWO `-YEARS `-AWAY (`-82) from `-AGE of `-DEATH (`-84)"!!!~'

(365 (-) 103) = (`-262) = Reciprocal-Sequencing-Numerology-RSN!!!~'

AMERICAN ACTRESS CAROL CHANNING `-DIED on JANUARY 15th within `-2019!!!~' `-SHE was `-BORN on JANUARY 31st in `-1921!!!~' `-SHE `-DIED at the `-AGE of (`-97)!!!~'

(1 (-) 5) = (`-4) = (3 + 1) = (`-4)!!!~'

`-DEATH/DAY = (1/15) = RECIPROCAL = (51/1) = (5 (-) 1) (1) = (4 x 1) = (`-4)!!!~'

`-BIRTH/DAY = (1/31) = RECIPROCAL = (13/1) = (1 + 3) (1) = (4 x 1) = (`-4)!!!~'

(51/1) = (5 + 1) (1) = (6) x (1) = (`-6)!!!~' /||\ (13/1) = (1 x 3) (1) = (3 x 1) = (`-3)!!!~'

(`-63) = (9 x 7) = (`-97) = "AGE of `-DEATH for AMERICAN ACTRESS CAROL CHANNING (`-97)"!!!~'

`-BIRTH/YEAR = (`-1921) = "FLIP EVERY (`-2) OVER to a (`-7)" = (`-1971) = (1 x 9) (7 x 1) = (`-97) = "AGE of `-DEATH for AMERICAN ACTRESS CAROL CHANNING (`-97)"!!!~'

`-DEATH/YEAR = (`-2019) = "FLIP EVERY (`-2) OVER to a (`-7)" = (`-7019) = (7 + 0) (1 x 9) = (`-79) = RECIPROCAL = (`-97) = "AGE of `-DEATH for AMERICAN ACTRESS CAROL CHANNING (`-97)"!!!~'

AMERICAN ACTRESS CAROL CHANNING `-BIRTHDAY # `-NUMBER = `-EQUALS = (1 + 31 + 19 + 21) = (`-72) = RECIPROCAL

= (`-27) = (72 + 27) = (`-99) = "TWO `-YEARS `-AWAY (`-99) from `-AGE of `-DEATH (`-97)"!!!~'

AMERICAN ACTRESS CAROL CHANNING `-DEATH/DAY # `-NUMBER = `-EQUALS = (1 + 15 + 20 + 19) = (`-55)!!!~'

`-AGE of `-DEATH = (`-97) = (-) MINUS (-) = (`-55) = (`-42) = (6 x 7) = (`-67) = "FLIP EVERY (`-6) OVER to a (`-9)" = (`-97) = "AGE of `-DEATH for AMERICAN ACTRESS CAROL CHANNING (`-97)"!!!~'

AMERICAN ACTRESS CAROL CHANNING had `-DIED (`-16) `-DAYS before `-HER `-NEXT `-BIRTHDAY!!!~'

(`-16) = "AGE of `-DEATH" = (`-97) = (9 + 7) = (`-16)!!!~'

(365 (-) 16) = (`-349) = RECIPROCAL = (`-943) = (9) (4 + 3) = (`-97) = "AGE of `-DEATH for AMERICAN ACTRESS CAROL CHANNING (`-97)"!!!~'

AMERICAN THEATRE ACTRESS KAYE BALLARD `-DIED on *JANUARY 21ˢᵗ* within `-*2019*!!!!!~' `-SHE was `-BORN on *NOVEMBER 20ᵗʰ* in `-*1925*!!!!!~' `-SHE `-DIED at the `-AGE of (`-93)!!!!!~'

`-AGE of `-DEATH = (`-93) = (9 + 3) = (`-12)!!!~'

`-DEATH/DAY = (1/21) = (112) = (12 x 1) = (`-12)!!!~'

`-BIRTH/DAY = (11/20) = (112) (0) = (112) = (12 x 1) = (`-12)!!!~'

(12 x 3) = (`-36) = RECIPROCAL = (`-63) = "FLIP EVERY (`-6) OVER to a (`-9) = (`-93) = "AGE of `-DEATH for AMERICAN THEATRE ACTRESS KAYE BALLARD (`-93)"!!!~'

`-DEATH/YEAR** = (`-2019**) = RECIPROCAL = (`-**9102**) = (91) + (02) = (`-**93**) = **"AGE of `-DEATH for AMERICAN THEATRE ACTRESS KAYE BALLARD (`-93)"**!!!~'

`-DEATH/YEAR** = (`-2019**) = (20 + 19) = (`-**39**) = RECIPROCAL = (`-**93**) = **"AGE of `-DEATH for AMERICAN THEATRE ACTRESS KAYE BALLARD (`-93)"**!!!~'

`-BIRTH/YEAR** = (`-1925**) = (1 x 9) (2 (-) 5) = (`-**93**) = **"AGE of `-DEATH for AMERICAN THEATRE ACTRESS KAYE BALLARD (`-93)"**!!!~'

AMERICAN THEATRE ACTRESS KAYE BALLARD `-**BIRTHDAY # `-NUMBER** = `-EQUALS = (11 + 20 + 19 + 25) = (`-**75**) = "FLIP EVERY (`-**7**) OVER to a (`-**2**)" = (`-**25**) = `-**BIRTH/YEAR** = (`-**25**)!!!~'

AMERICAN THEATRE ACTRESS KAYE BALLARD `-**DEATH/DAY # `-NUMBER** = `-EQUALS = (1 + 21 + 20 + 19) = (`-**61**) = "FLIP EVERY (`-**6**) OVER to a (`-**9**)" = (`-**91**) = **"TWO `-YEARS `-AWAY (`-91) from `-AGE of `-DEATH (`-93)"**!!!~'

(75 + 61) = (`-**136**) = RECIPROCAL = (`-**631**) = "FLIP EVERY (`-**6**) OVER to a (`-**9**)" = (`-**931**) = (93 x 1) = (`-**93**) = **"AGE of `-DEATH for AMERICAN THEATRE ACTRESS KAYE BALLARD (`-93)"**!!!~'

AMERICAN THEATRE ACTRESS KAYE BALLARD had `-**DIED** (`-**62**) `-**DAYS after `-HER `-LAST `-BIRTHDAY**!!!~'

(`-**62**) = "FLIP EVERY (`-**6**) OVER to a (`-**9**)" = (`-**92**) = **"ONE `-YEAR `-AWAY (`-92) from `-AGE of `-DEATH (`-93)"**!!!~'

(365 (-) 62) = (`-**303**) = <u>**R**eciprocal-**S**equencing-**N**umerology-**RSN**</u>!!!~'

99

DWAYNE W. ANDERSON

AMERICAN BUSINESSMAN PETER A. MAGOWAN `-DIED on *JANUARY 27th* within `-*2019*!!!~' `-HE was `-BORN on *APRIL 5th* in `-*1942*!!!~' `-HE `-DIED at the `-AGE of (`-**76**)!!!~'

`-**DEATH/DAY** = (**1/27**) = (1 (-) 27) = (`-**26**) = "FLIP EVERY (`-**2**) OVER to a (`-**7**)" = (`-**76**) = "AGE of `-DEATH for AMERICAN BUSINESSMAN PETER A. MAGOWAN (`-**76**)"!!!~'

`-**DEATH/DAY** = (**1/27**) = RECIPROCAL = (**72/1**) = "FLIP EVERY (`-**2**) OVER to a (`-**7**)" = (**77/1**) = (77 (-) 1) = (`-**76**) = "AGE of `-DEATH for AMERICAN BUSINESSMAN PETER A. MAGOWAN (`-**76**)"!!!~'

`-**BIRTH/YEAR** = (`-**42**) = (7 x 6) = (`-**76**) = "AGE of `-DEATH for AMERICAN BUSINESSMAN PETER A. MAGOWAN (`-**76**)"!!!~'

`-**BIRTH/YEAR** = (`-**42**) = RECIPROCAL = (`-**24**) = "FLIP EVERY (`-**2**) OVER to a (`-**7**)" = (`-**74**) = "TWO `-YEARS `-AWAY (`-**74**) from `-AGE of `-DEATH (`-**76**)"!!!~'

`-**DEATH/YEAR** = (`-**2019**) = "FLIP EVERY (`-**2**) OVER to a (`-**7**)" = (`-**7019**) = "FLIP EVERY (`-**9**) OVER to a (`-**6**)" = (`-**7016**) = (7 + 0) (1 x 6) = (`-**76**) = "AGE of `-DEATH for AMERICAN BUSINESSMAN PETER A. MAGOWAN (`-**76**)"!!!~'

AMERICAN BUSINESSMAN PETER A. MAGOWAN `-**BIRTHDAY** # `-**NUMBER** = `-EQUALS = (4 + 5 + 19 + 42) = (`-**70**)!!!~'

AMERICAN BUSINESSMAN PETER A. MAGOWAN `-**DEATH/ DAY** # `-**NUMBER** = `-EQUALS = (1 + 27 + 20 + 19) = (`-**67**) = RECIPROCAL = (`-**76**) = "AGE of `-DEATH for AMERICAN BUSINESSMAN PETER A. MAGOWAN (`-**76**)"!!!~'

(70 + 67) = (`-**137**) = RECIPROCAL = (`-**731**) = (73 + 1) = (`-**74**) = "TWO `-YEARS `-AWAY (`-**74**) from `-AGE of `-DEATH (`-**76**)"!!!~'

AMERICAN BUSINESSMAN PETER A. MAGOWAN had `-**DIED** (`-**68**) `-DAYS before `-HIS `-NEXT `-BIRTHDAY!!!~'

`-DEATH CIPHERS/CYPHERS FOR LIFE & DEATH!!!~'

(365 (-) 68) = (`-**297**) = (2 (-) 9) (7) = (`-**77**) = "ONE `-YEAR `-AWAY (`-**77**) from `-AGE of `-DEATH (`-**76**)"!!!~'

AMERICAN SINGER/SONGWRITER JAMES INGRAM `-DIED on *JANUARY 29th* within `-*2019*!!!~' `-HE was `-BORN on *FEBRUARY 16th* in `-*1952*!!!~' `-HE `-DIED at the `-AGE of (`-**66**)!!!~'

`-**DEATH/DAY** = (**1/29**) = "FLIP EVERY (`-**9**) OVER to a (`-**6**)" = (**1/26**)!!!~'

`-**BIRTH/DAY** = (**2/16**) = "SWIPE ONE (`-**1**) to the `-LEFT" = (**1/26**)!!!~'

`-**DEATH/DAY** = (**1/29**) = `-**DEATH/YEAR** = (`-**2019**) = "SWIPE ONE (`-**1**) to the `-LEFT" = (129) (0) = (**1/29**)!!!~'

`-**DEATH/DAY** = (**1/29**) = (1 x 29) = (`-**29**) = "FLIP EVERY (`-**9**) OVER to a (`-**6**)" = (`-**26**) = 2(6's) = (`-**66**) = "AGE of `-DEATH for AMERICAN SINGER/SONGWRITER JAMES INGRAM (`-**66**)"!!!~'

`-**BIRTH/YEAR** = (`-**1952**) = (52 (-) 19) = (`-**33**) = `-TIMES "**X**" (`-**2**) = (`-**66**) = "AGE of `-DEATH for AMERICAN SINGER/SONGWRITER JAMES INGRAM (`-**66**)"!!!~'

`-**DEATH/YEAR** = (`-**2019**) = (2 + 1) (0 + 9) = (`-**39**) = "FLIP EVERY (`-**9**) OVER to a (`-**6**)" = (`-**36**) = (6 x 6) = (`-**66**) = "AGE of `-DEATH for AMERICAN SINGER/SONGWRITER JAMES INGRAM (`-**66**)"!!!~'

`-**DEATH/YEAR** = (`-**2019**) = (20 + 19) = (`-**39**) = "FLIP EVERY (`-**9**) OVER to a (`-**6**)" = (`-**36**) = (6 x 6) = (`-**66**) = "AGE of `-DEATH for AMERICAN SINGER/SONGWRITER JAMES INGRAM (`-**66**)"!!!~'

`-**BIRTH/DAY** = (**2/16**) = (2 + 1) (6) = (`-**36**) = (6 x 6) = (`-**66**) = "AGE of `-DEATH for AMERICAN SINGER/SONGWRITER JAMES INGRAM (`-**66**)"!!!~'

`-**BIRTH/DAY** = (**2/16**) = RECIPROCAL = (**61/2**) = (6) (1 + 2) = (`-**63**) = RECIPROCAL = (`-**36**) = (6 x 6) = (`-**66**) = **"AGE of `-DEATH for AMERICAN SINGER/SONGWRITER JAMES INGRAM (`-66)"**!!!~'

AMERICAN SINGER/SONGWRITER JAMES INGRAM `-**BIRTHDAY** # `-**NUMBER** = `-EQUALS = (2 + 16 + 19 + 52) = (`-**89**) = "FLIP EVERY (`-**8**) OVER to a (`-**3**)" = (`-**39**) = "FLIP EVERY (`-**9**) OVER to a (`-**6**)" = (`-**36**) = (6 x 6) = (`-**66**) = **"AGE of `-DEATH for AMERICAN SINGER/SONGWRITER JAMES INGRAM (`-66)"**!!!~'

AMERICAN SINGER/SONGWRITER JAMES INGRAM `-**DEATH/ DAY #** `-**NUMBER** = `-EQUALS = (1 + 29 + 20 + 19) = (`-**69**) = "FLIP EVERY (`-**9**) OVER to a (`-**6**)" = (`-**66**) = **"AGE of `-DEATH for AMERICAN SINGER/SONGWRITER JAMES INGRAM (`-66)"**!!!~'

(89 + 69) = (`-**158**) = (1 + 5) (8) = (`-**68**) = **"TWO `-YEARS `-AWAY (`-68) from `-AGE of `-DEATH (`-66)"**!!!~'

(8 x 9) = (`-**72**)!!!~' /||\ (6 x 9) = (`-**54**)!!!~'

(72 + 54) = (`-**126**)!!!~'

`-**DEATH/DAY** = (**1/29**) = "FLIP EVERY (`-**9**) OVER to a (`-**6**)" = (**1/26**)!!!~'

`-**BIRTH/DAY** = (**2/16**) = **"SWIPE ONE (`-1) to the `-LEFT"** = (**1/26**)!!!~'

AMERICAN SINGER/SONGWRITER JAMES INGRAM had `-**DIED** (`-**18**) `-**DAYS before `-HIS `-NEXT `-BIRTHDAY**!!!~'

(`-**18**) = RECIPROCAL = (`-**81**) = (9 x 9) = (`-**99**) = "FLIP EVERY (`-**9**) OVER to a (`-**6**)" = (`-**66**) = **"AGE of `-DEATH for AMERICAN SINGER/SONGWRITER JAMES INGRAM (`-66)"**!!!~'

AMERICAN ACTOR KRISTOFF ST. JOHN `-DIED on *FEBRUARY 3rd* within `-*2019*!!!~' `-HE was `-BORN on *JULY 15th* in `-*1966*!!!~' `-HE `-DIED at the `-AGE of (`-**52**)!!!~'

`-**DEATH/DAY** = (**2/3**) = "FLIP EVERY (`-**3**) OVER to an (`-**8**)" = (**2/8**) = "DAYS in the **MONTH** of `-**FEBRUARY** (`-**28**)"!!!~'

(**28**) (-) (**3**) for (*FEB.3*) = (`-**25**) = RECIPROCAL = (`-**52**) = "AGE of `-DEATH for AMERICAN ACTOR KRISTOFF ST. JOHN (`-**52**)"!!!~'

`-**BIRTH/DAY** = (**7/15**) = "FLIP EVERY (`-**7**) OVER to a (`-**2**)" = (**2/15**) = RECIPROCAL = (**51/2**) = (52 x 1) = (`-**52**) = "AGE of `-DEATH for AMERICAN ACTOR KRISTOFF ST. JOHN (`-**52**)"!!!~'

`-**DEATH/YEAR** = (`-**2019**) = "FLIP EVERY (`-**9**) OVER to a (`-**6**)" = (`-**2016**) = RECIPROCAL = (`-**6102**) = (6 (-) 1) (0 + 2) = (`-**52**) = "AGE of `-DEATH for AMERICAN ACTOR KRISTOFF ST. JOHN (`-**52**)"!!!~'

`-**BIRTH/YEAR** = (`-**1966**) = RECIPROCAL = (`-**6691**) = (6 (-) 1) (6 (-) 9) = (`-**53**) = "ONE `-YEAR `-AWAY (`-**53**) from `-AGE of `-DEATH (`-**52**)"!!!~'

`-**BIRTH/YEAR** = (`-**1966**) = (66 (-) 19) = (`-**47**) = RECIPROCAL = (`-**74**)!!!~'

`-**BIRTH/DAY** = (**7/15**) = (7) (1 (-) 5) = (`-**74**)!!!~'

AMERICAN ACTOR KRISTOFF ST. JOHN `-**BIRTHDAY** # `-**NUMBER** = `-**EQUALS** = (7 + 15 + 19 + 66) = (`-**107**)!!!~'

AMERICAN ACTOR KRISTOFF ST. JOHN `-**DEATH/DAY** # `-**NUMBER** = `-**EQUALS** = (2 + 3 + 20 + 19) = (`-**44**)!!!~'

(107 + 44) = (`-**151**) = (51 + 1) = (`-**52**) = "AGE of `-DEATH for AMERICAN ACTOR KRISTOFF ST. JOHN (`-**52**)"!!!~'

AMERICAN ACTOR KRISTOFF ST. JOHN had `-**DIED** (`-**162**) `-**DAYS before** `-**HIS** `-**NEXT** `-**BIRTHDAY**!!!~`

(`-**162**) = (1 (-) 6) (2) = (`-**52**) = "**AGE of** `-**DEATH for AMERICAN ACTOR KRISTOFF ST. JOHN** (`-**52**)"!!!~`

(365 (-) 162) = (`-**203**) = (23 + 0) = (`-**23**) = `-**DEATH/DAY** = (**2/3**) = (**FEBRUARY 3**rd)!!!~`

AMERICAN ACTOR **KRISTOFF ST. JOHN** = `-**RECIPROCAL of** = AMERICAN SINGER/SONGWRITER **JAMES INGRAM** = `-**66** to `-**52** = `-**52** to `-**66** = "**AGE of** `-**DEATH to** `-**YEAR of** `-**BIRTH to** `-**YEAR of** `-**BIRTH to** `-**AGE of** `-**DEATH**"!!!~`

BASEBALL GREAT FRANK ROBINSON `-DIED on *FEBRUARY 7th* within `-*2019*!!!~` `-HE was `-BORN on *AUGUST 31st* in `-*1935*!!!~` `-HE `-DIED at the `-AGE of (`-**83**)!!!~`

`-**BIRTH/DAY** = (**8/31**) = (83 x 1) = (`-**83**) = "**AGE of** `-**DEATH for BASEBALL GREAT FRANK ROBINSON** (`-**83**)"!!!~`

`-**BIRTH/DAY** = (**8/31**) = RECIPROCAL = (**13/8**) = (1 (-) 3) (8) = (**2/8**) = `-**DIED the** `-**DAY** `-**PRIOR on** (**2/7**) = (**FEBRUARY 7**th)!!!~`

`-**DEATH/DAY** = (**2/7**) (+) `-**BIRTH/DAY** = (**8/31**) = (2 + 7 + 8 + 31) = (`-**48**) = RECIPROCAL = (`-**84**) = "**ONE** `-**YEAR** `-**AWAY** (`-**84**) from `-**AGE of** `-**DEATH** (`-**83**)"!!!~`

`-**BIRTH/YEAR** = (`-**35**) = "FLIP EVERY (`-**3**) OVER to an (`-**8**)" = (`-**85**) = "**TWO** `-**YEARS** `-**AWAY** (`-**85**) from `-**AGE of** `-**DEATH** (`-**83**)"!!!~`

`-**BIRTH/YEAR** = (`-**1935**) = (19 + 35) = (`-**54**) / `-**DIVIDED** `-**by** / (`-**2**) = (`-**27**) = (**2/7**) = `-**DEATH/DAY** = (**FEBRUARY 7**th)!!!~`

`-**DEATH/YEAR** = (`-**2019**) = RECIPROCAL = (`-**9102**) = (9 (-) 1) (0 + 2) = (`-**82**) = "ONE `-YEAR `-AWAY (`-**82**) from `-AGE of `-DEATH (`-**83**)"!!!~'

BASEBALL GREAT FRANK ROBINSON `-**BIRTHDAY # **`-**NUMBER** = `-EQUALS = (8 + 31 + 19 + 35) = (`-**93**) = (9 x 3) = (`-**27**) = `-**DEATH/ DAY** = (**2/7**) = (**FEBRUARY 7**th)!!!~'

BASEBALL GREAT FRANK ROBINSON `-**DEATH/DAY # **`-**NUMBER** = `-EQUALS = (2 + 7 + 20 + 19) = (`-**48**) = RECIPROCAL = (`-**84**) = "ONE `-YEAR `-AWAY (`-**84**) from `-AGE of `-DEATH (`-**83**)"!!!~'

(93 + 48) = (`-**141**) = (1 + 1) (4) = (`-**24**) = (8 x 3) = (`-**83**) = "AGE of `-DEATH for BASEBALL GREAT FRANK ROBINSON (`-**83**)"!!!~'

(93 (-) 48) = (`-**45**) = RECIPROCAL = (`-**54**) / `-**DIVIDED** `-by / (`-**2**) = (`-**27**) = (**2/7**) = `-**DEATH/DAY** = (**FEBRUARY 7**th)!!!~'

BASEBALL GREAT FRANK ROBINSON had `-**DIED** (`-**205**) `-**DAYS** before `-**HIS** `-**NEXT** `-**BIRTHDAY**!!!~'

(`-**205**) = (20 + 5) = (`-**25**) = (**2/5**) = `-**DIED** `-**TWO** (`-**2**) `-**DAYS** `-**LATER** on (**2/7**) = (**FEBRUARY 7**th)!!!~'

(365 (-) 205) = (`-**160**) = (16 + 0) = (`-**16**) = (8 x 2) = (`-**82**) = "ONE `-YEAR `-AWAY (`-**82**) from `-AGE of `-DEATH (`-**83**)"!!!~'

FORMER UNITED STATES REPRESENTATIVE JOHN DINGELL `-DIED on *FEBRUARY 7*<sup>th</sup> within `-*2019*!!!~' `-HE was `-BORN on *JULY 8*th in `-*1926*!!!~' `-HE `-DIED at the `-AGE of (`-**92**)!!!~'

`-**DEATH/YEAR** = (`-**2019**) = RECIPROCAL = (`-**9102**) = (9 x 1) (0 + 2) = (`-**92**) = "AGE of `-DEATH for FORMER UNITED STATES REPRESENTATIVE JOHN DINGELL (`-**92**)"!!!~'

`-**BIRTH/DAY** = (**7/8**) = "FLIP EVERY (`-**8**) OVER to a (`-**3**)" = (**7/3**)!!!~'

`-**DEATH/DAY** = (**2/7**) = RECIPROCAL = (**7/2**)!!!~'

`-**BIRTH/YEAR** = (`-**26**) = RECIPROCAL = (`-**62**) = "FLIP EVERY (`-**6**) OVER to a (`-**9**)" = (`-**92**) = "AGE of `-DEATH for FORMER UNITED STATES REPRESENTATIVE JOHN DINGELL (`-**92**)"!!!~'

BASEBALL PITCHER DON NEWCOMBE `-DIED on *FEBRUARY 19th* within `-*2019*!!!~' `-HE was `-BORN on *JUNE 14th* in `-*1926*!!!~' `-HE `-DIED at the `-AGE of (`-**92**)!!!~'

`-**BIRTH/DAY** = (**6/14**) = RECIPROCAL = (**41/6**) = (`-**416**) / `-DIVIDED `-by / (`-**2**) = (`-**208**) = (20 + 8) = (`-**28**) = `-**DEATH/DAY** = (**2/19**) = (2) (1 (-) 9) = (`-**28**)!!!~'

`-**DEATH/DAY** = (**2/19**) = `-**DIED** within (`-**2019**)!!!~'

`-**BIRTH/DAY** = (**6/14**) = "FLIP EVERY (`-**6**) OVER to a (`-**9**)" = (**9/14**) = (94 (-) 1) = (`-**93**) = "ONE `-YEAR `-AWAY (`-**93**) from `-AGE of `-DEATH (`-**92**)"!!!~'

`-**DEATH/DAY** = (**2/19**) = RECIPROCAL = (**91/2**) = (92 x 1) = (`-**92**) = "AGE of `-DEATH for BASEBALL PITCHER DON NEWCOMBE (`-**92**)"!!!~'

`-**DEATH/YEAR** = (`-**2019**) = RECIPROCAL = (`-**9102**) = (9 x 1) (0 + 2) = (`-**92**) = "AGE of `-DEATH for BASEBALL PITCHER DON NEWCOMBE (`-**92**)"!!!~'

`-**BIRTH/YEAR** = (`-**26**) = RECIPROCAL = (`-**62**) = "FLIP EVERY (`-**6**) OVER to a (`-**9**)" = (`-**92**) = "AGE of `-DEATH for BASEBALL PITCHER DON NEWCOMBE (`-**92**)"!!!~'

`-**BIRTH/YEAR** = (`-**1926**) = (1 x 9) (2 (-) 6) = (`-**94**) = "TWO `-YEARS `-AWAY (`-**94**) from `-AGE of `-DEATH (`-**92**)"!!!~'

`-DEATH CIPHERS/CYPHERS FOR LIFE & DEATH!!!~'

BASEBALL PITCHER DON NEWCOMBE `-BIRTHDAY # `-NUMBER = `-EQUALS = (6 + 14 + 19 + 26) = (`-65)!!!~'

BASEBALL PITCHER DON NEWCOMBE `-DEATH/DAY # `-NUMBER = `-EQUALS = (2 + 19 + 20 + 19) = (`-60)!!!~'

(65 + 60) = (`-125) = (1 + 5) (2) = (`-62) = "FLIP EVERY (`-6) OVER to a (`-9)" = (`-92) = "AGE of `-DEATH for BASEBALL PITCHER DON NEWCOMBE (`-92)"!!!~'

MUSICIAN PETER TORK from THE MUSICAL GROUP "THE MONKEYS" `-DIED on *FEBRUARY 21st* within `-*2019*!!!~' `-HE was `-BORN on *FEBRUARY 13th* in `-*1942*!!!~' `-HE `-DIED at the `-AGE of (`-77)!!!~'

`-BIRTH/DAY = (2/13) = (2) (1 (-) 3) = = (`-22) = "FLIP EVERY (`-2) OVER to a (`-7)" = (`-77) = "AGE of `-DEATH for MUSICIAN PETER TORK from THE MUSICAL GROUP "THE MONKEYS" (`-77)"!!!~'

`-DEATH/DAY = (2/21) = (2) (2 x 1) = (`-22) = "FLIP EVERY (`-2) OVER to a (`-7)" = (`-77) = "AGE of `-DEATH for MUSICIAN PETER TORK from THE MUSICAL GROUP "THE MONKEYS" (`-77)"!!!~'

`-DEATH/DAY = (2/21) = "FLIP EVERY (`-2) OVER to a (`-7)" = (7/71) = (77 x 1) = (`-77) = "AGE of `-DEATH for MUSICIAN PETER TORK from THE MUSICAL GROUP "THE MONKEYS" (`-77)"!!!~'

MUSICIAN PETER TORK from THE MUSICAL GROUP "THE MONKEYS" `-BIRTHDAY # `-NUMBER = `-EQUALS = (2 + 13 + 19 + 42) = (`-76) = "ONE `-YEAR `-AWAY (`-76) from `-AGE of `-DEATH (`-77)"!!!~'

MUSICIAN PETER TORK from THE MUSICAL GROUP "THE MONKEYS" `-BIRTHDAY # `NUMBER = `-EQUALS = (2 + 13 + 19 + 42) = (`-76) = RECIPROCAL = (`-67)!!!~'

MUSICIAN PETER TORK from THE MUSICAL GROUP "THE MONKEYS" `-DEATH/DAY # `-NUMBER = `-EQUALS = (2 + 21 + 20 + 19) = (`-62) = "FLIP EVERY (`-2) OVER to a (`-7)" = (`-67)!!!~'

`-DEATH/YEAR = (`-2019) = "FLIP EVERY (`-2) OVER to a (`-7)" = (`-7019) = (7 + 0) (1 (-) 9) = (`-78) = "ONE `-YEAR `-AWAY (`-78) from `-AGE of `-DEATH (`-77)"!!!~'

`-BIRTH/YEAR = (`-1942) = (9 (-) 2) (1 + 4) = (`-75) = "TWO `-YEARS `-AWAY (`-75) from `-AGE of `-DEATH (`-77)"!!!~'

`-BIRTH/YEAR = (`-1942) = (42 (-) 19) = (`-23) = "FLIP EVERY (`-2) OVER to a (`-7)" = (`-73) = "FLIP EVERY (`-3) OVER to an (`-8)" = (`-78) = "ONE `-YEAR `-AWAY (`-78) from `-AGE of `-DEATH (`-77)"!!!~'

AMERICAN ACTRESS KATHERINE HELMOND `-DIED on *FEBRUARY 23rd* within `-*2019*!!!~' `-SHE was `-BORN on *JULY 5th* in `-*1929*!!!~' `-SHE `-DIED at the `-AGE of (`-89)!!!~'

`-DEATH/DAY = (2/23) = "FLIP EVERY (`-2) OVER to a (`-7)" = (7/23) = (7) (2 + 3) = (7/5) = `-BIRTH/DAY = (JULY 5th)!!!~'

`-DEATH/DAY = (2/23) = RECIPROCAL = (32/2) = "FLIP EVERY (`-3) OVER to an (`-8)" = (82/2) = "FLIP EVERY (`-2) OVER to a (`-7)" = (87/2) = (87 + 2) = (`-89) = "AGE of `-DEATH for AMERICAN ACTRESS KATHERINE HELMOND (`-89)"!!!~'

`-DEATH/YEAR = (`-2019) = (20 + 19) = (`-39) = "FLIP EVERY (`-3) OVER to an (`-8)" = (`-89) = "AGE of `-DEATH for AMERICAN ACTRESS KATHERINE HELMOND (`-89)"!!!~'

`-DEATH/YEAR = (`-2019) = "FLIP EVERY (`-2) OVER to a (`-7)" = (`-7019) = (7 + 1) (0 + 9) = (`-89) = "AGE of `-DEATH for AMERICAN ACTRESS KATHERINE HELMOND (`-89)"!!!~'

`-**BIRTH/YEAR** = (`-**1929**) = "FLIP EVERY (`-**9**) OVER to a (`-**6**)" = (`-**1926**) = (1 x 9) (2 + 6) = (`-**98**) = RECIPROCAL = (`-**89**) = "**AGE of** `-**DEATH for AMERICAN ACTRESS KATHERINE HELMOND** (`-**89**)"!!!~'

`-**BIRTH/YEAR** = (`-**1929**) = (99 (-) 12) = (`-**87**) = "**TWO** `-**YEARS** `-**AWAY** (`-**87**) from `-**AGE of** `-**DEATH** (`-**89**)"!!!~'

AMERICAN ACTRESS KATHERINE HELMOND `-**BIRTHDAY #** `-**NUMBER** = `-**EQUALS** = (7 + 5 + 19 + 29) = (`-**60**)!!!~'

AMERICAN ACTRESS KATHERINE HELMOND `-**DEATH/DAY #** `-**NUMBER** = `-**EQUALS** = (2 + 23 + 20 + 19) = (`-**64**)!!!~'

(64 + 60) = (`-**124**) = "FLIP EVERY (`-**2**) OVER to a (`-**7**)" = (`-**174**) = (74 + 1) = (`-**75**) = `-**BIRTH/DAY** = (**7/5**) = (**JULY 5**[th])!!!~'

AMERICAN ACTRESS KATHERINE HELMOND had `-**DIED** (`-**132**) `-**DAYS before** `-**HER** `-**NEXT** `-**BIRTHDAY**!!!~'

(`-**132**) = "FLIP EVERY (`-**3**) OVER to an (`-**8**)" = (`-**182**) = "FLIP EVERY (`-**2**) OVER to a (`-**7**)" = (`-**187**) = (87 + 1) = (`-**88**) = "**ONE** `-**YEAR** `-**AWAY** (`-**88**) from `-**AGE of** `-**DEATH** (`-**89**)"!!!~'

(365 (-) 132) = (`-**233**) = "FLIP EVERY (`-**3**) OVER to an (`-**8**)" = (`-**288**) = (88 + 2) = (`-**90**) = "**ONE** `-**YEAR** `-**AWAY** (`-**90**) from `-**AGE of** `-**DEATH** (`-**89**)"!!!~'

MUSIC ARTIST RAPPER NIPSEY HUSSLE `-DIED on **MARCH 31**[st] within `-**2019**!!!~' `-HE was `-BORN on **AUGUST 15**[th] in `-**1985**!!!~' `-HE `-DIED at the `-AGE of (`-**33**)!!!~'

`-**DEATH/DAY** = (**3/31**) = (33 x 1) = (`-**33**) = "AGE of `-DEATH for **MUSIC ARTIST RAPPER NIPSEY HUSSLE** (`-**33**)"!!!~'

`-**BIRTH/DAY** = (**8/15**) = "FLIP EVERY (`-**8**) OVER to a (`-**3**)" = (**3/15**) = (3) (1 (-) 5) = (`-**34**) = "**ONE** `-**YEAR** `-**AWAY** (`-**34**) from `-**AGE** of `-**DEATH** (`-**33**)"!!!~'

`-**DEATH/DAY** = (**3/31**) = (3) (3 + 1) = (`-**34**) = "**ONE** `-**YEAR** `-**AWAY** (`-**34**) from `-**AGE** of `-**DEATH** (`-**33**)"!!!~'

`-**BIRTH/DAY** = (**8/15**) = "**SWIPE** `-**ONE** to the `-**LEFT**" = `-**BIRTH/YEAR** = (`-**1985**)!!!~'

`-**BIRTH/DAY** = (**8/15**) = "FLIP EVERY (`-**8**) OVER to a (`-**3**)" = (**3/15**) = (35 x 1) = (`-**35**) = "**TWO** `-**YEARS** `-**AWAY** (`-**35**) from `-**AGE** of `-**DEATH** (`-**33**)"!!!~'

`-**BIRTH/YEAR** = (`-**85**) = "FLIP EVERY (`-**8**) OVER to a (`-**3**)" = (`-**35**) = "**TWO** `-**YEARS** `-**AWAY** (`-**35**) from `-**AGE** of `-**DEATH** (`-**33**)"!!!~'

`-**BIRTH/YEAR** = (`-**1985**) = (85 (-) 19) = (`-**66**) / `-**DIVIDED** `-**by** / (`-**2**) = (`-**33**) = "**AGE** of `-**DEATH** for MUSIC ARTIST RAPPER NIPSEY HUSSLE (`-**33**)"!!!~'

MUSIC ARTIST RAPPER NIPSEY HUSSLE `-**BIRTHDAY #** `-**NUMBER** = `-**EQUALS** = (8 + 15 + 19 + 85) = (`-**127**) = RECIPROCAL = (`-**721**) = (72 + 1) = (`-**73**) = `-**DEATH/DAY #** `-**NUMBER** (`-**73**)!!!~'

MUSIC ARTIST RAPPER NIPSEY HUSSLE `-**DEATH/DAY #** `-**NUMBER** = `-**EQUALS** = (3 + 31 + 20 + 19) = (`-**73**)!!!~'

MUSIC ARTIST RAPPER NIPSEY HUSSLE had `-**DIED** (`-**137**) `-**DAYS** before `-**HIS** `-**NEXT** `-**BIRTHDAY**!!!~'

(`-**137**) = "FLIP EVERY (`-**7**) OVER to a (`-**2**)" = (`-**132**) = (32 + 1) = (`-**33**) = "**AGE** of `-**DEATH** for MUSIC ARTIST RAPPER NIPSEY HUSSLE (`-**33**)"!!!~'

(365 (-) 137) = (`-**228**) = "FLIP EVERY (`-**8**) OVER to a (`-**3**)" = (`-**223**) = RECIPROCAL = (`-**322**) = (32 + 2) = (`-**34**) = "ONE `-YEAR `-AWAY (`-**34**) from `-AGE of `-DEATH (`-**33**)"!!!~'

AMERICAN HISTORIAN SCHOLAR OF SLAVERY DAVID BRION DAVIS `-DIED on **APRIL 14**th within `-**2019**!!!~' `-HE was `-BORN on **FEBRUARY 16**th in `-**1927**!!!~' `-HE `-DIED at the `-AGE of (`-**92**)!!!~'

`-**DEATH/DAY** = (**4/14**) = (4 + 14) = (`-**18**) = (9 x 2) = (`-**92**) = "AGE of `-DEATH for AMERICAN HISTORIAN SCHOLAR OF SLAVERY DAVID BRION DAVIS (`-**92**)"!!!~'

`-**BIRTH/DAY** = (**2/16**) = (2 + 16) = (`-**18**) = (9 x 2) = (`-**92**) = "AGE of `-DEATH for AMERICAN HISTORIAN SCHOLAR OF SLAVERY DAVID BRION DAVIS (`-**92**)"!!!~'

`-**BIRTH/DAY** = (**2/16**) = RECIPROCAL = (**61/2**) = "FLIP EVERY (`-**6**) OVER to a (`-**9**)" = (**91/2**) = (92 x 1) = (`-**92**) = "AGE of `-DEATH for AMERICAN HISTORIAN SCHOLAR OF SLAVERY DAVID BRION DAVIS (`-**92**)"!!!~'

`-**DEATH/YEAR** = (`-**2019**) = RECIPROCAL = (`-**9102**) = (9 x 1) (0 + 2) = (`-**92**) = "AGE of `-DEATH for AMERICAN HISTORIAN SCHOLAR OF SLAVERY DAVID BRION DAVIS (`-**92**)"!!!~'

AMERICAN HISTORIAN SCHOLAR OF SLAVERY DAVID BRION DAVIS `-BIRTHDAY # `-NUMBER = `-EQUALS = (2 + 16 + 19 + 27) = (`-**64**) = RECIPROCAL = (`-**46**) = `-**BIRTH/YEAR** = (19 + 27) = (`-**46**) = RECIPROCAL = (`-**64**)!!!~'

AMERICAN HISTORIAN SCHOLAR OF SLAVERY DAVID BRION DAVIS `-**DEATH/DAY #** `-NUMBER = `-EQUALS = (4 + 14 + 20 + 19) = (`-**57**) = `-**DIED** this `-**MANY** `-**DAYS** (`-**57**) after `-**HIS** `-**LAST** `-**BIRTHDAY**!!!~'

DWAYNE W. ANDERSON

AMERICAN HISTORIAN SCHOLAR OF SLAVERY DAVID BRION
DAVIS had `-**DIED** (`-**57**) `-**DAYS after** `-**HIS** `-**LAST** `-**BIRTHDAY**!!!~'

(`-**57**) = "**HIS** `-**DEATH/DAY** # `-**NUMBER** (`-**57**)!!!~'

AMERICAN ACTRESS GEORGIA ENGEL `-DIED on *APRIL 12th*
within `-*2019*!!!~' `-SHE was `-BORN on *JULY 28th* in `-*1948*!!!~'
`-SHE `-DIED at the `-AGE of (`-**70**)!!!~'

`-**DEATH/DAY** = (**4/12**) = (4 x 12) = (`-**48**) = "**BORN in the** `-**YEAR**
of (`-**48**)"!!!~'

`-**BIRTH/DAY** = (**7/28**) = (7) (2 + 8) = (7) (10) = (7 x 10) = (`-**70**) =
"**AGE of** `-**DEATH for AMERICAN ACTRESS GEORGIA ENGEL**
(`-**70**)"!!!~'

`-**DEATH/DAY** = (**4/12**) = RECIPROCAL = (**21/4**) = "FLIP EVERY
(`-**2**) OVER to a (`-**7**)" = (**71/4**) = (7 x 1) (4) = (**74**)!!!~'

`-**BIRTH/DAY** = (**7/28**) = (7) (8 (/) 2) = (**74**)!!!~'

`-**DEATH/YEAR** = (`-**2019**) = "FLIP EVERY (`-**2**) OVER to a (`-**7**)"
= (`-**7019**) = (7 + 0) (1 + 9) = (7) (10) = (7 x 10) = (`-**70**) = "**AGE of**
`-**DEATH for AMERICAN ACTRESS GEORGIA ENGEL** (`-**70**)"!!!~'

`-**BIRTH/YEAR** = (`-**1948**) = "FLIP EVERY (`-**8**) OVER to a (`-**3**)"
= (`-**1943**) = (1 + 9) (4 + 3) = (10) (7) = (10 x 7) = (`-**70**) = "**AGE of**
`-**DEATH for AMERICAN ACTRESS GEORGIA ENGEL** (`-**70**)"!!!~'

AMERICAN ACTRESS GEORGIA ENGEL `-**BIRTHDAY** #
`-**NUMBER** = `-**EQUALS** = (7 + 28 + 19 + 48) = (`-**102**) = "FLIP
EVERY (`-**2**) OVER to a (`-**7**)" = (`-**107**) = `-**DIED** this `-**MANY**
`-**DAYS** (`-**107**) before `-**HER** `-**NEXT** `-**BIRTHDAY**!!!~'

AMERICAN ACTRESS GEORGIA ENGEL `-**DEATH/DAY** #
`-**NUMBER** = `-**EQUALS** = (4 + 12 + 20 + 19) = (`-**55**)!!!~'

AMERICAN ACTRESS GEORGIA ENGEL had `-**DIED** (`-**107**) `-**DAYS** before `-**HER** `-**NEXT** `-**BIRTHDAY**!!!~'

(`-**107**) `-**TIMES** "**X**" (`-**2**) = (`-**214**) = RECIPROCAL = (`-**4/12**) = (**APRIL 12**th) = "**DEATH/DAY**"!!!~'

(365 (-) 107) = (`-**258**) = "FLIP EVERY (`-**2**) OVER to a (`-**7**)" = (`-**758**) = "FLIP EVERY (`-**8**) OVER to a (`-**3**)" = (`-**753**) = (75 (-) 3) = (`-**72**) = "**TWO** `-**YEARS** `-**AWAY** (`-**72**) from `-**AGE** of `-**DEATH** (`-**70**)"!!!~'

AMERICAN BASKETBALL PLAYER of the BOSTON CELTICS JOHN HAVLICEK `-DIED on **APRIL 25**th within `-**2019**!!!~' `-HE was `-BORN on **APRIL 8**th in `-**1940**!!!~' `-HE `-DIED at the `-AGE of (`-**79**)!!!~'

`-**DEATH/DAY** = (**4/25**) = (4) (2 + 5) = (**4/7**) = "**Was** `-**BORN** the `-**VERY** `-**NEXT** `-**DAY**" on (**4/8**) = (**APRIL 8**th)!!!~'

`-**DAY** of `-**DEATH** = (`-**25**th) = "FLIP EVERY (`-**2**) OVER to a (`-**7**)" = (`-**75**) = (+) **PLUS** (+) `-**MONTH** of `-**DEATH** (`-**4**) = (75 + 4) = (`-**79**) = "**AGE** of `-**DEATH** for AMERICAN BASKETBALL PLAYER of the BOSTON CELTICS JOHN HAVLICEK (`-**79**)"!!!~'

`-**DEATH/YEAR** = (`-**2019**) = "FLIP EVERY (`-**2**) OVER to a (`-**7**)" = (`-**7019**) = (7 x 1) (0 + 9) = (`-**79**) = "**AGE** of `-**DEATH** for AMERICAN BASKETBALL PLAYER of the BOSTON CELTICS JOHN HAVLICEK (`-**79**)"!!!~'

AMERICAN BASKETBALL PLAYER of the BOSTON CELTICS JOHN HAVLICEK `-**BIRTHDAY #** `-**NUMBER** = `-EQUALS = (4 + 8 + 19 + 40) = (`-**71**) = `-**BIRTH/YEAR** = (**1940**) = (40 (-) 19) = (`-**21**) = "FLIP EVERY (`-**2**) OVER to a (`-**7**)" = (`-**71**)!!!~'

AMERICAN BASKETBALL PLAYER of the BOSTON CELTICS JOHN HAVLICEK `-**DEATH/DAY #** `-**NUMBER** = `-EQUALS = (4 + 25 + 20 + 19) = (`-**68**) = "FLIP EVERY (`-**8**) OVER to a (`-**3**)" = (`-**63**) =

(7 x 9) = (`-**79**) = "AGE of `-DEATH for AMERICAN BASKETBALL PLAYER of the BOSTON CELTICS JOHN HAVLICEK (`-**79**)"!!!~'

(71 + 68) = (`-**139**) = "FLIP EVERY (`-**3**) OVER to an (`-**8**)" = (`-**189**) = (1 (-) 8) (9) = (`-**79**) = "AGE of `-DEATH for AMERICAN BASKETBALL PLAYER of the BOSTON CELTICS JOHN HAVLICEK (`-**79**)"!!!~'

AMERICAN BASKETBALL PLAYER of the BOSTON CELTICS JOHN HAVLICEK had `-**DIED** (`-**17**) `-**DAYS** after `-**HIS** `-**LAST** `-**BIRTHDAY**!!!~'

(`-**17**) = RECIPROCAL = (`-**71**) = `-**BIRTH/DAY** # `-**NUMBER** (`-**71**)!!!~'

(365 (-) 17) = (`-**348**) = (3 + 4) (8) = (`-**78**) = "ONE `-YEAR `-AWAY (`-**78**) from `-AGE of `-DEATH (`-**79**)"!!!~'

FORMER US REPRESENTATIVE ELLEN TAUSCHER `-DIED on *APRIL 29*[th] within `-*2019*!!!~' `-SHE was `-BORN on *NOVEMBER 15*[th] in `-*1951*!!!~' `-SHE `-DIED at the `-AGE of (`-**67**)!!!~'

`-**DEATH/DAY** = (**4/29**) = (4) (2 + 9) = (**4/11**) = RECIPROCAL = (**11/4**)!!!~'

`-**BIRTH/DAY** = (**11/15**) = (11) (1 (-) 5) = (**11/4**)!!!~'

`-**BIRTH/DAY** = (**11/15**) = (11 + 15) = (`-**26**) = "FLIP EVERY (`-**2**) OVER to a (`-**7**)" = (`-**76**) = RECIPROCAL = (`-**67**) = "AGE of `-DEATH for FORMER US REPRESENTATIVE ELLEN TAUSCHER (`-**67**)"!!!~'

`-**DAY** of `-**BIRTH** = (`-**15**[th]) = RECIPROCAL = (`-**51**) = "**YEAR** of `-**BIRTH**"!!!~'

`-**DEATH/YEAR** = (`-**2019**) = "FLIP EVERY (`-**2**) OVER to a (`-**7**)" = (`-**7019**) = "FLIP EVERY (`-**9**) OVER to a (`-**6**)" = (`-**7016**) = (7 +

0) (1 x 6) = (`-**76**) = RECIPROCAL = (`-**67**) = "AGE of `-DEATH for **FORMER US REPRESENTATIVE ELLEN TAUSCHER (`-67)**"!!!~'

`-**BIRTH/YEAR** = (`-**1951**) = "FLIP EVERY (`-**9**) OVER to a (`-**6**)" = (`-**1651**) = (6) (1 + 5 + 1) = (`-**67**) = "AGE of `-DEATH for **FORMER US REPRESENTATIVE ELLEN TAUSCHER (`-67)**"!!!~'

FORMER US REPRESENTATIVE ELLEN TAUSCHER `-**BIRTHDAY # `-NUMBER** = `-EQUALS = (11 + 15 + 19 + 51) = (`-**96**) = RECIPROCAL = (`-**69**) = "**TWO `-YEARS `-AWAY (`-69) from `-AGE of `-DEATH (`-67)**"!!!~'

FORMER US REPRESENTATIVE ELLEN TAUSCHER `-**DEATH/ DAY # `-NUMBER** = `-EQUALS = (4 + 29 + 20 + 19) = (`-**72**)!!!~'

(96 + 72) = (`-**168**) = (6) (1 (-) 8) = (`-**67**) = "**AGE of `-DEATH for FORMER US REPRESENTATIVE ELLEN TAUSCHER (`-67)**"!!!~'

FORMER US REPRESENTATIVE ELLEN TAUSCHER had `-**DIED** (`-**165**) `-**DAYS** after `-**HER `-LAST `-BIRTHDAY**!!!~'

(`-**165**) = (65 + 1) = (`-**66**) = "**ONE `-YEAR `-AWAY (`-66) from `-AGE of `-DEATH (`-67)**"!!!~'

AMERICAN PROFESSIONAL ZOOLOGIST & AMERICAN TV HOST of "MUTUAL of OMAHA'S WILD KINGDOM" JIM FOWLER `-DIED on *MAY 8[th]* within `-*2019*!!!~' `-HE was `-BORN on *APRIL 9th* in `-*1932*!!!~' `-HE `-DIED at the `-AGE of (`-**87**)!!!~'

`-**BIRTH/YEAR** = (`-**32**) = "FLIP EVERY (`-**3**) OVER to an (`-**8**)" = (`-**82**) = "FLIP EVERY (`-**2**) OVER to a (`-**7**)" = (`-**87**) = "**AGE of `-DEATH for AMERICAN PROFESSIONAL ZOOLOGIST & AMERICAN TV HOST of "MUTUAL of OMAHA'S WILD KINGDOM" JIM FOWLER (`-87)**"!!!~'

`-**DEATH/DAY** = (**5/8**) = (5 + 8) = (`-**13**)!!!~'

DWAYNE W. ANDERSON

`-BIRTH/DAY = (**4/9**) = (4 + 9) = (`-**13**)!!!~`

`-BIRTH/YEAR = (`-**1932**) = (32 (-) 19) = (`-**13**)!!!~`

(13 x 3) = (`-**39**) = "FLIP EVERY (`-**3**) OVER to an (`-**8**)" = (`-**89**) = "TWO `-YEARS `-AWAY (`-**89**) from `-AGE of `-DEATH (`-**87**)"!!!~`

`-DEATH/YEAR = (`-**2019**) = (20 + 19) = (`-**39**)!!!~`

`-DEATH/YEAR = (`-**2019**) = RECIPROCAL = (`-**9102**) = "FLIP EVERY (`-**2**) OVER to a (`-**7**)" = (`-**9107**) = (9 (-) 1) (0 + 7) = (`-**87**) = "AGE of `-DEATH for AMERICAN PROFESSIONAL ZOOLOGIST & AMERICAN TV HOST of "MUTUAL of OMAHA'S WILD KINGDOM" JIM FOWLER (`-**87**)"!!!~`

`-DEATH/DAY = (**5/8**) = RECIPROCAL = (**8/5**) = (`-**85**) = "TWO `-YEARS `-AWAY (`-**85**) from `-AGE of `-DEATH (`-**87**)"!!!~`

AMERICAN PROFESSIONAL ZOOLOGIST & AMERICAN TV HOST of "MUTUAL of OMAHA'S WILD KINGDOM" JIM FOWLER `-BIRTHDAY # `-NUMBER = `-EQUALS = (4 + 9 + 19 + 32) = (`-**64**) = (8 x 8) = (`-**88**) = "ONE `-YEAR `-AWAY (`-**88**) from `-AGE of `-DEATH (`-**87**)"!!!~`

`-BIRTH/YEAR = (`-**32**) = `-TIMES "X" (`-**2**) = (`-**64**)!!!~`

AMERICAN PROFESSIONAL ZOOLOGIST & AMERICAN TV HOST of "MUTUAL of OMAHA'S WILD KINGDOM" JIM FOWLER `-DEATH/DAY # `-NUMBER = `-EQUALS = (5 + 8 + 20 + 19) = (`-**52**)

`-BIRTH/YEAR = (`-**1932**) = (19 + 32) = (`-**51**)!!!~`

AMERICAN PROFESSIONAL ZOOLOGIST & AMERICAN TV HOST of "MUTUAL of OMAHA'S WILD KINGDOM" JIM FOWLER had `-DIED (`-**29**) `-DAYS after `-HIS `-LAST `-BIRTHDAY!!!~`

(`-**29**) = `-DIED within the `-YEAR of (`-**2019**)!!!~`

(365 (-) 29) = (`-**336**) = (3 + 36) = (`-**39**) = (20 + 19) = `-**DEATH/YEAR of** (`-**2019**)!!!~'

AMERICAN FOOTBALL COACH & PLAYER DICK TOMEY `-DIED on *MAY 10<sup>th</sup>* within `-*2019*!!!~' `-HE was `-BORN on *JUNE 20th* in `-*1938*!!!~' `-HE `-DIED at the `-AGE of (`-**80**)!!!~'

`-**BIRTH/DAY** = (**6/20**) = (6 + 2) (0) = (`-**80**) = "AGE of `-DEATH for AMERICAN FOOTBALL COACH & PLAYER DICK TOMEY (`-**80**)"!!!~'

`-**DIED** in the `-**MONTH** of (`-**5**); and, was `-**BORN** in the `-**MONTH** of (`-**6**) = (5 x 6) = (`-**30**) = "FLIP EVERY (`-**3**) OVER to an (`-**8**)" = (`-**80**) = "AGE of `-DEATH for AMERICAN FOOTBALL COACH & PLAYER DICK TOMEY (`-**80**)"!!!~'

`-**BIRTH/DAY** = (**6/20**) = "FLIP EVERY (`-**6**) OVER to a (`-**9**)" = (**9/20**) = (9 x 20) = (`-**180**) = (80 x 1) = (`-**80**) = "AGE of `-DEATH for AMERICAN FOOTBALL COACH & PLAYER DICK TOMEY (`-**80**)"!!!~'

`-**DEATH/DAY** = (**5/10**) = (5 x 10) = (`-**50**)!!!~'

`-**BIRTH/DAY** = (**6/20**) = (6 x 20) = (`-**120**)!!!~'

(50 + 120) = (`-**170**) = (1 + 7) (0) = (`-**80**) = "AGE of `-DEATH for AMERICAN FOOTBALL COACH & PLAYER DICK TOMEY (`-**80**)"!!!~'

`-**DEATH/YEAR** = (`-**2019**) = RECIPROCAL = (`-**9102**) = (9 (-) 1) (0 + 2) = (`-**82**) = "TWO `-YEARS `-AWAY (`-**82**) from `-AGE of `-DEATH (`-**80**)"!!!~'

AMERICAN FOOTBALL COACH & PLAYER DICK TOMEY `-**BIRTHDAY # `-NUMBER** = `-EQUALS = (6 + 20 + 19 + 38) = (`-**83**)

= RECIPROCAL = (`-**38**) = `-**BIRTH/YEAR** (`-**38**) = RECIPROCAL = (`-**83**)!!!~`

AMERICAN FOOTBALL COACH & PLAYER DICK TOMEY `-**DEATH/DAY #** `-**NUMBER** = `-EQUALS = (5 + 10 + 20 + 19) = (`-**54**)!!!~`

(83 + 54) = (`-**137**) = (1 + 7) (3) = (`-**83**) = `-**BIRTH/DAY #** `-**NUMBER** (`-**83**)!!!~`

(83 (-) 54) = (`-**29**) = RECIPROCAL = (`-**92**) = "FLIP EVERY (`-**9**) OVER to a (`-**6**)" = (`-**62**)!!!~`

`-**BIRTH/DAY** = (**6/20**) = (62 + 0) = (`-**62**)!!!~`

AMERICAN FOOTBALL COACH & PLAYER DICK TOMEY had `-**DIED** (`-**41**) `-**DAYS before** `-**HIS** `-**NEXT** `-**BIRTHDAY**!!!~`

(`-**41**) = `-**TIMES "X"** (`-**2**) = (`-**82**) = "TWO `-**YEARS** `-**AWAY** (`-**82**) from `-**AGE of** `-**DEATH** (`-**80**)"!!!~`

(365 (-) 41) = (`-**324**) = (3 + 2) (4) = (`-**54**) = `-**DEATH/DAY #** `-**NUMBER** (`-**54**)!!!~`

AMERICAN COMEDY LEGEND TIM CONWAY `-DIED on *MAY 14th* within `-*2019*!!!~` `-HE was `-BORN on *DECEMBER 15th* in `-*1933*!!!~` `-HE `-DIED at the `-AGE of (`-**85**)!!!~`

`-**BIRTH/DAY** = (**12/15**) = (1 + 2 + 1) (5) = (**45**) = RECIPROCAL = (**54**) = `-**DEATH/DAY** = (**5/14**) = (54 x 1) = (`-**54**)!!!~`

`-**BIRTH/DAY** = (**12/15**) = RECIPROCAL = (**51/21**) = (5 x 1) (2 x 1) = (`-**52**)!!!~`

`-**BIRTH/YEAR** = (`-**1933**) = (19 + 33) = (`-**52**)!!!~'

`-**BIRTH/DAY** = (**12/15**) = RECIPROCAL = (**51/21**) = (5) (1 + 2 + 1) = (`-**54**)!!!~'

`-**DEATH/DAY** = (**5/14**) = (54 x 1) = (`-**54**)!!!~'

`-**DEATH/YEAR** = (`-**2019**) = "FLIP EVERY (`-**2**) OVER to a (`-**7**)" = (`-**7019**) = "FLIP EVERY (`-**9**) OVER to a (`-**6**)" = (`-**7016**) = (7 + 1) (0 + 6) = (`-**86**) = "ONE `-YEAR `-AWAY (`-**86**) from `-AGE of `-DEATH (`-**85**)"!!!~'

`-**BIRTH/YEAR** = (`-**1933**) = (1 (-) 9) (3 + 3) = (`-**86**) = "ONE `-YEAR `-AWAY (`-**86**) from `-AGE of `-DEATH (`-**85**)"!!!~'

`-**BIRTH/YEAR** = (`-**33**) = "FLIP EVERY (`-**3**) OVER to an (`-**8**)" = (`-**83**) = "TWO `-YEARS `-AWAY (`-**83**) from `-AGE of `-DEATH (`-**85**)"!!!~'

AMERICAN COMEDY LEGEND TIM CONWAY `-**BIRTHDAY #** `-**NUMBER** = `-EQUALS = (12 + 15 + 19 + 33) = (`-**79**)!!!~'

AMERICAN COMEDY LEGEND TIM CONWAY `-**DEATH/DAY #** `-**NUMBER** = `-EQUALS = (5 + 14 + 20 + 19) = (`-**58**) = RECIPROCAL = (`-**85**) = "AGE of `-DEATH for AMERICAN COMEDY LEGEND TIM CONWAY (`-**85**)"!!!~'

(79 + 58) = (`-**137**) = (1 + 7) (3) = (`-**83**) = "TWO `-YEARS `-AWAY (`-**83**) from `-AGE of `-DEATH (`-**85**)"!!!~'

AMERICAN COMEDY LEGEND TIM CONWAY had `-**DIED** (`-**150**) `-**DAYS after** `-**HIS** `-**LAST** `-**BIRTHDAY!!!~'**

(`-**150**) = (15 + 0) = (`-**15**) = (8 + 7) = (`-**87**) = "TWO `-YEARS `-AWAY (`-**87**) from `-AGE of `-DEATH (`-**85**)"!!!~'

(365 (-) 150) = (`-**215**) = "FLIP EVERY (`-**2**) OVER to an (`-**7**)" = (`-**715**)
= (7 + 1) (5) = (`-**85**) = "**AGE of `-DEATH for AMERICAN COMEDY
LEGEND TIM CONWAY (`-85)**"!!!~'

AMERICAN FOOTBALL PLAYER & COACH BART STARR `-DIED
on **MAY 26**[th] within `-**2019**!!!~' `-HE was `-BORN on **JANUARY 9**[th]
in `-**1934**!!!~' `-HE `-DIED at the `-AGE of (`-**85**)!!!~'

`-**AGE of `-DEATH** = (`-**85**) = RECIPROCAL = (`-**58**) = `-**DEATH/
DAY** = (**5/26**) = (5) (2 + 6) = (`-**58**)!!!~'

`-**DEATH/DAY** = (**5/26**) = RECIPROCAL = (**62/5**) = (6 + 2) (5) = (`-
85) = "**AGE of `-DEATH for AMERICAN FOOTBALL PLAYER &
COACH BART STARR (`-85)**"!!!~'

`-**BIRTH/YEAR** = (`-**34**) = "FLIP EVERY (`-**3**) OVER to an (`-**8**)"
= (`-**84**) = "**ONE `-YEAR `-AWAY (`-84) from `-AGE of `-DEATH
(`-85)**"!!!~'

`-**DEATH/DAY** = (**5/26**) = (5 x 26) = (`-**130**)!!!~' /||\

`-**BIRTH/DAY** = (**1/9**) = (1 x 9) = (`-**9**)!!!~' /||\

(130 + 9) = (`-**139**) = (39 x 1) = (`-**39**) = (20 + 19) = `-**DEATH/
YEAR**!!!~'

`-**DEATH/YEAR** = (`-**2019**) = "FLIP EVERY (`-**2**) OVER to a (`-**7**)"
= (`-**7019**) = RECIPROCAL = (`-**9107**) = (9 (-) 1) (0 + 7) = (`-**87**) =
"**TWO `-YEARS `-AWAY (`-87) from `-AGE of `-DEATH (`-85)**"!!!~'

`-**BIRTH/YEAR** = (`-**1934**) = (1 (-) 9) (3 + 4) = (`-**87**) = "**TWO `-YEARS
`-AWAY (`-87) from `-AGE of `-DEATH (`-85)**"!!!~'

AMERICAN FOOTBALL PLAYER & COACH BART STARR
`-BIRTHDAY # `-NUMBER = `-EQUALS = (1 + 9 + 19 + 34) =
(`-**63**)!!!~'

AMERICAN FOOTBALL PLAYER & COACH BART STARR `-DEATH/DAY # `-NUMBER = `-EQUALS = (5 + 26 + 20 + 19) = (`-**70**)!!!~'

(70 + 63) = (`-**133**) = "FLIP EVERY (`-**3**) OVER to an (`-**8**)" = (`-**183**) = (83 + 1) = (`-**84**) = "ONE `-YEAR `-AWAY (`-**84**) from `-AGE of `-DEATH (`-**85**)"!!!~'

AMERICAN FOOTBALL PLAYER & COACH BART STARR had `-**DIED** (`-**137**) `-DAYS after `-HIS `-LAST `-BIRTHDAY!!!~'

(`-**137**) = "FLIP EVERY (`-**3**) OVER to an (`-**8**)" = (`-**187**) = (87 (-) 1) = (`-**86**) = "ONE `-YEAR `-AWAY (`-**86**) from `-AGE of `-DEATH (`-**85**)"!!!~'

(365 (-) 137) = (`-**228**) = RECIPROCAL = (`-**822**) = (82 + 2) = (`-**84**) = "ONE `-YEAR `-AWAY (`-**84**) from `-AGE of `-DEATH (`-**85**)"!!!~'

AMERICAN COMPOSER CHICK COREA `-DIED on *FEBRUARY 9th* within `-**2021**!!!~' `-HE was `-BORN on *JUNE 12th* in `-**1941**!!!~' `-HE `-DIED at the `-AGE of (`-**79**)!!!~'

`-**AGE** of `-**DEATH** = (`-**79**) = "FLIP EVERY (`-**7**) OVER to a (`-**2**)" = (`-**29**) = `-**DEATH/DAY** (**2/9**)!!!~'

`-**DEATH/DAY** = (**2/9**) = "FLIP EVERY (`-**2**) OVER to a (`-**7**)" = (`-**79**) = "AGE of `-DEATH for AMERICAN COMPOSER CHICK COREA (`-**79**)"!!!~'

`-**BIRTH/YEAR** = (`-**41**) = (20 + 21) = `-**DEATH/YEAR**!!!~'

`-**DEATH/DAY** = (**2/9**) = (2 x 9) = (`-**18**)!!!~' /|||\

`-**BIRTH/DAY** = (**6/12**) = (6 + 12) = (`-**18**)!!!~' /|||\

121

`-BIRTH/DAY = (6/12) = (6 x 12) = (`-72) = "Was `-MARRIED to GAYLE MORAN in (`-72)"!!!~'

`-BIRTH/DAY = (6/12) = RECIPROCAL = (21/6) = (26 x 1) = (`-26) = "FLIP EVERY (`-6) OVER to a (`-9) = (`-29) = (2/9) = `-DEATH/ DAY!!!~'

`-DEATH/YEAR = (`-2021) = "FLIP EVERY (`-2) OVER to a (`-7)" = (`-7071) = (7 + 0) (7 + 1) = (`-78) = "ONE `-YEAR `-AWAY (`-78) from `-AGE of `-DEATH (`-79)"!!!~'

`-BIRTH/YEAR = (`-1941) = (41 (-) 19) = (`-22) = "FLIP EVERY (`-2) OVER to a (`-7)" = (`-77) = "TWO `-YEARS `-AWAY (`-77) from `-AGE of `-DEATH (`-79)"!!!~'

`-DEATH/YEAR = (`-2021) = "FLIP EVERY (`-2) OVER to a (`-7)" = (`-7071) = (7 + 0) (7 + 1) = (`-78) = `-BIRTH/DAY # `-NUMBER (`-78)"!!!~'

AMERICAN COMPOSER CHICK COREA `-BIRTHDAY # `-NUMBER = `-EQUALS = (6 + 12 + 19 + 41) = (`-78) = "ONE `-YEAR `-AWAY (`-78) from `-AGE of `-DEATH (`-79)"!!!~'

AMERICAN COMPOSER CHICK COREA `-DEATH/DAY # `-NUMBER = `-EQUALS = (2 + 9 + 20 + 21) = (`-52)!!!~'

(78 (-) 52) = (`-26) = "FLIP EVERY (`-2) OVER to a (`-7)" = (`-76) = "FLIP EVERY (`-6) OVER to a (`-9)" = (`-79) = "AGE of `-DEATH for AMERICAN COMPOSER CHICK COREA (`-79)"!!!~'

AMERICAN COMPOSER CHICK COREA had `-DIED (`-123) `-DAYS after `-HIS `-LAST `-BIRTHDAY!!!~'

(`-123) = "FLIP EVERY (`-3) OVER to an (`-8)" = (`-128) = "FLIP EVERY (`-2) OVER to a (`-7)" = (`-178) = (78 + 1) = (`-79) = "AGE of `-DEATH for AMERICAN COMPOSER CHICK COREA (`-79)"!!!~'

(365 (-) 123) = (`-**242**) = **R**eciprocal-**S**equencing-**N**umerology-**RSN**!!!~'

`-**DIED** in the `-**MONTH** of (`-**2**); and, was `-**BORN** in the `-MONTH of (`-**6**) = (`-**26**) = "FLIP EVERY (`-**2**) OVER to a (`-**7**)" = (`-**76**) = "FLIP EVERY (`-**6**) OVER to a (`-**9**)" = (`-**79**) = "**AGE of `-DEATH for AMERICAN COMPOSER CHICK COREA (`-79)**"!!!~'

AMERICAN NOVELIST JUDITH KRANTZ `-DIED on JUNE 22[nd] within `-20**19**!!!~' `-SHE was `-BORN on *JANUARY 9th* in `-1928!!!~' `-SHE `-DIED at the `-AGE of (`-**91**)!!!~'

`-**BIRTH/DAY** = (**1/9**) = (`-**19**) = RECIPROCAL = (`-**91**) = "**AGE of `-DEATH for AMERICAN NOVELIST JUDITH KRANTZ (`-91)**"!!!~'

`-**DEATH/YEAR** = (`-**19**) = RECIPROCAL = (`-**91**) = "**AGE of `-DEATH for AMERICAN NOVELIST JUDITH KRANTZ (`-91)**"!!!~'

LET'S GET SUPER SIMPLE MINDED HERE!~' IF ONE ASKS HOW CREATION GOT STARTED AND SAYS THE "BIG BANG"; then, WHAT EXISTED BEFORE THE "BIG BANG"!~' IF ONE SAYS GOD was CREATED, THEN WHAT EXISTED before `-GOD!~' KNOW YOURSELF; by ANATOMY, PHYSIOLOGY & BIOLOGY and SEE the GLORY of GOD!!!~'

DWAYNE W. ANDERSON

DEATH CIPHERS

FORMULAS - CODE BREAKERS OF LIFE/death (based on the
RECIPROCALS of TRIGONOMETRY_)

DEATH/CYPHER

Our Understanding; Of The World, Is;
`-About To Change, `-Forever!!!~'

`-DEATH CIPHERS/CYPHERS FOR LIFE & DEATH!!!~'

The "RETURN OF THE DRAGON"!!!!~' (SPIRITUALLY SPEAKING)!!!!~'

FOR SHANNON LEE!!!!~' The "PROPHET'S" BROTHER'S NAME is `-SHANNON with his `-MIDDLE NAME being `-LEE!!!!~'

The `-PROOF that a `-GOD EXISTS!!!!~' The `-NUMBERS; don't, `-LIE!!!!~' We're `-ALL a part of a `-NUMERICAL `-MATRIX!!!!~'

If The COSMOS could be divided into QUADRANTS of CONSTELLATIONS, look for LIFE on OTHER PLANETS; in, QUADRANTS `-23, `-32; and, `-13!!!!~

There are `-MANY Cardinal Numbers; but, look for these `-three numbers (`-13, `-23, & `-32) as stated above; to be everywhere, in the `-LIFE that is; -all- around `-US!!!!~'

I loved the Movie "Return Of The Dragon"!!!!~' I wrote about Bruce Lee's Birth, Marriage; and, Death in my NEW BOOK – "The REAL Prophet Of Doom (Kismet) – Introduction – Pendulum Flow"; and, `-OTHERS; on how it relates to the Deaths of Actor Robin Williams; and, Comedienne Joan Rivers!!!!~' I didn't write about Chuck Norris, yet!!!!~' The following in is my book about the Martial Artist Bruce Lee:

Birth Day: (11.27) November 27th, `-1940!!!!~'

Married: At `-23 Years of Age!!!!~' Age of Death: `-32 Years of Age !!!!~' (`-23 = RECIPROCAL = `-32)!!!!~'

Death Day: (07.20) July 20th, `-1973!!!!~' (`-27 = RECIPROCAL = `-72)!!!!~' (BIRTH & DEATH 27/72)!!!!~'

Height: 5' 7" (1.71 m) = RECIPROCAL-SEQUENCING-NUMEROLOGY-!!!!~'

11.27.1940 (-) 07.20.1973 = `-22 = This Number is Encapsulated; by, the number `-23!!!!~'

125

07 + 20 + 19 + 73 = `-119 (Death Date)!!!!!~'

11 + 27 + 19 + 40 = `-97 (Birth Date)!!!!!~'

`-119 (-) `-97 = `-22 (Difference – Birth to Death)!!!!!~'

`-119 (+) `-97 = `-216 = `-21.6 = `-22 ("Rounded Up")!!!!!~'

A "NEW" `-KIND OF "NUMEROLOGY"; CALLED "PENDULUM FLOW", that I'VE CREATED - IT'S WITH `-GOD'S INNER/ OUTER WORKINGS `-WITH; AND, `-FROM; HIS `-DIVINE "HOLYSPIRIT"!!!!!~

This is a `-NUMEROLOGY for `-CHRISTIANS!!!!!~' This; `-is a, `-

NUMEROLOGY for ALL `-RELIGIONS; AND, -for the `-WORLD!!!!!~'

Regards,

The "PROPHET"!!!!!~'

Dwayne W. Anderson!!!!!~'

A RETURN of the `-DRAGON!!!!!~' (SPIRITUALLY SPEAKING)!~'

Numerological Numbers and the American Alphabet System!!!!!~'

1 = a, j, s
2 = b, k, t
3 = c, l, u
4 = d, m, v
5 = e, n, w
6 = f, o, x
7 = g, p, y
8 = h, q, z
9 = i, r

Bruce Lee / Linda Lee

29335 355 / 39541 355

29335 + 39541 = 68876 = 6 + 8 + 8 + 7 + 6 = `-35 = Bruce + Linda = `-Lee!!!!!~' `-55 = `-WE!!!!!~'

11.27.1940 (-) 07.20.1973 = `-22 = This Number is Encapsulated; by, the number `-23!!!!!~'

`-22 = Bucket!!!!!~' `-23 = bc / `-23 = kL / `-23 = tu!!!!!~'

07 + 20 + 19 + 73 = `-119 (Death Date)!!!!!~'

`-119 = as(ir_)!!!!!~'

11 + 27 + 19 + 40 = `-97 (Birth Date)!!!!!~'

`-97 = ir_(y,p,g)

`-119 (-) `-97 = `-22 (Difference – Birth to Death)!!!!!~'

`-22 = Bucket!!!!!~'

`-119 (+) `-97 = `-216 = `-21.6 = `-22 ("Rounded Up")!!!!!~'

`-216 = fat bos job tao tax!!!!!~'

Greek Numbers; and, the Greek Alphabet - Tau; and, the Warrior Number `-300!!!!~'

Tao = Bruce Lee = `-213!!!!!~'

`-213 = Tau = is the `-19th letter of the Greek Alphabet; and, in the system of Greek Numerals; it, has a Value of `-300!!!!!~'

From: The "PROPHET"!!!!~'

Dwayne W. Anderson!!!!~'

COPYRIGHT 03/19/2015 / AUTHOR: DWAYNE W. ANDERSON / THE "PROPHET"!!!!~' /

The "PROPHET'S" CREATIVE `-NEW `-TYPE Of `-NUMEROLOGY VIA `-GOD'S HOLY SPIRIT!!!!~' The ORIGINAL DATE OF DEATH CYPHERS = CODE BREAKERS!!!!~'

If The COSMOS could be divided into QUADRANTS of CONSTELLATIONS, look for LIFE on OTHER PLANETS; in, QUADRANTS `-**23**, `-**32**; and, `-**13**!!!!~

ROBIN WILLIAM'S BIRTH DATE & YEAR; FROM, BRUCE LEE'S DAY & DATE OF DEATH EQUALS `-**21** YEARS!!!!~ `-1 DAY AWAY FROM `-**22** YEARS; `-EXACTLY!!!!~' ENCAPSULATED BY THE NUMBER `-**23**!!!!~'

ROBIN WILLIAMS COMMITS SUICIDE!!!!~ COMMITS SUICIDE `-**21** DAYS AFTER HIS BIRTHDAY THAT WAS ON THE **21**ˢᵗ; OF JULY!!!!~ NEWLY TURNED `-**63** YEARS OF AGE!!!!~ HE DIED AT THE VERY SAME TENDER AGE; OF `-**63**, AS MARY TODD LINCOLN, FRANKLIN DELANO ROOSEVELT; AND, TOO; THE REAL PROPHET OF DOOM'S MOTHER!!!!~'

AT THE TIME OF ROBIN WILLIAMS DEATH DATE; AND, JOAN RIVERS DEATH DATE; THE "PROPHET" WAS `-**44** YEARS OF AGE WITH THE "PROPHET'S" BROTHER BEING `-**46** YEARS OF AGE!!!!~' THE "PROPHET'S" BROTHER'S BIRTH DATE BEING `-**44** DAYS AWAY FROM ROBIN WILLIAMS DEATH DATE; AND, `-**21** DAYS AWAY FROM JOAN RIVER'S DEATH DATE!!!!~'

JOAN RIVERS WAS BORN ON **JUNE 8**th OF; AND, IN `-**1933**!!!!!~
JUNE 8th = 6 + 8 = `-**14** = **RECIPROCAL** = `-**41** = The **NUMBER** of
YEARS; SINCE, the DEATH of BRUCE LEE!!!!!~

SEPTEMBER 4th = `-**41** years & `-**46** days from the date of **DEATH**
of **BRUCE LEE**!!!!!~' `-**46** = `-**23** x **2**!!!!!~' `-**232**!!!!!~'

JOAN RIVER'S DATE OF DEATH = `-0**9** + `-0**4** = `-**13** = **EQUALS**
= "A VERY PIVOTAL NUMBER"!!!!!~'

`-**1933** = 19 - 33 = 33 - 19 = `-**14** = **YEAR OF DEATH**!!!!!~'

JOAN RIVERS DIES IN THE CALENDAR YEAR OF `-20**14**!!!!!~

JOAN RIVERS DIES AT THE AGE OF `-**81**!!!!!~ ROBIN WILLIAMS
DIES ON THE VERY DAY OF **8/11**!!!!!~ BOTH COMEDIANS!!!!!~
MALE & FEMALE!!!!!~ `-_DEUTERONOMY 18:11_ !!!!!~

ROBIN WILLIAMS WAS BORN ON **JULY 21**st, IN `-**1951**!~ JULY 21st
= 7 - 21 = 21 - 7 = `-**14** =

-TRIGONOMETRY- REFERENCED `-**RECIPROCALS** = `-**41** Years
& `-**23** days (D to D) = August 11th from Bruce Lee's Date of
DEATH!!!!!~

ROBIN WILLIAMS DIES IN THE CALENDAR YEAR OF `-20**14**!!!!!~
JOAN RIVERS & ROBIN WILLIAMS HAVE / `-**23** - / `DAYS _IN_
`-**BETWEEN** THEIR DEATHS!!!!!~ / / `-**23** = **RECIPROCAL** = `-**32**
/-...' -

`-**1951** = 1**9** - **5**1 = 51 - 19 = `-**32** = -a PROPHETIC NUMBER!!!!!~

MARTIAL ARTS MASTER-ARTIST **BRUCE LEE** MARRIED HIS
WIFE LINDA C. LEE AT THE YOUTHFUL AGE OF `-**23** ON **AUGUST**
`-**17**th OF `-19**64**!!!!!~ BRUCE LEE LIVED FOR `-**32** YEARS!!!!!~

08/17 (Bruce Lee/Linda Lee) - **08/11** (Robin Williams) = `-**17** (-)
`-**11** = `-**6** = **2** x **3** = `-**23**!!!!!~'

08/17 (Bruce Lee/Linda Lee) - 08/11 (Robin Williams) = `-17 (-)
`-11 = `-6 = 3 x 2 = `-32!!!!!~'

`-19**64** = `-**64** = **2** x `-**32** = `-**232**!!!!!~'

FIRST LADY ELEANOR ROOSEVELT DIED ON 11/7/ FIRST
LADY LADY BIRD JOHNSON DIED ON 7/11 = RECIPROCAL-
SEQUENCED-NUMEROLOGY/19**62**!!!!!~ SHE DIED THE VERY
SAME YEAR AS MARI**LYN** MONROE IN `-19**62** - JUST SOME `-**94**
DAYS LATER!!!!!~ PRESIDENT LYNDON B. JOHNSON'S WIFE,
FIRST LADY LADY BIRD JOHNSON, DIED AT THE TENDER AGE
OF `-**94**!!!!!~'

PRESIDENT THEODORE ROOSEVELT'S 2nd WIFE, FIRST LADY
EDITH KERMIT CAROW ROOSEVELT DIED `-**94** DAYS AWAY
FROM `-19**49**!!!!!~' `-**94** = RECIPROCAL = `-**49**!!!!!~' (JOAN RIVERS
9/4)!!!!!~'

FIRST LADY LADY BIRD JOHNSON HAD DIED `-**44** YEARS `-**34**0
DAYS; AND, WITH `-**24** DAYS LYING IN BETWEEN THE DEATH
DAYS; FROM, THE DEATH DATE OF MARILYN MONROE!!!!!~'
THE NUMBER `-**23**!!!!!~' `-**25** DAYS (D to D - SUBTRACTION) =
`-**25** = RECIPROCAL = `-**52**!!!!!~' `-**26** DAYS (INCLUDING D to D)
= `-**26** / `-**2** = `-**13** = EQUALS = "A VERY PIVOTAL NUMBER"!!!!!~'

PRESIDENT THEODORE ROOSEVELT WAS MARRIED TO FIRST
LADY EDITH KERMIT CAROW ROOSEVELT FOR `-**32** YEARS AT
THE TIME OF HIS UNTIMELY DEATH!!!!!~' FIRST LADY ELEANOR
ROOSEVELT DIED AT THE AGE OF `-**78**; WHILE, FIRST LADY
EDITH KERMIT CAROW ROOSEVELT DIED AT THE AGE OF
`-**87**!!!!!~ `-**78** = RECIPROCAL = `-**87**!!!!!~

LADY BIRD JOHNSON DIED 7/11 / ELEANOR ROOSEVELT DIED
11/7 / 7/11 = RECIPROCAL = 11/7! THERE IS A `-**44** YEARS
DIFFERENCE IN TIME!!!!!~ `-**94** (-) `-**44** = `-**50** = "THE HAND OF
`-GOD"!!!!!~'

11 x 7 = `-**77** / 7 x 11 = `-**77** / `-**77** = `**77** / OVERLAY **7**=**7**=**7** / **7** x **3** = `-**21** (ROBIN WILLIAMS)!!!!!~'

MARILYN MONROE DIED ON **AUGUST** **5**th 19**62**!!!!!~'
0**8**/0**5**/19**62**!!!!!~'

0**8** + 0**5** = `-**13** = **EQUALS** = "A VERY PIVOTAL NUMBER"!!!!!~'
09 + 04 = `**13** = JOAN RIVERS!!!!!~'

MARILYN MONROE'S DEATH; AND, **JOAN RIVER'S DEATH DATE** SPAN'S `-**52** YEARS (ROBIN WILLIAMS BIRTH DATE)!!!!!~'
`-**52** YEARS & `-**29** DAYS!!!!!~ `-**52** + `-**29** = `-**81** (AGE AT JOAN RIVER'S DEATH)!!!!!~'

`-**29** = **RECIPROCAL** = `-**92**

`-**92** (/) **2** = `-**46** = `-**23** x **2** = `-**232**!!!!!~'

MARILYN MONROE WAS BORN IN `-19**26**; AND AGAIN, SHE DIED IN `-19**62**!!!!!~

`-**26** = `-**13** x **2** = `-**132**!!!!!~'

`-**26** = **RECIPROCAL** = `-**62**

MARILYN MONROE BORN: 0**6**/0**1**/19**26**
MARILYN MONROE DIED: 0**8**/0**5**/19**62** / 0**8** + 0**5** = `-**13** = **EQUALS** = "A VERY PIVOTAL NUMBER"!!!!!~

06/01 = `-**61** / 08/05 = `-**85**

`-**6** x `-**1** = `-**6** = **3** x **2** = `-**32**!!!!!~'
`-**6** x `-**1** = `-**6** = **2** x **3** = `-**23**!!!!!~'

`-61 (+) `-85 = `-**146** = `-**46** = "AGE AT WHICH '**TIME** '/ PRESIDENT (JOHN **F**ITZGERALD KENNEDY) / WAS SHOT; AND, KILLED"!!!!!!~

DWAYNE W. ANDERSON

SNL'S Jan Hooks dead at `-**57**!!!!!~ Born on **April** `-**23**ʳᵈ `-19**57**!!!!!~ `-**58** days in between Robin William's; and, `-**34** days (Joan River's); and, hers; dates of death!!!!~ `-**41** years & `-**81** days from the Death Date of the Martial Arts Artist BRUCE LEE!!!!!~ **5** + **8** = `-**13** = **"A Very Pivotal Number"**!!!!!~ **7,9,12** = `-**23**!!!!!~ Pete Wilson - Former Governor of (CA) was `-**81** at this time/ born Aug. **23**ʳᵈ; and, Pete Wilson (Broadcaster) died `-**34** years exactly after Bruce Lee's Day of Death in `-**2007**/Born **4/5/45**!~ The "PROPHET" met this 2ⁿᵈ Pete Wilson (`-ABC7 NEWS) as a `-Kid at Channel `-40 in Sacramento!!!!!~'

SINCERELY; and, REGARDS,

THE "PROPHET"!!!!!~'

Dwayne W. Anderson!!!!!~'

132

KEY CYPHERS - OUR DEATH DATES -VIA- RSN-Reciprocal-Sequenced/Sequencing-Numerology!!!!!~'

DEATH DATE CYPHERS - CODE BREAKERS!!!!!~'

(PROPHET'S) MOM – BIRTH – 11/15/1944

1115 = RECIPROCAL = 1511

4419 – 1511 = `-2908

1944 – 1115 = `-829

`-2908 + `-829 = `-3737

4491 – 5111 = `-620 = NEAR AGE OF DEATH!!!!!~'

`-94 (-) `-62 = `-32

`-44 + `-19 = `-63 = AGE AT TIME OF DEATH!!!!!~' THE NUMBER `-**32**!!!!!~'

`-62 = 6 + 2 = `-8

`-62 = 6 x 2 = `-12

`-12 + `-8 = `-20

`-20 / 2 = `-10

`-32 + `-12 + `-8 + `-10 = `-62 = ONE YEAR AWAY FROM AGE OF DEATH!!!!!!~'

TWO APPEARS TWICE = DIVIDE BY `-2 = 6 / 2 = `-3

`-8 x `-12 = `-96 (9-3)(6-3) = `-63 = AGE AT TIME OF DEATH!!!!!~'

`-62 = 6 + 2 + 0 = `-8

`-62 = 6 x 2 x 0 = `-0

08 = YEAR OF DEATH!!!!!~'

11 + 15 + 19 + 44 = `-89 = AGE AT TIME OF DEATH FOR MOTHER'S MOTHER!!!!!~'

`-89 / `-8 = `-11.125

`-89 = RECIPROCAL = `-98

`-98 (-) `-44 = `-54

`-54 + `-8 = `-62 = ONE YEAR AWAY –NEAR AGE OF DEATH!!!!!~'

`-8 + `-11.125 = `-19.125

`-DEATH CIPHERS/CYPHERS FOR LIFE & DEATH!!!~'

`-19.125 / `-2 = `-9.5625

`-54 + `-9.5625 = `-63.5625 = AGE AT TIME OF DEATH!!!!!~'

(RECIPROCAL) IN TIME OF FRACTION (0.5625) – IS THE EXACT TIME OF DEATH!!!!!~'

`-94/2 = `-47

`-47 + `-15 = `-62 = ONE YEAR AWAY –NEAR AGE OF DEATH!!!!!~'

DEATH – 04/16/2008 – 10PM

(PROPHET'S) DAD – BIRTH – 0**9**/0**1**/**19**41

`-91 = RECIPROCAL = `-19

0901 = RECIPROCAL = `-0109 = `-19

1941 = 41 = RECIPROCAL = `-14

`-19 + `-14 = `-33 / 2 = `-16.5 = 16th OF THE MONTH – ½ DAY OF TIME OF DEATH = `-6AM/6PM!!!!!~'

1491 – 1090 = `-401

`-401 = 4 + 0 + 1 = `-5

`-401 = 4 x 0 x 1 = `-0

`-19 + `-41 = `-60

`-60 + `-5 = `-65 = ONE YEAR AWAY - NEAR AGE OF DEATH!!!!!~'

`-91 (-) `19 = `-72

135

`-72 (-) `-41 = `-31

`-31 (+) `-5 = `-36

`-**3** x (**2**) = `-6 = THE NUMBER `-**32**!!!!!~'

`-94 / `-2 = `-47

`-47 + `19 = `-66 = AGE AT TIME OF DEATH!!!!!~'

09 + 01 + 19 + 41 = `-70

`-70 (-) 5 = `-65 = ONE YEAR AWAY - NEAR AGE OF DEATH!!!!!~'

DEATH – 04/16/2008 – 6PM

(FIRST LADY) LADY BIRD JOHNSON – BIRTH – 1**2**/**22**/1912

`-19 (-) `-12 = `-7 = `-2007 = YEAR OF DEATH!!!!!~'

12/22 = 22 – (1 x 2) = `-20 + `-7 = `-2007 = YEAR OF DEATH!!!!!~'

2191 – 2221 = `-30

`-30 = 3 + 0 = `-3

`-30 = 3 x 0 = `-0

= `-91 + `-3 = `-94 = AGE AT TIME OF DEATH!!!!!~'

`-19 + `-12 = `-31

`-31 x 3 = `-93 = ONE YEAR AWAY - NEAR AGE OF DEATH!!!!!~'

12 + 22 + 19 + 12 = `-65

`-65 + 30 = `-95 = ONE YEAR AWAY - NEAR AGE OF DEATH!!!!!~'

DEATH – 07/11/2007

(PRESIDENT) LYNDON B. JOHNSON – BIRTH – 08/27/1908

08 + 27 + 19 + 08 = `-62 = TWO YEARS FROM AGE OF DEATH!!!!!~'

8091 – 7280 = `-811

DOUBLE (SIDE BY SIDE) NUMBERS ADDED (1 + 1) = `-2 = ADD BY `-2

`-62 + `-2 = `-64 = AGE AT TIME OF DEATH!!!!!~'

`-811 = 8 + 1 + 1 = `-10

`-811 = 8 x 1 x 1 = `-8

`-10 + `-8 = `-18

`-90 / `-2 = `-45

`45 + `-18 = `-63 = ONE YEAR FROM AGE OF DEATH!!!!!~'

08/08 = BEGINNING; AND, END NUMBERS; OF, BIRTHDATE = 8 x 8 = `-64 = AGE AT TIME OF DEATH!!!!!~'

`-811 = RECIPROCAL = `-118

`-118 (-) `-62 = `-56

`-56 = RECIPROCAL = `-65 = ONE YEAR AWAY - NEAR AGE OF DEATH!!!!!~'

DEATH – 01/22/1973

(PRESIDENT) ABRAHAM LINCOLN – BIRTH – 02/12/1809

02 + 12 + 18 + 09 = `-41

9081 – 2120 = `-6961

`-6961 = 6 + 9 + 6 + 1 = `-22

`-6961 = 6 x 9 x 6 x 1 = `-324

`-324 / `-22 = `-14.727272 = ROUNDED = `-15

`-41 + 15 = `-56 = AGE AT TIME OF DEATH!!!!!~'

`-324 (-) `-22 = `-30**2** = THE NUMBER `-**32**!!!!!~'

`-80/2 = `-40

`-40 + `-15 = `-55 = ONE YEAR AWAY - NEAR AGE OF DEATH!!!!!~'

DEATH – 04/15/1865

(PRESIDENT) GEORGE WASHINGTON – BIRTH – 0**2**/**22**/1732

02 + 22 + 17 + 32 = `-73

1799 = 99 (-) 17 = `-82

1732 = 32 (-) 17 = `-15

`-82 (-) `-15 = `-67 = AGE AT TIME OF DEATH

2371 – 2220 = `-151 = DOUBLE NUMBER `-1 (1 + 1 = 2) = DOUBLE NUMBERS SEPARATED - DIVIDE BY `-2.

151 = 1 x 5 x 1 = `-5

151 = 1 + 5 + 1 = `-7

`-5 + `-7 = `-12 / `-2 = `-6!!!!!~'

`-73 - `-6 = `-67 = AGE AT TIME OF DEATH!!!!!~'

`-151 (-) `-17 = `-134

`-134/`-2 = `-67 = AGE AT TIME OF DEATH!!!!!~'

DEATH – 12/14/1799

(PRESIDENT) WOODROW WILSON – BIRTH – 12/28/1856

12 + 28 + 18 + 56 = `-114

6581 – 8221 = `-1640

`-1640 = 1 + 6 + 4 + 0 = `-11

`-1640 = 1 x 6 x 4 x 0 = `-0

`-114 (-) `-85 = `-29

`-85 + `-11 = `-96

`-96 (-) `-29 = `-67 = AGE AT TIME OF DEATH!!!!!~'

`-85 / `-2 = `-42.5

139

`-42.5 = RECIPROCAL = `-24.5

`-42.5 + `-24.5 = `-67 = AGE AT TIME OF DEATH!!!!!~'

DEATH – 02/03/1924

MARILYN MONROE – BIRTH – 06/01/1926

06 + 01 + 19 + 26 = `-52

6291 – 1060 = `-5231

`-5231 = 5 + 2 + 3 + 1 = `-11

`-5231 = 5 x 2 x 3 x 1 = `-30

(30(-)11)/2= `-19/2 = `-9.5

`-92/2 = `-46

`-46 (-) `-9.5 = `-36.5 = AGE AT TIME OF DEATH!!!!!~'

(.5 = 5)

`-12 MONTHS TO A YEAR!!!!!~'

(RECIPROCAL) IN TIME OF FRACTION (12/5=`-2.4 MONTHS) – IS THE EXACT TIME OF DEATH!!!!!~'

EXACT MONTH; AND, THE EXACT TIME WITHIN THE MONTH!!!!!~'

`-52 = RECIPROCAL = `-25

`-52 DUPLICATED = CANCEL OUT THE OTHER NUMBER!!!!!~'

`-DEATH CIPHERS/CYPHERS FOR LIFE & DEATH!!!~'

`-25 + `-11 = `-36 = AGE AT TIME OF DEATH!!!!!~'

DEATH – 08/05/1962

BRUCE LEE – BIRTH – 11/27/1940

11 + 27 + 19 + 40 = `-97

`-97 (-) `-94 = `-3 = NUMBER OF DECADES LIVING!!!!!~'

0491 – 7211 = `-6720

`-6720 = 6 + 7 + 2 + 0 = `-15

`-6720 = 6 x 7 x 2 x 0 = `-0

`-94/2 = `-47

`-47 (-) `-15 = `-32 = AGE AT TIME OF DEATH!!!!!~'

`-94 = RECIPROCAL = `-49

`-94 (-) `-49 = `-45

`-45 (-) `-15 = `-30 = TWO YEARS FROM AGE OF DEATH!!!!!~'

DEATH = 07/20/1973

ROBIN WILLIAMS – BIRTH – 07/21/1951

07 + 21 + 19 + 51 = `-98

`-98 (-) `-95 = `-3

`-98 = RECIPROCAL = `-89

`-95 (-) `-89 = `-6 = NUMBER OF DECADES LIVING!!!!!~'

1591 – 1270 = `-321

`-321 = PROPHETIC LINEAR PROGRESSION!!!!!~'

`-321 = 3 + 2 + 1 = `6

`-321 = 3 x 2 x 1 = `-6

`-95/2 = `-47.5

`-47.5 + `-12 + 3 = `-62.5 = ROUNDED = `-63 = AGE AT TIME OF DEATH!!!!!~'

`-6 x `-2 = `-12/2 = `-6

`-98 (-) `-95 = `-3

`-6 / `-3 = `-63 = AGE AT TIME OF DEATH!!!!!~'

DEATH – 08/11/2014

JOAN RIVERS – BIRTH – 06/08/1933

06 + 08 + 19 + 33 = `-66

`-93 (-) `-66 = `-27

3391 – 8060 = `-4669

`-4669 = 4 + 6 + 6 + 9 = `-25

`-4669 = 4 x 6 x 6 x 9 = `-1296

`-1296 + `-25 = `-1321 = ROBIN WILLIAMS!!!!!~' `-**23** DAYS IN BETWEEN THEIR DEATHS!!!!!~'

`-1296/`-25 = `-51.84

`-51.84 = RECIPROCAL = `-48.15

`-51.84 (-) `-48.15 = `-3.69 / 3 = `-1.23 = THE NUMBER `-**23**!!!!!~'

`-51.84 + `-48.15 = `-99.99

`-99.99 + `-66 = `-165.99

`-165.99/2 = `-82.995 = TWO YEARS FROM AGE OF DEATH!!!!!~'

`-82.000 (-) `-0.995 = `-81.005 = AGE AT TIME OF DEATH!!!!!~'

`-68 + `-66 + `-27 = `-161

`-161/2 = `-80.5 = ROUNDED = `-81 = AGE AT TIME OF DEATH!!!!!~'

`-93/2 = `-46.5

`-66/2 = `-33

`-46.5 + `-33 = `-79.5 = ROUNDED = `-80 = ONE YEAR FROM AGE OF DEATH!!!!!~'

`-68/2 = `-34

`-46.5 + `-34 = `-80.5 = ROUNDED = `-81 = AGE AT TIME OF DEATH!!!!!~'

DEATH 09/04/2014

PARENTS, PRESIDENTS, FIRST LADIES; AND, CELEBRITIES!!!!!~'

DEATH DATE CYPHERS – A CODE BREAKER/BREAKERS/A `-CODE OF `-DAYS!!!!!~'/

COPYRIGHT 3/23/2015!!!!!~' / Dwayne W. Anderson!!!!!~' / The "PROPHET"!!!!!~' /

HENRY GONZALEZ (AKA/LIZARD) – BIRTH - 04/12/1978 (36) YEARS OF AGE AT TIME OF DEATH!!!!!~'

DIED ON `-18 Days before his Next Birthday!!!!!~'

The "PROPHET"; Was Informed of his Death, `-13 DAYS; before his next `-BIRTHDAY!!!!!~'

04 + 12 + 19 + 78 = `-113

8791 – 2140 = `-6651

`-6651 = 6 + 6 + 5 + 1 = `-18

`-6651 = 6 x 6 x 5 x 1 = `-180

`180 / `-18 = `-10

`-97/2 = `-48.5

`-48.5 (-) `-10 = `-38.5 = 2 ½ YEARS AWAY FROM DEATH DATE!!!!!~'

`-113 + `-10 = `-123 = THE NUMBER `-23!!!!!~'

`-DEATH CIPHERS/CYPHERS FOR LIFE & DEATH!!!~'

`-113 (-) `-48.5 = `-64.5

`-64.5 / 2 = `-32.25

`-38.5 + `-32.25 = `-70.75

`-70.75 / `-2 = `-35.375 = WITHIN ONE INTEGER OF AGE OF DEATH!!!!!~'

`-48.5 (-) `-12 = `-36.5 = AGE AT TIME OF DEATH!!!!!~'

`-36.5 = (ROUNDED) = `-18 DAYS NEAR `-37 YEARS OF AGE AT TIME OF DEATH!!!!!~'

DEATH – 03/26/2014

CHARLES TAZE RUSSEL – BIRTH – 02/16/1852 (64) YEARS OF AGE AT TIME OF DEATH!!!!!~'

02 + 16 + 18 + 52 = `-88

2581 – 6120 = `-3539

`-3539 = 3 + 5 + 3 + 9 = `-20

`-3539 = 3 x 5 x 3 x 9 = `-405

`-405 / `-20 = `-20.25

`-88 / 2 = `-44

`-44 + `-20.25 = `-64.25 = EXACT AGE AT TIME OF DEATH!!!!!~'

RECIPROCAL OF 0.25 = IN TIME OF 0.75 = EXACT TIME OF DEATH AT AGE `-64!!!!!~'

`-85 / 2 = `-42.5

`-42.5 + `-20.25 = 62.75 = ROUNDED = `-63 = ONE YEAR AWAY
FROM EXACT TIME OF DEATH!!!!!~'

`-42.5 + `-18 + `-2 = `-62.5 = ROUNDED = `-63 = ONE YEAR AWAY
FROM EXACT TIME OF DEATH!!!!!~'

DEATH – 10/31/1916

JOSEPH FRANKLIN RUTHERFORD – BIRTH – 11/08/1869 (72)
YEARS OF AGE AT TIME OF DEATH!!!!!~'

11 + 08 + 18 + 69 = `-106

9681 – 8011 = `-1670

`-1670 = 1 + 6 + 7+ 0 = `-14

`-1670 = 1 x 6 x 7 x 0 = `-0

`-106 / `-2 = `-53

`-53 + `-14 = `-67

`-67 = RECIPROCAL = `-76 = FOUR YEARS AWAY FROM EXACT
TIME OF DEATH!!!!!~'

`-86 / `-2 = `-43

`-43 + `-14 = `-57

`-57 = RECIPROCAL = `-75 = THREE YEARS AWAY FROM EXACT
TIME OF DEATH!!!!!~'

`-43 + `-18 + `-11 = `-72 = EXACT TIME OF DEATH AT AGE `-72!!!!!~'

DEATH – 01/08/1942

NATHAN HOMER KNORR – BIRTH – 04/23/1905 (72) YEARS OF AGE AT TIME OF DEATH!!!!!~'

JUDGE RUTHERFORD + NATHAN KNORR = 72 + 72 = `-144 = `-144,000

04 + 23 + 19 + 05 = `-51

`-51 = RECIPROCAL = `-15

5091 - 3240 = `-1851

`-1851 = 1 + 8 + 5 + 1 = `-15

`-1851 = 1 x 8 x 5 x 1 = `-40

`-40 (-) `-15 = `-25

`-51 + `-25 = `-76 = FOUR YEARS AWAY FROM EXACT TIME OF DEATH!!!!!~'

`-40 + `-15 = `-55

`-55 + `-15 = `-70 = TWO YEARS AWAY FROM EXACT TIME OF DEATH!!!!!~'

`-90 / `-2 = `-45

`-45 + `-25 = `-70 = TWO YEARS AWAY FROM EXACT TIME OF DEATH!!!!!~'

`-45 + `-55 + `-51 = `-151

`-151 / `-2 = `-75.5 = ROUNDED = `-76 = FOUR YEARS AWAY FROM EXACT TIME OF DEATH!!!!!~'

`-45 + `-23 + `-4 = `-72 = EXACT TIME OF DEATH AT AGE `-72!!!!!~'

DEATH – 06/08/1977

FREDERICK WILLIAM FRANZ – BIRTH – 09/12/1893 (99) YEARS OF AGE AT TIME OF DEATH!!!!!~'

09 + 12 + 18 + 93 = `-1**32** = THE NUMBER `-**32**!!!!!~'

`-90, `-91, `-92, `-93 = "PROPHETIC LINEAR PROGRESSION"!!!!!~'

3981 – 2190 = `-1791

`-1791 = 1 + 7 + 9 + 1 = `-18

`-1791 = 1 x 7 x 9 x 1 = `-63

`-63 (-) `-18 = `-45

`-63 + `-18 = `-81

`-81 + `-12 + `-09 = `-102 = THREE YEARS AWAY FROM EXACT TIME OF DEATH!!!!!~'

`-81 + `-18 = `-99 = EXACT AGE AT TIME OF DEATH!!!!!~'

`-89 / `-2 = `-44.5

`-DEATH CIPHERS/CYPHERS FOR LIFE & DEATH!!!~'

`-44.5 + `-45 + `-12 = `-101.5 = ROUNDED = `-102 = THREE YEARS AWAY FROM TIME OF DEATH!!!!!~'

DEATH – 12/22/1992

FIRST WATCHTOWER WAS PUBLISHED IN `-1879!!!!!~ `-1914 (-) `-1879 = `-**35**!!!!!~

`-**35** = **RECIPROCAL** = `-**53**

`-**53** = "**WAR OF THE WORLDS**" = SEE BOOK: "THE REAL PROPHET OF DOOM (KISMET) – INTRODUCTION – PENDULUM FLOW" – BOOK - = "**FOR EXPLANATION**"!!!!!~'

/ AUTHOR/MEDIATOR/ARBITRATOR/: DWAYNE W. ANDERSON / 03/31/2015 / The "PROPHET"!!!!!~' /

149

DWAYNE W. ANDERSON

DEATH CIPHERS

FORMULAS - CODE BREAKERS OF LIFE/death (based on the
RECIPROCALS of TRIGONOMETRY_)

DEATH/CYPHER

DEATH CIPHERS

FORMULAS - CODE BREAKERS OF LIFE/death (based on the RECIPROCALS of TRIGONOMETRY_)

DEATH/CYPHER

Our Understanding; Of The World, Is;
`-About To Change, `-Forever!!!~'

II

Noted `-ONES of `-HISTORY!!!!!~' Death Cypher for `-DUMMIES!!!!!~' It doesn't get any easier than this!!!!!~' Calculate ANYONE'S "AGE" of "DEATH" simply by their `-BIRTHDAY; and, `-YEAR of `-BIRTH!!!!!~ Listed; in this `-LETTER, for `-EASY `-USE; of the `-CYPHER: Bruce Lee, Mahatma Gandhi, President Nelson Mandela, Martin Luther King, Jr.; and, Mr. Malcolm X!!!!!~' Enjoy the `-READ!!!!!~'

Death Ciphers / Death Cypher / Death Formula / `-The `-GOD `-Equation!!!!!~'

BRUCE LEE – BIRTH – **11**/**27**/1**94**0 **(32) YEARS OF AGE AT TIME OF DEATH!!!!!~'**

*(**2**/**3**) - 94; or, 97 times `-2; Divided by `-3; Divided by `-2 = `-**32**!~'*

11 + 27 + 19 + 40 = `-**97**

`-97 (-) `-94 = `-**3** = *NUMBER OF DECADES LIVING!!!!!~'*

`-97 / `-2 = `-**48.5**

`-27 + `-19 (-) `-11 = `-**35** = *THREE YEARS AWAY FROM THE EXACT TIME OF DEATH AGE!!!!!~'*

`-40 + `-19 (-) `-27 = `-**32** = *EXACT TIME OF AGE AT TIME OF DEATH!!!!!~'*

0491 – 7211 = `-**6720**

`-**04** = **RECIPROCAL** = `-**40**

`-**04**91 = `-40 (-) `-9 + 1 = `-**32** = *EXACT TIME OF AGE AT TIME OF DEATH!!!!!~'*

`-6720 = 72 (-) 6 = `-**66**

`-66 / `-2 = `-**33** = *ONE YEAR AWAY FROM THE EXACT TIME OF DEATH AGE!!!!!~'*

`-6720 = 6 + 7 + 2 + 0 = `-15

`-6720 = 6 x 7 x 2 x 0 = `-0

`-15 + `-0 = `-**15**

`-94/2 = `-**47**

`-47 (-) `-15 = `-**32** = *EXACT TIME OF AGE AT TIME OF DEATH!!!!!~'*

`-**94** = **RECIPROCAL** = `-**49**

`-94 (-) `-49 = `-45

`-45 (-) `-15 = `-**30** = *TWO YEARS AWAY FROM EXACT TIME OF DEATH AGE!!!!!~'*

`-**19** = **RECIPROCAL** = `-**91**

`-91 (-) `-27 (-) `-11 (-) `-19 = `-**34** = *TWO YEARS AWAY FROM EXACT TIME OF DEATH AGE!!!!!~'*

`-**27** = **RECIPROCAL** = `-**72**

`-94 (-) `-72 + `-11 = `-**33** = *ONE YEAR AWAY FROM THE EXACT TIME OF DEATH AGE!!!!!~'*

`-72 (-) `-40 = `-**32** = *EXACT TIME OF AGE AT TIME OF DEATH!!!!!~'*

`-72 (-) `-11 (-) `-27 = `-`-**34** = *TWO YEARS AWAY FROM EXACT TIME OF DEATH AGE!!!!!~'*

`-90` (-) `-27 (-) `-11 (-) `-19 = `-**33** = *ONE YEAR AWAY FROM THE EXACT TIME OF DEATH AGE!!!!!~'*

`-90 (-) `-41 (-) 27 + `-11 = `-**33** = *ONE YEAR AWAY FROM THE EXACT TIME OF DEATH AGE!!!!!~'*

`-27 + `-19 (-) `-11 (-) `-04 = `-**31** = *ONE YEAR AWAY FROM THE EXACT TIME OF DEATH AGE!!!!!~'*

`-48.5 (-) `-15 = `-**33**.**5** = *ONE; AND, A HALF YEARS AWAY FROM THE EXACT TIME OF AGE AT TIME OF DEATH!!!!!~'*

`-19 + `-11 = `-**30** = *TWO YEARS AWAY FROM THE EXACT TIME OF DEATH AGE!!!!!~'*

`-27 + `-11 (-) `-19 + `-04 = `-**23**

2/**3**rds = *The NUMBER `-23!!!!!~'*

`-**23** = **RECIPROCAL** = `-**32**

`-94 x `-2 = `-188

`-188 / `-3 = `-62.66

`-62.66 / `-2 = `-**31**.**33** = *NEAR ONE YEAR AWAY FROM THE EXACT TIME OF DEATH AGE!!!!!~'*

`-97 x `-2 = `-194

`-194 / `-3 = `-64.66

`-64.66 / `-2 = `-**32**.**33** = *EXACT TIME OF AGE AT TIME OF DEATH!!!!!~'*

DEATH = 07/20/1973

Death Ciphers / Death Cypher / Death Formula / `-The `-GOD `-Equation!!!!!~'

(Example: MAHATMA GANDHI & PRESIDENT NELSON MANDELA): *- Death Formula -*

MAHATMA GANDHI – Birth – **10/02/186**9 **(78) YEARS OF AGE AT TIME OF DEATH!!!!!~'**

10 + 02 + 18 + 69 = `-**99**

`-99 / `-2 = `-**49.5**

`-99 + `-49.5 = `-148.50

`-148.50 / `-2 = `-**74.25** = *THREE; AND, THREE QUARTER YEARS FROM THE EXACT TIME OF AGE AT TIME OF DEATH!!!!!~'*

96**8**1 (-) **2**00**1** = `-**7**6**8**0

98 (-) 21 = `-**77** = *ONE YEAR AWAY FROM THE EXACT TIME OF DEATH AGE!!!!!~'*

`-7680 = 7 + 6 + 8 + 0 = `-21

`-7680 = 7 x 6 x 8 x 0 = `-0

`-21 + `-0 = `-**21**

`-**99** (-) `-**21** = `-**78** = *EXACT TIME OF AGE AT TIME OF DEATH!!!!!~'*

`-86 / `-2 = `-**43**

`-43 + `-21 + `-18 (-) `-2 = `-**80** = *TWO YEARS AWAY FROM EXACT TIME OF DEATH AGE!!!!!~'*

`-91 (-) `-10 (-) `-2 = `-**79** = *ONE YEAR AWAY FROM THE EXACT TIME OF DEATH AGE!!!!!~'*

`-**18** = **RECIPROCAL** = `-**81**

`-81 (-) `-2 = `-**79** = *ONE YEAR AWAY FROM THE EXACT TIME OF DEATH AGE!!!!!~'*

`-69 + `-18 + `-2 (-) `-10 = `-**79** = *ONE YEAR AWAY FROM THE EXACT TIME OF DEATH AGE!!!!!~'*

`-89 (-) `-10 = `-**79** = *ONE YEAR AWAY FROM THE EXACT TIME OF DEATH AGE!!!!!~'*

`-86 + `-02 (-) `-10 = `-**78** = *EXACT TIME OF AGE AT TIME OF DEATH!!!!!~'*

`-49.5 + `-21 + `-10 (-) `-2 = `-**78**.**5** = *EXACT TIME OF AGE AT TIME OF DEATH!!!!!~'*

DEATH – 01/30/1948

PRESIDENT NELSON MANDELA – Birth – 0**7**/**18**/19**1**8 **(95) YEARS OF AGE AT TIME OF DEATH!!!!!~'**

07 + 18 + 19 + 18 = `-**62**

`-62 + `-18 + `-19 = `-**99** = *FOUR YEARS AWAY FROM EXACT TIME OF DEATH AGE!!!!!~'*

`-62 / `-2 = `-**31**

`-62 + `-31 = `-**93** = *TWO YEARS AWAY FROM EXACT TIME OF DEATH AGE!!!!!~'*

8191 (-) 8170 = `-**21**

`-8191 = 89 + 11 = `-**100** = *FIVE YEARS AWAY FROM EXACT TIME OF DEATH AGE!!!!!~'*

`-8170 = 87 + 10 = `-**97** = *TWO YEARS AWAY FROM EXACT TIME OF DEATH AGE!!!!!~'*

`-8191 = 2 + 1 = `-3

`-8191 = 2 x 1 = `-2

`-DEATH CIPHERS/CYPHERS FOR LIFE & DEATH!!!~'

`-3 + `-2 = `-**5**

`-91 + `-5 = `-**96** = *ONE YEAR AWAY FROM EXACT TIME OF DEATH AGE!!!!!~'*

`-**2**, `-**3**, `-**4** = *-PROPHETIC-LINEAR-PROGRESSION!!!!!~'*

`-91 + `-4 = `-**95** = *EXACT TIME OF AGE AT TIME OF DEATH!!!!!~'*

`-62 + `-21 + `-7 + `-5 = `-**95** = *EXACT TIME OF AGE AT TIME OF DEATH!!!!!~'*

`-31 + `-7 + `-18 + `-19 + `-18 + `-2 = `-**95** = *EXACT TIME OF AGE AT TIME OF DEATH!!!!!~'*

`-91 + `-7 = `-**98** = *THREE YEARS AWAY FROM THE EXACT TIME OF DEATH AGE!!!!!~'*

`-81 + `-11 = `-**92** = *THREE YEARS AWAY FROM THE EXACT TIME OF DEATH AGE!!!!!~'*

`-**18** = **RECIPROCAL** = `-**81**

`-91 + `-81 + `-7 + 18 = `-197

`-197 / `-2 = **98**.**5** = *THREE; AND, A HALF PLUS YEARS FROM THE EXACT TIME OF AGE AT TIME OF DEATH!!!!!~'*

`-91 / `-2 = `-**45**.**5**

`-45.5 + `-31 + `-21 = `-97.5 = *TWO; AND, A HALF PLUS YEARS FROM THE EXACT TIME OF AGE AT TIME OF DEATH!!!!!~'*

DEATH – 12/05/2013

(End of `-EXAMPLE)!~'

Death Ciphers / Death Cypher / Death Formula / `-The `-GOD `-Equation!!!!!~'

(Example: MARTIN LUTHER KING, JR. & MALCOLM X): *- Death Formula -*

MARTIN LUTHER KING, JR. – Birth – 0<u>1</u>/<u>15</u>/1<u>92</u>9 **(39) YEARS OF AGE AT TIME OF DEATH!!!!!~'**

01 + 15 + 19 + 29 = `-**64**

`-64 / `-2 = `-**32** = *-a Prophetic Number!!!!!~'*

9291 (-) 5110 = `-**4181**

`-4181 = `-41 (-) `-81 = `-**40** = *ONE YEAR AWAY FROM EXACT TIME OF DEATH AGE!!!!!~'*

`-48 (-) `-11 = `-**37** = *TWO YEARS AWAY FROM EXACT TIME OF DEATH AGE!!!!!~'*

`-4181 = 4 + 1 + 8 + 1 = `-14

`-4181 = 4 x 1 x 8 x 1 = `-32

`-14 + `-32 = `-**46** = **23** x **2** = `-**232** = *Reciprocal-Sequenced-Numerology-RSN!!!!!~'*

`-32 (-) `-14 = `-18

`-92 / `-2 = `-**46** = **23** x **2** = `-**232** = *Reciprocal-Sequenced-Numerology-RSN!!!!!~'*

`-46 / `-2 = `-**23** = *-a Prophetic Number!!!!!~'*

`-32 / `-2 = `-16

`-23 + `-16 = `-**39** = *EXACT TIME OF AGE AT TIME OF DEATH!!!!!~'*

`-**19** = **RECIPROCAL** = `-**91**

`-**15** = **RECIPROCAL** = `-**51**

`-91 (-) `-51 (-) `-1 = `-**39** = *EXACT TIME OF AGE AT TIME OF DEATH!!!!!~'*

`-99 (-) `-51 (-) `-29 + `-19 + `-1 = `-**39** = *EXACT TIME OF AGE AT TIME OF DEATH!!!!!~'*

DEATH – 04/04/1968

MALCOLM X – Birth – 0**5**/**19**/19**2**5 **(39) YEARS OF AGE AT TIME OF DEATH!!!!!~'**

05 + 19 + 19 + 25 = `-**68**

`-68 / `-2 = `-**34** = *FIVE YEARS AWAY FROM EXACT TIME OF DEATH AGE!!!!!~'*

`-34 + `-25 (-) `-19 = `-**40** = *ONE YEAR AWAY FROM THE EXACT TIME OF DEATH AGE!!!!!~'*

5291 (-) 9150 = `-**3859**

`-89 (-) `-53 = `-**36** = *THREE YEARS AWAY FROM EXACT TIME OF DEATH AGE!!!!!~'*

`-3859 = 3 + 8 + 5 + 9 = `-25

`-3859 = 3 x 8 x 5 x 9 = `-1080

`-1080 / `-25 = `-**43**.**2**

`-43.2 + `-19 = `-62.2

`-62.2 (-) `-25 = `-**37**.**2** = *NEAR TWO YEARS AWAY FROM EXACT TIME OF DEATH AGE!!!!!~'*

`-92 / `-2 = `-**46** = **23** x **2** = `-**232** = *Reciprocal-Sequenced-Numerology-RSN!!!!!~'*

`-46 + `-34 = `-80

`-80 / `-2 = `-**40** = *ONE YEAR AWAY FROM THE EXACT TIME OF DEATH AGE!!!!!~'*

`-**19** = RECIPROCAL = `-**91**

`-**15** = RECIPROCAL = `-**51**

`-91 (-) `-51 = `-**40** = *ONE YEAR AWAY FROM THE EXACT TIME OF DEATH AGE!!!!!~'*

`-92 (-) `-51 (-) `-5 = `-**36** = *THREE YEARS AWAY FROM EXACT TIME OF DEATH AGE!!!!!~'*

`-46 (-) `-25 + `-19 = `-**40** = *ONE YEAR AWAY FROM THE EXACT TIME OF DEATH AGE!!!!!~'*

`-19 + `-19 = `-**38** = *ONE YEAR AWAY FROM THE EXACT TIME OF DEATH AGE!!!!!~'*

`-25 + `-19 = `-44

`-44 (-) `-5 = `-**39** = *EXACT TIME OF AGE AT TIME OF DEATH!!!!!~'*

.

`-95 (-) `-51 = `-44

`-44 (-) `-5 = `-**39** = *EXACT TIME OF AGE AT TIME OF DEATH!!!!!~'*

DEATH – 02/21/1965

(End of `-EXAMPLE)!~'

'-DEATH CIPHERS/CYPHERS FOR LIFE & DEATH!!!~'

Fyi,

Regards, Author,

Dwayne W. Anderson

The "PROPHET"!!!!!~'

("PROPHET'S BLOG" on `-WEBSITE)

DWAYNE W. ANDERSON

I was `-WONDERING; if, `-CHILDREN; could be done!!!!!~' So I did JonBenet Ramsey; and, here it is!!!!!~'

Death Ciphers / Death Cypher / Death Formula / `-The `-GOD `-Equation!!!!!~'

(Example: JonBenet Ramsey): **- *Death Formula* -**

JonBenet Ramsey – Birth – 0**8**/0**6**/1**90**0 **(6) YEARS OF AGE AT TIME OF DEATH!!!!!~'**

08 + 06 + 19 + 00 = `-**33**

`-33 / `-2 = `-**16**.5

`-16.5 (-) `-10 = `-**6.5** = *EXACT TIME OF AGE AT TIME OF DEATH!!!!!~'*

0091 (-) 6080 = `-**5989**

00**9**1 (-) **6**0**8**0 = `-14 (-) `-9 = `-5 + `-1 = `-**6** = `- *EXACT TIME OF AGE AT TIME OF DEATH!!!!!~'*

0**09**1 = 09 (-) 01 = `-**8** = *TWO YEARS AWAY FROM EXACT TIME OF DEATH AGE!!!!!~'*

6080 = `-80 (-) `-60 = `-20

0091 = `-90 (-) `-10 = `-80

`-80 (-) `-20 = `-60 = 6 + 0 = `-**6** = `- *EXACT TIME OF AGE AT TIME OF DEATH!!!!!~'*

`-5989 = 5 + 9 + 8 + 9 = `-31

`-5989 = 5 x 9 x 8 x 9 = `-3240

`-3240 / `-31 = `-**104.516**

`-516 (-) `-104 = `-**412**

`-412 = (4 + 2) x 1 = `-**6** = `- *EXACT TIME OF AGE AT TIME OF DEATH!!!!!~'*

`-3240 = `-40 (-) `-32 = `-8

`-31 = `-3 (-) `-1 = `-2

`-8 (-) `-2 = `-**6** = *EXACT TIME OF AGE AT TIME OF DEATH!!!!!~'*

`-516 + `-104 = `-**620**

`-620 (-) `-412 = `-208

`-208 = `-8 (-) `-2 = `-**6** = `- *EXACT TIME OF AGE AT TIME OF DEATH!!!!!~'*

`-90 / `-2 = `-**45**

`-45 (-) `-33 = `-12 / `-2 = `-**6** = `- *EXACT TIME OF AGE AT TIME OF DEATH!!!!!~'*

`-14 (-) `-9 = `-**5** = *ONE YEAR AWAY FROM EXACT TIME OF DEATH AGE!!!!!~'*

`-19 (-) `-14 = `-**5** = *ONE YEAR AWAY FROM EXACT TIME OF DEATH AGE!!!!!~'*

`-91 (-) `-86 = `-**5** = *ONE YEAR AWAY FROM EXACT TIME OF DEATH AGE!!!!!~'*

`-80 + `-60 = `-140

`-90 (-) `-10 = `-80

`-140 (-) `-80 = `-60 = `-6 + `-0 = `-**6** = `- *EXACT TIME OF AGE AT TIME OF DEATH!!!!!~'*

`-80 (-) `-60 = `-20

`-90 (-) `-10 = `-80

`-80 (-) `-20 = `-60 = `-6 + `-0 = `-**6** = `- *EXACT TIME OF AGE AT TIME OF DEATH!!!!!~'*

DEATH – 12/25/1996

(End of `-EXAMPLE)!~'

Fyi,

`-DEATH CIPHERS/CYPHERS FOR LIFE & DEATH!!!~'

Regards, Author,

Dwayne W. Anderson

The "PROPHET"!!!!!~'

Death Ciphers / Death Cypher/Death Formula / `-The `-GOD `-Equation!!!!!~'

(Example: BISON DELE – Brian Williams): - *Death Formula* -

BISON DELE – Brian Williams – NBA STAR – Birth – 0**4**/0**6**/1**96**9 **(33) YEARS OF AGE AT TIME OF DEATH!!!!!~' Cousin; Of, "The Real Prophet Of Doom!!!!!~'**

`-**46** = **23** x **2** = `-**232** = *Reciprocal-Sequenced-Numerology-RSN!!!!!~'*

04 + 06 + 19 + 69 = `-**98**

`-98 / `-2 = `-49

`-49 (-) `-19 = `-30

`-30 + `-04 = `-**34** = *ONE YEAR AWAY FROM EXACT TIME OF DEATH AGE!!!!!~'*

9691 (-) 6040 = `-3651

`-**3651** = `-65 (-) `-31 = `-**34** = *ONE YEAR AWAY FROM EXACT TIME OF DEATH AGE!!!!!~'*

`-3651 = 3 + 6 + 5 + 1 = `-15

`-3651 = 3 x 6 x 5 x 1 = `-90

`-90 (-) `-15 = `-**75**

`-90 / `-15 = `-**6**

`-96 / `-2 = `-**48**

`-75 (-) `-48 = `-27

`-27 + `-6 = `-**33** = *EXACT TIME OF AGE AT TIME OF DEATH!!!!!~'*

`-48 (-) `-19 = `-29

`-29 + `-4 = `-**33** = *EXACT TIME OF AGE AT TIME OF DEATH!!!!!~'*

DEATH – 07/07/2002

(End of `-EXAMPLE)!~'

Fyi,

Regards, Author,

Dwayne W. Anderson

The "PROPHET"!!!!!~'

("PROPHET'S BLOG" on `-WEBSITE)

I think that `-LEARNING any of the `-SCIENCES is just another way to `-LEARN more about `-GOD, for these `-LAWS might not be in the `-BIBLE; but, they are OMNIPRESENT; and, `-self-evident; and, are `-TRUE to `-GOD'S very OWN `-NATURE!!!!!~' I truly feel that the `-LAWS; used in formulation by `-GOD, for the `-SCIENCES; and, for `-ALL of `-NATURE; and, for that of all `-WEATHER; `-ALL truly show a clear `-SIGN of `-GOD'S OMNIPOTENT `-HAND!!!!!~' Here is another CLEAR `-SIGN of `-GOD'S RIGHT `-HAND!!!!!~' Here is `-the `-GOD `-Equation!!!!!~' A `-SYSTEM of `-FORMULAS that `-CALCULATE anyone's `-AGE of `-DEATH; simply, by their `-BIRTHDAY; and, `-YEAR of `-BIRTH!!!!!~' I've never studied `-NUMEROLOGY, `-before; or, will I `-EVER!!!!~' This; is my, VERY `-OWN `-INVENTION!!!!!~'

Death Ciphers/Death Cypher/Death Formula/`-The `-GOD `-Equation!!!!!~'

(Example: Pope John Paul II): **- Death Formula -**

Pope John Paul II – Birth – 0**5**/**18**/1**92**0 **(84) YEARS OF AGE AT TIME OF DEATH!!!!!~'**

05 + 18 + 19 + 20 = `-**62**

`-**62** + `-0**5** + `-**18** = `-**85** = *YEAR OF EXACT TIME OF DEATH!!!!!~'*

0291 (-) 8150 = `-7**85**9

`-7859 = 7 + 8 + 5 + 9 = `-29

`-7859 = 7 x 8 x 5 x 9 = `-2520

`-2520 / `-29 = `-**86**.8965 = *TWO YEARS AWAY FROM TIME OF DEATH AGE!!!!!~'*

`-**86**.8965 (-) `-5 = `-**81**.**8965**= *TWO PLUS YEARS AWAY FROM TIME OF DEATH AGE!!!!!~'*

`-7859 = `-78 + `-59 = `-137

`-137 / `-2 = `-**68**.5

`-**68** = RECIPROCAL = `-**86** = *TWO YEARS AWAY FROM TIME OF DEATH AGE!!!!!~'*

`-78**59** = 79(**85**) = 7 (-) 9(85) = 2 (-) 85 = `-**83** = *ONE YEAR AWAY FROM TIME OF DEATH AGE!!!!!~'*

`-**92** (-) `-**5** = `-**87** = *THREE YEARS AWAY FROM TIME OF DEATH AGE!!!!!~'*

`-**92** / `-2 = `-**46**

`-**46** + `-**20** + `-**18** = `-**84** = *EXACT TIME OF AGE AT TIME OF DEATH!!!!!~'*

`-46 + `-62 = `-108

`-108 (-) `-86 = `-**22** = *ENCAPSULATED BY THE NUMBER* `-**23**!!!!!~'

DEATH – 04/02/2005

(End of `-EXAMPLE)!~'

Death Ciphers/Death Cypher/Death Formula/`-The `-GOD `-Equation!!!!!~'

(Example: L. Ron Hubbard): *- Death Formula -*

L. Ron Hubbard – Birth – 03/13/1911 **(74) YEARS OF AGE AT TIME OF DEATH!!!!!~'**

03 + 13 + 19 + 11 = `-**46** = **23** x **2** = `-**232** = *Reciprocal-Sequenced-Numerology-RSN!!!!!~'*

1191 (-) 3130 = `-1**939** = *Reciprocal-Sequenced-Numerology-RSN!!!!!~'*

`-1**939** = 1 + 9 + 3 + 9 = `-22

`-DEATH CIPHERS/CYPHERS FOR LIFE & DEATH!!!~'

`-1939 = 1 x 9 x 3 x 9 = `-243

`-243 / `-22 = `-11.04545 = `-**11**

`-46 + `-11 = `-**57**

`-**57** = **RECIPROCAL** = `-**75** = *YEAR OF EXACT TIME OF DEATH!!!!!~'*

`-**91** / `-2 = `-**45**.**5** = ROUNDED = `-**46** = = **23** x **2** = `-**232** = *Reciprocal-Sequenced-Numerology-RSN!!!!!~'*

`-46 + `-3 + `-13 + `-11 = `-**73** = *ONE YEAR AWAY FROM EXACT TIME OF DEATH!!!!!~'*

`-**46** + `-**46** = `-**92**

`-92 (-) `-19 = `-**73** = *ONE YEAR AWAY FROM EXACT TIME OF DEATH!!!!!~'*

`-1939 = **93** (-) **19** = `-**74** = *EXACT TIME OF AGE AT TIME OF DEATH!!!!!~'*

DEATH – 01/24/1986

(End of `-EXAMPLE)!~'

Fyi,

Regards, Author,

Dwayne W. Anderson

The "PROPHET"!!!!!~'

("PROPHET'S BLOG" on `-WEBSITE)

Death Ciphers / Death Cypher / Death Formula / `-The `-GOD `-Equation!!!!!~'

(Example: ADOLF HITLER & NAZI LEADER HERMANN GORING): - *Death Formula* -

ADOLF HITLER – Birth – 0**4**/**20**/1**88**9 **(56) YEARS OF AGE AT TIME OF DEATH!!!!!~'**

04 + 20 + 18 + 89 = `-**131**

`-131 / `-2 = `-**65**.5

`-**65** = **RECIPROCAL** = `-**56** = *EXACT TIME OF AGE AT TIME OF DEATH!!!!!~'*

9881 (-) 0240 = `-**9641**

`-**9641** = 96 (-) 41 = `-**55** = *ONE YEAR AWAY FROM EXACT TIME OF DEATH AGE!!!!!~'*

`-9641 = 9 + 6 + 4 + 1 = `-20

`-9641 = 9 x 6 x 4 x 1 = `-216

`-216 / `-20 = `-**10**.8

`-216 + `-20 = `-236

`-236 / `-4 = `-**59** = *THREE YEARS AWAY FROM EXACT TIME OF DEATH AGE!!!!!~'*

`-88 / `-2 = `-**44**

`-**44** + `-10.8 = `-**54**.8 = ROUNDED = `-**55** = *ONE YEAR AWAY FROM EXACT TIME OF DEATH AGE!!!!!~'*

`-65.5 (-) `-10.8 = `-**54.7** = ROUNDED = `-**55** = *ONE YEAR AWAY FROM EXACT TIME OF DEATH AGE!!!!!~'*

`-44 + `-18 + `-4 (-) `-10 = `-**56** = *EXACT TIME OF AGE AT TIME OF DEATH!!!!!~'*

`-89 (-) `-20 (-) `-18 + `-4 = `-**55** = *ONE YEAR AWAY FROM EXACT TIME OF DEATH AGE!!!!!~'*

`-89 (-) `-20 (-) `-4 = `-**65**

`-**65** = **RECIPROCAL** = `-**56** = *EXACT TIME OF AGE AT TIME OF DEATH!!!!!~'*

DEATH – 04/30/1945

HERMANN GORING – Birth – 0**1**/**12**/1**89**3 **(53) YEARS OF AGE AT TIME OF DEATH!!!!!~'**

01 + 12 + 18 + 93 = `-**124**

`-124 / `-2 = `-**62**

`-62 (-) `-12 = `-50

`-50 + 1 = `-**51** = *TWO YEARS AWAY FROM EXACT TIME OF DEATH AGE!!!!!~'*

3981 (-) 2110 = `-**1871**

`-**1871** = `-18 (-) `-71 = `-**53** = *EXACT TIME OF AGE AT TIME OF DEATH!!!!!~'*

`-1871 = 1 + 8 + 7 + 1 = `-17

`-1871 = 1 x 8 x 7 x 1 = `-56

`-56 + `-17 = `-**73**

`-56 (-) `-17 = `-**39**

`-56 / `-17 = `-**3**.29

`-73 + `-39 = `-112

`-112 / `-2 = `-**56** = *THREE YEARS AWAY FROM EXACT TIME OF DEATH AGE!!!!!~'*

`-56 (-) `-3 = `-**53** = *EXACT TIME OF AGE AT TIME OF DEATH!!!!!~'*

`-89 (-) `-2 = `-**44**.5

`-44.5 + `-18 (-) `-12 + `-1 = **51**.5 = ROUNDED = `-**52** = *ONE YEAR AWAY FROM EXACT TIME OF DEATH AGE!!!!!~'*

`-**12** = **RECIPROCAL** = `-**21**

`-93 (-) `-18 (-) `-21 (-) `-1 = `-**53** = *EXACT TIME OF AGE AT TIME OF DEATH!!!!!~'*

DEATH – 10/15/1946

(End of `-EXAMPLE)!~'

Fyi,

Regards, Author,

Dwayne W. Anderson

The "PROPHET"!!!!!~'

("PROPHET'S BLOG" on `-WEBSITE)

COPYRIGHT 04/19/2015!!!!!~' / Dwayne W. Anderson!!!!!~' / The "PROPHET"!!!!!~' /

/ AUTHOR/MEDIATOR/ARBITRATOR/: DWAYNE W. ANDERSON / 04/19/2015 / The "PROPHET"!!!!!~' /

©Copyright: Dwayne W. Anderson!!!!!~'

The "PROPHET" has `-CREATED; `-The `-GOD `-Equation!!!!!~'

Message to '-ALL-' `-PROFESSORS of `-PHYSICS!!!!!~'

You; like to `-USE your `-MIND, `-too!!!!!~' I've; been very impressed, with; `-YOU, just As Well!!!!!~'

You (Bob Cargill); and, your `-PARTNER were married on my `-DATE of `-BIRTH!!!!!~' The very same `-DAY that Sir Isaac Newton HAD died `-ON (MARCH 20th)!!!!!~' When I had finished watching your `-SHOW from `-2011 – The Universe – "God and the Universe" / The Grand Design of `-THINGS, my `-UNCLE by `-MARRIAGE; lost his `-UNCLE by `- MARRIAGE – PERCY SLEDGE – "When A Man Loves A Woman"; just after `-MIDNIGHT!!!!!~'

Science must always be open to `-NEW DISCOVERIES!!!!!~' This is the Definitive Evidence of a `-GOD'S EXISTENCE!!!!!~'

I created the `-Death Cypher; and, You; like to `-USE your `-MINDS!!!!!~' Download; and, `-OPEN; the `-Death Cypher; and, tell me; for `-IF, it's not `-TRUE!!!!!~'

(Example: PERCY SLEDGE): - **Death Formula** -

PERCY SLEDGE – BIRTH – 11/**25**/**19**41 (73) YEARS OF AGE AT TIME OF DEATH!!!!!~'

11 + 25 + 19 + 41 = `-**96**

1491 – 5211 = `-3720

`-3720 = 3 + 7 + 2 + 0 = `-**12**

`-3720 = 3 x 7 x 2 x 0 = `-**0**

`-12 (-) `-0 = `-**12**

`-**94** / `-2 = `-**47**

`-**47** = **RECIPROCAL** = `-**74** = *YEAR OF EXACT TIME OF DEATH!!!!!~'*

`-47 + `-25 = `-72 = ONE YEAR AWAY FROM EXACT TIME OF DEATH!!!!!~'

`-47 + `-12 + `-11 = `-70 = THREE YEARS AWAY FROM EXACT TIME OF DEATH!!!!!~'

`-96 (-) `-25 = `-71 = TWO YEARS AWAY FROM EXACT TIME OF DEATH!!!!!~'

`-96 / `-2 = `-**48**

`-**48** + `-**25** = `-**73** = *EXACT TIME OF AGE AT TIME OF DEATH!!!!!~'*

DEATH – 04/14/2015

(End of `-EXAMPLE)!~'

A Start-Up!!!!!~' A Reciprocal Start-up; of, `-Beautiful; and, `-Mesmerizing `-NUMBERS!!!!!~' Please, choose; and, work these Reciprocal `-NUMBERS; within WORLD `-HISTORY!!!!!~' I've `-Never Studied `-NUMEROLOGY before; but, I have `-CREATED; my VERY `-OWN!!!!~' An APPS COMPANY could `-MAKE BILLIONS `-HERE!!!!!~' For the `-FORMULA, for a `-QUICK REFERENCE;

`-DEATH CIPHERS/CYPHERS FOR LIFE & DEATH!!!~'

note, the `-BIRTH DATE; and, `-death; of LEGENDARY Martial Artist, `-BRUCE LEE; within, `-the CYPHER of `-DEATH!!!!!~'

Here; is, the `-DEATH CIPHER!!!!!~' You can `-PREDICT; your `-AGE, -of `-DEATH, for a `-REAL `-CERTAINTY; *simply from,* Your `-BIRTH `-DATE of `-RECORD!!!!!~' **What does this `-MEAN about `-GOD'S PLAN?????~'**

I've created a Formula/Death Cipher calculating the death age from anyone's birthday! It's my own creation that is based on the `-RECIPROCALS of `-TRIGONOMETRY!!!!!~' `-23; celebs completed, `-so far! Review my (Www.TheRealProphetOfDoom. Com) website; and, download on the `-FRONT PAGE; or, hit the "PROPHET'S BLOG"; for a lead-up, `-to the Formula!~'

These `-FORMULAS could be utilized; and, created; into `-SOFTWARE `-APPS / CELLPHONE APPLICATIONS, in the very near; `-Future!!!!!~' For this very `-Investment - There could be `-$BILLIONS made `-HERE / to `-FEED, -the `-WORLD!!!!!~' I've taken the mathematical reference of the `-Reciprocals of `-TRIGONOMETRY; of which, I got an (A-) in; for when I took it in school!!!!!~' In using these `-RECIPROCALS of `-MINE, I've `-CREATED a `-FORMULA that `-CALCULATES the `-AGE of `-DEATH of `-ANYONE by JUST using their DATE of `-BIRTH!!!!!~' My `-DOCUMENT; on the `-WEBSITE, is `-ENTITLED "DATE - AGE OF DEATH - CIPHERS - FORMULAS - CODE BREAKERS OF LIFE/ death (based on the RECIPROCALS of TRIGONOMETRY)!!!!!~' Our Understanding; Of This World, Is; `-About To Change, `-Forever!!!~' My `-NEW BOOK discovering `-THIS new REVELATION is ENTITLED: "The Real Prophet of Doom (Kismet) - Introduction - Pendulum Flow - " for where I explain `-WORLD `-HISTORY, in using these `-RECIPROCALS of `-LIFE!!!!!~' **Enjoy; -the `-READ!!!!!~'**

Every Person that I've Tried, these `-NUMBERS with; `-works!!!!!~' NOW, `-you TRY, `-PICK; and, `-CALCULATE; virtually anyone's, `-AGES of `-DEATH!!!!!~' Everyone I've picked; `-works!!!!!~' NOW, YOU, `-SUGGEST, `-PICK; and, `-CALCULATE; individuals, from; `-WORLD `-HISTORY!!!!!~' *Be `-CAREFUL;* **about, `-DOING `-YOURSELF though; for there are `-MANY `-FORMULAS; and,**

YOU might not `-PICK the `-RIGHT `-ONE; but YOU will for SURE, match up; to AT LEAST `-ONE (`-1) of `-THEM!!!!!~'

Fyi,

Regards, Author,

Dwayne W. Anderson

©Copyright: Dwayne W. Anderson!!!!!~'

On February 1st of `-2003, the U.S. Space Shuttle Columbia blew up over San Francisco California raining down debris on top of the "PROPHET'S" ROOFTOP - breaking the roof tile on top of the roof of the "Prophet's" newly built home!~' It sounded like sands of rain for where the "Prophet" was sitting inside of his home!~' The roof tile that had broken off into the backyard was repaired due to the new home warranty!~' The "PROPHET" was to be on a flight that very same morning/day to Mexico, to where the "Prophet" was to be buying some land in Mexico- "FIDEICOMISO"!~' The "PROPHET" – Dwayne W. Anderson; also, emailed Oprah Winfrey via her email address encouraging her on starting her own new network station; and, to be calling it "OWN"!~' This Station was founded on January 1st of `-2011!~'

"The Real Prophet Of Doom (Kismet) - Introduction - <u>Pendulum Flow</u>" = Presented in this book is the undeniable **PROOF** that our Heavenly Father `-**GOD**; -Exists!!!!!~'

A _Holy Spirit Numerology_ = A Numerology of **_Reciprocal Sequencing_** that is at its <u>Source</u>; **_Guided_**, by `-**GOD'S HOLY SPIRIT**!!!!!~'

The "PROPHET" need not ask if a HEAVENLY `-GOD -EXISTS!!!!!~' The BIBLE says to have Faith, in His Reality; but, the "PROPHET" has indeed talked via `-GOD'S SPIRIT `-through the PROPHET'S very OWN `-BODY; with this `-UNIVERSAL `-BEING!!!!!~' There is, no need; for `-FAITH, -in `-HIS EXISTENCE!!!!!~' There is `-ONE THING; however, that the "PROPHET" MUST have`-FAITH

176

IN; and, that ONE THING is; that `-MAN HIMSELF will have an `-EVERLASTING LIFE as `-PROMISED in the `-BIBLE; and, not be `-DESTROYED ABSOLUTELY; much like that of the `-DINOSAURS, to have `-SERVED a `-PURPOSE; for some other, VARIED; and, WONDERFUL `-NEW CREATION of `-GOD'S; to OUR very OWN OMNIPOTENT UNIVERSAL LOVING HEAVENLY FATHER `-GOD'S (OWN) CURRENT LIKINGS; and, `-ULTIMATE OMNISCIENT PERFECT WELL MEANING; `-and `-LOVING, `-GIFTED `-PURPOSES!!!!!~' SINCERELY, The "PROPHET" - Dwayne W. Anderson!!!!!~' The `-ANOINTED `-ONE of `-GOD!!!!!~'

1 Timothy 2: (3) This is good and acceptable in the sight of God our Saviour; (4) who willeth that all men should be saved, and come to the knowledge of the truth. `-(ENGLISH REVISED EDITION - 1885)-'

1 Timothy 2:3,4 - Prophetic-Linear-Progression-Scripture!!!!!~'

"When `-GOD gives Prophecy to a `-Human with a look into the Future, `-HE Himself is now in a program to fulfill it (a self-imposed quest that `-HE Himself has `-Now `-Created for Himself to `-Fulfill)!!!!!~ `-GOD can `-Currently see the prophecy based on the potentials of how his creation will respond; `-to the "SPIRIT" WORLD's Communications, via the `-Brain as a `-Transducer; and, `-Paint a Picture of the `-FUTURE!!!!!~ From the prophecy; `-HE can `-Now, change only marginally a little bit; if `-HE so desires, `-Change `-Reality a whole lot; if, `-HE so desires; or, simply; `-Change nothing at all, about; and, from; `-The prophecy in concept, To the `-Actuality of being; `-In the `-Reality of `-LIFE!!!!!~ `If, `-HE so desires!!!!!~'" '(The REAL Prophet Of Doom (Kismet) - Introduction - Pendulum Flow)-"'~

DWAYNE W. ANDERSON

/|\ The "PROPHET" = Mr. Dwayne W. Anderson!!!!!~' /|

DEATH CIPHERS

FORMULAS - CODE BREAKERS OF LIFE/death (based on the RECIPROCALS of TRIGONOMETRY_)

II

DEATH CIPHERS

FORMULAS - CODE BREAKERS OF LIFE/death (based on the
RECIPROCALS of TRIGONOMETRY_)

DEATH/CYPHER

Our Understanding; Of The World, Is;
`-About To Change, `-Forever!!!~'

III

UPDATES for John P. Holdren – the `-President's Chief Science Advisor (The President's LETTER from EDWARD MOORE "TED" KENNEDY today) born `-Exactly `-200 years to the day/date of our/ the very first President of the United States of America: PRESIDENT: George Washington: `-00**32**!!!!!~'

Death Ciphers / Death Cypher / Death Formula / `-The `-GOD `-Equations!!!!!~'

(Example: **EDWARD MOORE "TED" KENNEDY** & **ROBERT F. KENNEDY**): *- Death Formula -*

EDWARD MOORE "TED" KENNEDY – DEATH AGE – **77** / ROBERT F. KENNEDY – DEATH AGE – **42**

`-**77** (-) `-**42** = `-**35** = **RECIPROCAL** = `-**53** = **"WAR OF THE WORLDS"!!!!!~'**

There are some `-1**97** days that lie in between the `-Birthday; and, the `-Assassination Day of Robert F. Kennedy!!!!!~' `-**97** = **RECIPROCAL** = `-**79**!!!!!~' There are some `-**79** days that lie in between the death dates of Robert F. Kennedy; and, Edward Moore "Ted" Kennedy!!!!!~'

What the "PROPHET" has learned by examining the `-KENNEDYS; and, the "PROPHET'S" Mother with First Lady - Mary Todd Lincoln; and, President Franklin Delano Roosevelt; is that `-OUR `-exact `-DAY of `-DEATH, is `-ALREADY set –by `-GOD!!!!!~'

EDWARD MOORE "TED" KENNEDY – Birth – 0**2**/**22**/19**3**2 **(77) YEARS OF AGE AT TIME OF DEATH!!!!!~'**

`-**32** = **RECIPROCAL** = `-**23**

`-23 (-) `-19 = `-**04** / `-04 / `-2 = `-**02** / `-20 (+) `-04 = `-**24** / `-24 + `-02 = `-**26**

`-22 (-) `-02 = `-**20**

`-20 (+) `-04 = `-**24** = DAYS IN THE MONTH BEFORE HIS `-DEATH!!!!!~'

`-32 (-) `-19 = `-**13**

`-13 / `-2 = `-**6.5**

`-22 (-) `-02 = `-**20**

`-20 + `-6.5 = `-**26.5** = ROUNDED DOWN = `-**26** = THE AMOUNT OF DAYS THAT DEATH WILL OCCUR IN!!!!!~'

02 + 22 + 19 + 32 = `-**75** = BIRTHDAY `-NUMBER!!!!!~'

`-75 + `-2 = `-**77** = *EXACT TIME OF AGE AT TIME OF DEATH!!!!!~'*

`-75 / `-2 = `-**37.5**

`-37.5 + `-22 + `-19 = `-**78.5** = *ONE YEAR AWAY FROM THE EXACT (EXACT) TIME OF DEATH AGE!!!!!~'*

`-37.5 + `-22 + `-19 (-) `-2 = `-**76.5** = *ONE YEAR AWAY FROM THE EXACT (EXACT) TIME OF DEATH AGE!!!!!~'*

`-37.5 + `-20 + `-22 = `-**79.5** = *TWO YEARS AWAY FROM THE EXACT (EXACT) TIME OF DEATH AGE!!!!!~'*

`-**93** = **RECIPROCAL** = `-**39**

`-39 + `-37.5 = `-**76.5** = *ONE YEAR AWAY FROM THE EXACT (EXACT) TIME OF DEATH AGE!!!!!~'*

2391 (-) 2220 = `-**171**

2391 = 92 (-) 13 = `-**79** = *TWO YEARS AWAY FROM EXACT TIME OF DEATH AGE!!!!!~'*

`-171 = 1 + 7 + 1 = `-9

`-171 = 1 x 7 x 1 = `-7

`-9 + `-7 = `-**16**

`-93 (-) `-16 = `-**77** = *EXACT TIME OF AGE AT TIME OF DEATH!!!!!~'*

`-9 (-) `-7 = `-**2**

`-75 + `-2 = `-**77** = *EXACT TIME OF AGE AT TIME OF DEATH!!!!!~'*

`-93 / `-2 = **46.5**

`-46.5 + `-32 = `-**78.5** = *ONE YEAR AWAY FROM THE EXACT (EXACT) TIME OF DEATH AGE!!!!!~'*

`-39 + `-2 = `-**41** = *ONE YEAR AWAY FROM THE EXACT TIME OF DEATH AGE (Robert F. Kennedy)!!!!!~'*

DEATH – 08/25/2009 / Another `-**54**; and, `-**36** (Marilyn Monroe); and, `-**63** (John F. Kennedy)!!!!!~'

08 + 25 + 20 + 09 = `-**62** / `-**94** = RECIPROCAL = `-**49**

`-**94** (-) `-**62** = `-**32** / `-**32** = RECIPROCAL = `-**23**

`-**62** (-) `-**49** = `-**13** / `-**13** = RECIPROCAL = `-**31**

`-**32** + `-**31** = `-**63** / `-63 + `-36 = `-**99**

`-13 + `-23 = `-**36**

`-**36** = RECIPROCAL = `-**63**

`-32 + `-13 = `-**45** / `-45 + `-54 = `-**99**

`-23 + `-31 = `-**54**

`-**45** = RECIPROCAL = `-**54**

182

`-32 + `-23 = `-**55** / `-55 + `-44 = `-**99**

`-13 + `-31 = `-**44**

`-**55** = `-**23** + `-**32**

`-**99** = **RECIPROCAL** = `-**66** / `-**96** = **RECIPROCAL** = `-**69** = "The CYCLE of `-LIFE"!!!!!~'

`-**99** ("Ted" Kennedy) (-) `-**77** (Robert F. Kennedy) = `-**22** = *Encapsulated by the `-NUMBER* `-**23**!!!!!~'

`-**77** (Robert F. Kennedy) (-) `-**54** ("Ted" Kennedy) = `-**23** = -a Prophetic Number!!!!!~'

`-**99** ("Ted" Kennedy) (-) `-**66** (Robert F. Kennedy) = `-**33** = (-) `-**1** = `-**32** = *-a Prophetic Number!!!!!~'*

Robert F. Kennedy; and, "Ted" Kennedy (`-**BOTH**) have the `-**BIRTHDAY** `-**NUMBER** of (`-**75**!)!!!!!~'

`-**75** = **RECIPROCAL** = `-**57**

`-**75** + `-**57** = `-**132** = (**1** x **32**) = `-**32** = -a Prophetic Number!!!!!~'

(`-**99**) Death Day `-NUMBER for Robert F. Kennedy (-) (`-**75**) Birthday `-NUMBER for "Ted" Kennedy = `-**24** = (-) `-**1** = `-**23** = *-a Prophetic Number!!!!!~'*

(`-**75**) Birthday `-NUMBER for Robert F. Kennedy (-) (`-**62**) Death Day `-NUMBER for "Ted" Kennedy = (`-**13**) = **"A VERY PIVOTAL NUMBER"**!!!!!~'

`-**13** = **RECIPROCAL** = `-**31** / `-**31** + `-**1** = `-**32** = -a Prophetic Number!!!!!~'

`-**77** + `-**77** = `-**154** = (1 x 54) = `-**54** *("Ted" Kennedy)!!!!!~'*

`-**23** = <u>RECIPROCAL</u> = `-**32**

"<u>The CYCLE of `-LIFE</u>"!!!!!~'

ROBERT F. KENNEDY – Birth – **11**/**20**/1**92**5 **(42) YEARS OF AGE AT TIME OF DEATH**!!!!!~' **(25 - 19) =** `-**6** = `-**DAY of `-DEATH**!!!!!~'

`-**25** = <u>RECIPROCAL</u> = `-**52**

`-52 (-) `-19 = `-**33**

`-33 / `-2 = `-**16**.**5**

`-20 (-) `-11 = `- **09**

`-16.5 (-) `-9 = `-**7**.**5**

`-**7**.**5** = <u>RECIPROCAL</u> = `-**5**.**7** = **DAY ROBERT F. KENNEDY WAS SHOT IN THE MONTH**!!!!!~'

`-25 (-) `-19 = `-**06**

`-06 / `-2 = `-**03**

`-20 (-) `-11 = `-**09**

`-09 (-) `-03 = `-**06** = **DAY OF DEATH**!!!!!~'

ROBERT F. KENNEDY was shot; and, KILLED by <u>**Sirhan/Sirhan**</u>; a `-**24** year old *<u>Palestinian</u>*!!!!!~' `-**42** = <u>RECIPROCAL</u> = `-**24**!!!!!~' **Born on March 19**th **in `-19**4**4**!!!!!~'

11 + 20 + 19 + 25 = `-**75** = **BIRTHDAY `-NUMBER**!!!!!~'

`-75 / `-2 = `-**37**.**5**

5291 (-) 0211 = `-**5080**

`-5080 = 50 (-) `-08 = `-**42** = *EXACT TIME OF AGE AT TIME OF DEATH!!!!!~'*

`-5080 = 5 + 0 + 8 + 0 = `-13

`-5080 = 5 x 0 x 8 x 0 = `-0

`-13 + `-0 = `-**13**

`-**92** = RECIPROCAL = `-**29**

`-29 + `-13 = `-**42** = *EXACT TIME OF AGE AT TIME OF DEATH!!!!!~'*

`-**13** = RECIPROCAL = `-**31**

`-75 (-) `-31 = `-**44** = *TWO YEARS AWAY FROM EXACT TIME OF DEATH AGE!!!!!~'*

`-20 + `-11 + `-13 = `-**44** = *TWO YEARS AWAY FROM EXACT TIME OF DEATH AGE!!!!!~'*

`-92 / `-2 = `-46

`-92 (-) `-**16** (**Ted Kennedy**) = `-**76** = *ONE YEAR AWAY FROM THE EXACT TIME OF DEATH AGE!!!!!~'*

`-**46** = RECIPROCAL = `-**64**

`-64 (-) `-13 (-) `-11 + `-02 = `-**42** = *EXACT TIME OF AGE AT TIME OF DEATH!!!!!~'*

`-92 (-) `-51 = `-**41** = *ONE YEAR AWAY FROM THE EXACT TIME OF DEATH AGE!!!!!~'*

`-75 (-) `-46 + `-11 = `-**40** = *TWO YEARS AWAY FROM EXACT TIME OF DEATH AGE!!!!!~'*

`-25 + `-19 = `-**44** = *TWO YEARS AWAY FROM EXACT TIME OF DEATH AGE!!!!!~'*

`-25 + `-20 = `-**45** = *THREE YEARS AWAY FROM EXACT TIME OF DEATH AGE!!!!!~'*

`-25 + `-11 + `-02 = `-**38** = *FOUR YEARS AWAY FROM EXACT TIME OF DEATH AGE!!!!!~'*

DEATH – 0**6**/0**6**/1968 /|\ "**ALPHA** `-**66**"-'!~' `-**99** = RECIPROCAL = `-**66** !!!!!~'

06 + 06 + 19 + 68 = `-**99** / `-**94** = **RECIPROCAL** = `-**49**

`-**94** (-) `-**99** = `-**05** / `-**05** = **RECIPROCAL** = `-**50**

`-**99** (-) `-**49** = `-**50** / `-**50** = **RECIPROCAL** = `-**05**

`-05 + `-05 = `-**10** / `-10 + `-100 = `-**110** = (110) = (11 + 0) = `-**11**

`-50 + `-50 = `-**100** / `-**11** = "Yin/Yang" = "The CYCLE of `-LIFE"!!!!!~'

`-DUPLICATIVE!!!!!~'

`-05 + `-50 = `-**55** / `-55 + `-55 = `-**110** = (110) = (11 + 0) = `-**11**

`-50 + `-05 = `-**55** / `-**11** = "Yin/Yang" = "The CYCLE of `-LIFE"!!!!!~'

`-DUPLICATIVE!!!!!~'

`-**94** (-) `-**99** = `-**05** / `-**05** = **RECIPROCAL** = `-**50**

`-**99** (-) `-**49** = `-**50** / `-**20** = **RECIPROCAL** = `-**02** / `-**23**/`-**32** = `-**50** (-) `-**2**0= `-**3**0

`-05 + `-20 = `-**25** / `-25 + `-52 = `-**77**

`-50 + `-02 = `-**52**

`-**52** = **RECIPROCAL** = `-**25**

`-05 + `-02 = `-**07** / `-07 + `-70 = `-**77**

`-20 + `-50 = `-**70**

`-**07** = **RECIPROCAL** = `-**70**

`-05 + `-50 = `-**77** / `-77 + `-22 = `-**99**

`-20 + `-02 = `-**22**

`-**99** = **RECIPROCAL** = `-**66** / `-**96** = **RECIPROCAL** = `-**69** = "The CYCLE of `-LIFE"!!!!!~'

`-**99** ("Ted" Kennedy) (-) `-**77** (Robert F. Kennedy) = `-**22** = *Encapsulated by the `-NUMBER `-23*!!!!!~'

`-**77** (Robert F. Kennedy) (-) `-**54** ("Ted" Kennedy) = `-**23** = -a Prophetic Number!!!!!~'

`-**99** ("Ted" Kennedy) (-) `-**66** (Robert F. Kennedy) = `-**33** = (-) `-**1** = `-**32** = *-a Prophetic Number!!!!!~'*

Robert F. Kennedy; and, "Ted" Kennedy (`-**BOTH**) have the `-**BIRTHDAY** `-**NUMBER** of (`-**75**!)!!!!!~'

`-**75** = **RECIPROCAL** = `-**57**

`-**75** + `-**57** = `-**132** = (**1** x **32**) = `-**32** = **-a Prophetic Number!!!!!~'**

(`-**99**) Death Day `-NUMBER for Robert F. Kennedy (-) (`-**75**) Birthday `-NUMBER for "Ted" Kennedy = `-**24** = (-) `-**1** = `-**23** = *-a Prophetic Number!!!!!~'*

(`-**75**) Birthday `-NUMBER for Robert F. Kennedy (-) (`-**62**) Death Day `-NUMBER for "Ted" Kennedy = (`-**13**) = **"A VERY PIVOTAL NUMBER"!!!!!~'**

`-**13** = <u>**RECIPROCAL**</u> = `-**31** / `-**31** + `-**1** = `-**32** = -a **Prophetic Number!!!!!~'**

`-**77** + `-**77** = `-**154** = (1 x 54) = `-**54** *("Ted" Kennedy)!!!!!~'*

`-**23** = <u>**RECIPROCAL**</u> = `-**32**

"<u>The CYCLE of `-LIFE</u>"!!!!!~'

(End of `-EXAMPLES)!~'

Fyi,

Regards, Author,

Dwayne W. Anderson

The "PROPHET"!!!!!~'

("PROPHET'S BLOG" on `-WEBSITE)

The Egyptians in building their `-Pyramids felt that the `-LIFE of a `-PHARAOH could not; or, never be; `-PREDICTED!!!!!~'

Abraham Lincoln, Mary Todd Lincoln, Marilyn Monroe, John F. Kennedy; and, Robert F. Kennedy; are much `-INCLUDED!!!!!~'

The `-"**MATRIX** might be more real than `-**IMAGINED**!!!!!~'

Does a `-"**PROPHET**"; see `-"**PROPHECY**", through a `-"**MATRIX**; that is to be `-"**FULFILLED**"?????~'

Death Ciphers / Death Cypher / Death Formula / `-The `-GOD `-Equations!!!!!~'

`-DEATH CIPHERS/CYPHERS FOR LIFE & DEATH!!!~'

New `-BOOK = The Real Prophet Of Doom (Kismet) – Introduction – Pendulum Flow –

Review my `-BOOK; for my `-DISCOVERY, of the `-WORLD'S `-IMPORTANCE, `-on **R**eciprocal-**S**equencing-**N**umerology!!!!!~' I have called it a `-**NUMEROLOGY**!!!!!~' It's a `-**NEW** `-**NUMEROLOGY**; that, `-**I** have just `-**CREATED**!!!!!~' And; It's **not**; of the `-**OCCULT**!!!!!~' Marilyn Monroe was born in `-19**26**; and, died in `-19**62**!!!!!~' `-**26** = **RECIPROCAL** = `-**62**!!!!!~'

Carnegie Mellon University - The Department of Religious Studies - the Study of New Religion; and, History – for your investigations; my name is Dwayne W. Anderson – "The Real Prophet Of Doom"!!!!!~' I have found; or, discovered what I can refer to as the `-GOD `-Equation!!!!!~' You can calculate anyone's "Age of Death" simply by using `-ONLY their `-BIRTHDAY; and, `-YEAR of `-BIRTH (Absolutely - It Really Works)!!!!!~' I've calculated the "Age of Death" for Singer Ben E. King!!!!!~' I've also done it for Guitarist BB King as he had recently been put into `-HOSPICE `-CARE; however, I couldn't post any of my `-PREDICTIONS; as, people might have thought that I was the `-CAUSE; or, the `-SOURCE; of his `-DEATH!!!!!~' Now I have included `-IT; the `-DATA!!!!!~' Can `-YOU do an `-INVESTIGATIVE `-REPORT on the `-GOD `-Equation / Death Formula / Death Cypher / Death Ciphers that I have `-CREATED!!!!!~' I need someone `-SMART to do `-THIS!!!!!!~' Can `-YOU handle `-IT!!!!!~' This can `-REVOLUTIONIZE the `-THOUGHT; of the `-WORLD, of `-ALL the `-RELIGIONS; that `-WE now `-KNOW `-OF!!!!!~' The `-WORLD of Religious Thought; and, Thought altogether; will be `-CHANGED `-FOREVER!!!!!~' What is `-GOD'S `-PLAN for `-US; in uncovering these, `-EQUATIONS?????~' I've attached two Ciphers: "CIPHER I"; and, "CIPHER II"!!!!!~' PLEASE; Enjoy, -The `-READ!!!!!~'

Noted `-ONES of `-HISTORY!!!!!~' Death Cyphers 1 & 2!!!!!~' It doesn't get any easier than within these `-Two `-Documents!!!!!~' Calculate ANYONE'S "AGE" of "DEATH" simply by `-USING `-ONLY their `-BIRTHDAY; and, `-YEAR of `-BIRTH!!!!!~ Listed; in the CYPHER 1, for `-EASE of `-USE; of the `-CYPHER: President Abraham Lincoln, President George Washington, President Lyndon B. Johnson, First Lady – Lady Bird Johnson, Actor Robin Williams, Comedian Joan

Rivers; and, Actress Marilyn Monroe!!!!!~' Listed; in the CYPHER 2, for `-EASE of `-USE; of the `-CYPHER: Bruce Lee, Mahatma Gandhi, President Nelson Mandela, Martin Luther King, Jr.; and, Mr. Malcolm X!!!!!~' Located at (**Www.TheRealProphetOfDoom. Com**)!!!!!~'

Isn't it `-IRONIC; the `-2 `-KINGS, so `-CLOSE in `-TIME?????~'

Death Ciphers / Death Cypher / Death Formula / `-The `-GOD `-Equations!!!!!~'

(Example: **BEN E. KING** & **BB KING**): - *Death Formula* -

BB KING – DEATH AGE – **89** / BEN E. KING – DEATH AGE – **76**

`-89 (-) `-76 = `-**13** = **"A VERY PIVOTAL NUMBER"**!!!!!~'

THERE WERE `-13 DAYS THAT LIE IN BETWEEN THEIR DAYS OF DEATH!!!!!~'

LETTERS OF THE ALPHABET ASSIGNED TO `-NUMBERS:

BEN E. KING = BE = `-**25** = EE = `-**55** = `-**5** / BB KING = BB = `-**22** = `-**2**

`-**25** = **RECIPROCAL** = `-**52** = **RECIPROCAL** = `-**25**

`-**55** + `-**22** = `-**77** = **BEN E. KING**

`-**77** + (`-**13** = DIFFERENCE IN AGES & DAYS IN DEATH) = `-**90** = **BB KING**

`-**77** + `-**90** = `-**167** = (`-1 x `-**67**) = `-**67** = **RECIPROCAL** = `-**76** = **DEATH AGE OF BEN E. KING!!!!!~'**

BB KING – BIRTH YEAR - `-**25** / BEN E. KING – BIRTH YEAR - `-**38**

`-**25** + `-**38** = `-**63**

CALENDAR YEAR OF `-**2015** (-) `-**63** = `-**1952** = `-**52**

BEN E. KING – BIRTH – 09/28/1938:

`-09 + `-28 = `-**37**

`-1938 = `-38 (-) `-1 = `-**37**

`-37 + `-9 = `-**46**

BB KING – BIRTH – 09/16/1925:

`-09 + `-16 = `-**25**

`-1925 = `-**25**

`-25 + `-19 = `-**44**

`-**46** + `-**44** = `-**90** = BB KING

`-**37** + `-**25** + (`-**13** = DIFFERENCE IN AGES & DAYS IN DEATH) = `-**75** = BEN E. KING

`-90 + `-75 = `-**165** = DEATH AGES COMBINED!!!!!~'

`-89 + `-76 = `-**165** = DEATH AGES COMBINED!!!!!~'

BEN E. KING – Birth – 0**9**/**28**/1**93**8 (76) YEARS OF AGE AT TIME OF DEATH!!!!!~'

`-**38** = **RECIPROCAL** = `-**83**

`-83 (-) `-19 = `-**64**

`-64 / `-2 = `-**32**

`-28 (-) `-09 = `-**19**

191

`-32 (-) `-19 = `-**13**

`-**13** = **RECIPROCAL** = `-**31** = DIED WITHIN `-**31** DAYS OF THE MONTH!!!!!~'

`-38 (-) `-19 = `-**19**

`-19 / `-2 = `-**9.5**

`-28 (-) `-09 = `-**19**

`-19 (+) `-9.5 = `-**28.5** = ROUNDED UP = `-**29** = DAYS IN THE MONTH BEFORE DEATH!!!!!~'

09 + 28 + 19 + 38 = `-**94** = ANOTHER `-Death on the `-NUMBER /'\ `-**94**!!!!!~ / BIRTHDAY `-NUMBER!!!!!~'

`-94 / `-2 = `-**47**

`-47 + `-28 = `-**75** = *ONE YEAR AWAY FROM EXACT TIME OF DEATH AGE!!!!!~'*

8391 (-) 8290 = `-**101**

8391 = 98 (-) 31 = `-**67** = **RECIPROCAL** = `-**76** = *EXACT TIME OF AGE AT TIME OF DEATH!!!!!~'*

8290 = 98 (-) 20 = `-**78** = *TWO YEARS AWAY FROM EXACT TIME OF DEATH AGE!!!!!~'*

`-**101** = 1 + 0 + 1 = `-2

`-**101** = 1 x 0 x 1 = `-0

`-2 + `-0 = `-**2**

`-93 / `-2 = **46**.5

`-46.5 + `-2 = `-48.5

`-48.5 + `-28 = `-<u>76</u>.5 = *EXACT (EXACT) TIME OF AGE AT TIME OF DEATH!!!!!~'*

`-46.5 + `-28 = `-<u>74</u>.5 = <u>ROUNDED</u> = `-<u>75</u> = *ONE YEAR AWAY FROM EXACT TIME OF DEATH AGE!!!!!~'*

`-09 + `-28 + `-38 = `-<u>75</u> = *ONE YEAR AWAY FROM EXACT TIME OF DEATH AGE!!!!!~'*

`-09 + `-28 + `-38 + `-2 = `-<u>77</u> = *ONE YEAR AWAY FROM EXACT TIME OF DEATH AGE!!!!!~'*

`-09 + `-28 + `-19 = `-<u>56</u> = <u>RECIPROCAL</u> = `-<u>65</u>

`-65 + `-2 = `-<u>67</u> = <u>RECIPROCAL</u> = `-<u>76</u> = *EXACT TIME OF AGE AT TIME OF DEATH!!!!!~'*

DEATH – 04/30/2015 / `-<u>69</u> = "Yin/Yang" = **"The CYCLE of `-LIFE"!!!!!~'**

04 + 30 + 20 + 15 = `-<u>69</u> / `-<u>94</u> = <u>RECIPROCAL</u> = `-<u>49</u>

`-<u>94</u> (-) `-<u>69</u> = `-<u>25</u> / `-<u>25</u> = <u>RECIPROCAL</u> = `-<u>52</u>

`-<u>69</u> (-) `-<u>49</u> = `-<u>20</u> / `-<u>20</u> = <u>RECIPROCAL</u> = `-<u>02</u>

`-<u>52</u> + `-<u>20</u> = `-<u>72</u> / `-72 + `-27 = `-<u>99</u>

`-<u>25</u> + `-<u>02</u> = `-<u>27</u>

`-<u>72</u> = <u>RECIPROCAL</u> = `-<u>27</u>

`-<u>25</u> + `-<u>20</u> = `-<u>45</u> / `-45 + `-54 = `-<u>99</u>

`-<u>52</u> + `-<u>02</u> = `-<u>54</u>

`-**45** = RECIPROCAL = `-**54**

`-25 + `-52 = `-**77** / `-77 + `-22 = `-**99**

`-20 + `-02 = `-**22**

`-**99** = RECIPROCAL = `-**66** / `-**96** = RECIPROCAL = `-**69** = "The CYCLE of `-LIFE"!!!!!~'

(`-**94**) Ben E. King's **Birthday** `-NUMBER (-) (`-**69**) Ben E. King's **Death Day** `-NUMBER = `-**25** = RECIPROCAL = `-**52** !!!!!~' (**25**+**52**) = `-**1** YR AWAY from `-**76**!!!!!~'

(`-**69**) BEN E. KING Death Day `-NUMBER; and, (`-**69**) BB KING Birthday `-NUMBER are `-EXACTLY the `-SAME!!!!!~' They both `-SHARE this very same `-NUMBER (**RECIPROCALLY**) in the **"CYCLE of LIFE"**!!!!!~'

BB KING – Birth – 0**9**/**16**/1**92**5 **(89) YEARS OF AGE AT TIME OF DEATH!!!!!~'**

`-**25** = RECIPROCAL = `-**52**

`-52 (-) `-19 = `-**33**

`-33 / `-2 = `-**16.5**

`-16 (-) `-09 = `-**07**

`-16.5 (-) `-07 = `-**9.5**

`-**9.5** = RECIPROCAL = `-**5.9** = (`-**9.5** + `-**5.9** = `-**15.4** = ROUNDED = `-**15** = DIED WITHIN `-**15** DAYS OF THE MONTH!!!!!~'

`-25 (-) `-19 = `-**06**

`-16 (-) `-09 = `-**07**

`-06 (+) `-07 = `-**13** = DAYS IN THE MONTH BEFORE DEATH!!!!!~'

`-25 (-) `-19 = `-**06**

`-06 / `-2 = `-**03**

`-07 (-) `-03 = `-**04** = DIE ON A `-**4** OF THE MONTH!!!!!~'

09 + 16 + 19 + 25 = `-**69** = "Yin/Yang" = **"The CYCLE of `-LIFE"!!!!!~'**
/ BIRTHDAY `-NUMBER!!!!!~'

`-69 / `-2 = `-**34**.**5**

5291 (-) 6190 = `-**899**

`-899 = `-**89**9 = *EXACT TIME OF AGE AT TIME OF DEATH!!!!!~'*

`-899 = 98 (-) 9 = `-**89** = *EXACT TIME OF AGE AT TIME OF DEATH!!!!!~'*

`-899 = 8 + 9 + 9 = `-26

`-899 = 8 x 9 x 9 = `-648

`-648 / `-26 = `-**24**.**92**

`-69 + `-24.92 = `-**93**.**92** = *NEAR FIVE YEARS AWAY FROM EXACT TIME OF DEATH AGE!!!!!~'*

`-34.5 + `-24.92 + `-19 + `-9 = `-**87**.**42** = *NEAR TWO YEARS AWAY FROM THE EXACT TIME OF DEATH AGE!!!!!~'*

`-24.92 = `-**2**.**492**

`-92 (-) `-2.492 = `-**89**.**508** = *EXACT (EXACT) TIME OF AGE AT TIME OF DEATH!!!!!~'*

`-92 / `-2 = `-46

`-46 + `-24.92 + `-19 = `-**89**.**92** = *EXACT TIME OF AGE AT TIME OF DEATH!!!!!~'*

`-95 (-) `-9 = `-**86** = *THREE YEARS AWAY FROM THE EXACT TIME OF DEATH AGE!!!!!~'*

`-59 + `-21 + `-9 = `-**89** = *EXACT TIME OF AGE AT TIME OF DEATH!!!!!~'*

DEATH – 05/14/2015 / `-**54** = "EARTHQUAKES"!!!!!~'

05 + 14 + 20 + 15 = `-**54** / `-**94** = RECIPROCAL = `-**49**

`-**94** (-) `-**54** = `-**40** / `-**40** = RECIPROCAL = `-**04**

`-**54** (-) `-**49** = `-**05** / `-**05** = RECIPROCAL = `-**50**

`-05 + `-04 = `-**09** / `-09 + `-90 = `-**99**

`-40 + `-50 = `-**90**

`-**09** = RECIPROCAL = `-**90**

`-40 + `-05 = `-**45** / `-45 + `-54 = `-**99**

`-04 + `-50 = `-**54**

`-**45** = RECIPROCAL = `-**54**

`-40 + `-04 = `-**44** / `-44 + `-55 = `-**99**

`-05 + `-50 = `-**55**

`-**99** = RECIPROCAL = `-**66** / `-**96** = RECIPROCAL = `-**69** = "The CYCLE of `-LIFE"!!!!!~'

(`-**69**) BB KING'S **Birthday** `-**NUMBER** (+) (`-**54**) BB KING'S **Death Date** `-**NUMBER** = `-**123** = (**1** x **23**) = `-**23** = -a Prophetic **Number!!!!!~'**

(`-**69**) BEN E. KING Death Day `-NUMBER; and, (`-**69**) BB KING Birthday `-NUMBER are `-EXACTLY the `-SAME!!!!!~' They both `-SHARE this very same `-NUMBER (**RECIPROCALLY**) in the **"CYCLE of LIFE"!!!!!~'**

(End of `-EXAMPLES)!~'

Fyi,

Regards, Author,

Dwayne W. Anderson

The "PROPHET"!!!!!~'

("PROPHET'S BLOG" on `-WEBSITE)

Carnegie Mellon University - The Department of Religious Studies - the Study of New Religion; and, History – for your investigations; here is the quick snapshot, of my `-NEW `-BOOK!!!!!~' `-NOTICE the `-SEQUENCING of `-ALL of the `-NUMBERS!!!!!~' It's `-ALL by `-GOD'S `-DIRECTION!!!!!~' Notice `-THIS `-PATTERN; **and,** there are some `-488 pages `-MORE in my `-NEW `-BOOK!!!!!~' The `-NUMBERS; are, in the `-UNIVERSE; just as well!!!!!~'

Mary Todd Lincoln's birthday is just about exactly `-**94** years in difference from Lady Bird Johnson's birthday; plus the `-"key number" of `-**9** days!!!!!~ Edith Kermit Carow Roosevelt died `-**94** days away from `-1**949**!!!!!~' `-**94** = **RECIPROCAL** = `-**49**!!!!!~' Lady Bird Johnson lived to be `-**94** years of age; while, Jacqueline Lee Kennedy died in `-19**94**!!!!!~' Comedian Joan Rivers died on **9/4** (September 4<sup>th</sup>)!!!!!~' Grace Kelly died on 0**9**/1**4**; while, Harry Houdini was married in `-18**94**!!!!!~'

President Lyndon B. Johnson married Lady Bird Johnson in `-**1934**!!!!!~ Lady Bird Johnson died `-**34** years; after, the death of President Lyndon B. Johnson!!!!!~ Jacqueline Lee Kennedy was `-**34** years of age at the time of her husband's assassination; that of, President John F. Kennedy; and, the inauguration of President Lyndon B. Johnson!!!!!~ Lady Bird Johnson died `-**34**0 days; and, `-**44** years after the death of Marilyn Monroe!!!!!~'

President John F. Kennedy was assassinated at the age of `-**46**!!!!!~ Mary Todd Lincoln was `-**46** years of age when President Abraham Lincoln was assassinated!!!!!~ President John F. Kennedy was assassinated in `-19**63**!!!!!~ Mary Todd Lincoln died at the age of `-**63**!!!!!~ President John F. Kennedy died at the tender age of `-**46**; with his spouse, Jacqueline Lee Kennedy dying at the **reciprocal** tender age of `-**64**!!!!!~ John F. Kennedy's Vice-President also died at tender reciprocal age of `-**64** just as well!!!!!~' Both Lyndon B. Johnson; and, Abraham Lincoln were the tallest Presidents ever at the height of **6' 4**"!!!!!~' Abraham Lincoln was born in `-18**09**; while, Lyndon B. Johnson was born in the Reciprocal Year of `-19**08**!!!!!~ The Civil Rights Act was implemented; and, signed by Lyndon B. Johnson on **7/2** (July 2ⁿᵈ) in`**1964**!!!!!~ **1964** = **RECIPROCAL** = **1865**!!!!!~ `-**1865** was Abraham Lincoln's `-**13**ᵗʰ Amendment Abolishing Slavery!!!!!~'

Notice the age differences; and, similarities in how long the First Lady's Outlived their Presidential Husbands!!!!!~ Two First Ladies were at `-17 years of living in difference!!!!!~ One was at a `-29 years in living in difference; while, another one was just at (only) one year more in difference at a `-30 years in difference after the `-DEATHS of their `-PRESIDENTS!!!!!~'

Notice the `-KEY `-AGES of `-DEATH for the `-RUSSIAN `-PRESIDENTS having died in a `-SEQUENCE of `-74, `-75, `-76, `-77, etc., etc. etc.!!!!!~ Notice the Presidents being of the same `-AGES for the `-AMERICAN `-PRESIDENTS; and, the `-KEY `-NUMBER for American Presidents at `-AGE of `-DEATH being at `-93 `-Years of `-Age!!!!!~'

President Nelson Mandela served `-**27** years in prison; and, was released at what `-AGE?????~' **27** = **RECIPROCAL** = **72**!!!!!~' President Nelson Mandela was released at `-AGE `-**72**!!!!!~' Civil Rights Act of `-19**64** (`-**72**)!!!!!~' Nelson Mandela was arrested in `-19**64**!!!!!~' Lady Bird Johnson died in `-**2007**!!!!!~' Bruce Lee was born on the **27**th of November; and, died on July 20th (0**7**/**20**)!!!!!~' There are `-1**27** years that span in between the deaths of The Real Prophet Of Doom's Mother; and, Mary Todd Lincoln; of which, they both died at the tender `-AGE of `-**63**!!!!!~' There is a span of some `-**63** years in between the deaths of The Real Prophet Of Doom's Mother; and, Franklin Delano Roosevelt; of which, they both died at the tender `-AGE of `-**63**!!!!!~' There is a span of some `-**63** years in between the deaths of Mary Todd Lincoln; and, Franklin Delano Roosevelt; of which, they both died at the tender `-AGE of `-**63**!!!!!~' In between their days; and, months of dates of death there is a span of some `-**94** days that lies in between these two individuals - President & First Lady!!!!!~' `-**90** days; and, `-**4** days for the Prophet's Mother's Death Date; and, these two same individuals!!!!!~' `-**90** + `-**4** = `-**94**!!!!!~' When taking the acronyms on these three individual's names MTL, ELM; and, FDR; and, matching them up to the English Alphabet; you get a `-NUMBER of `-**40**!!!!!~' This Number of `-**40** is arrived at by each; and, every Number of; and, `-from; these three acronym initials being added up together - one by one - to each other for; `-All of these three `-fine individuals!!!!!~' For, `-ALL of these `-THREE fine `-Individuals; their `-AGES of `-DEATH equals the Number `-**63**!!!!!~' `-**63** (-) `-**40** = `-**23** = -a Prophetic Number!!!!!~'

Mary Todd Lincoln = the `-**16**th President

Franklin Delano Roosevelt = the `-**32**nd President (`-**16** x `-**2** = `-**32**)!!!!!~'

Ethelyn Lee McFadden (**Stanford University Patient**) = the `-**43**rd President

A	B	C	D	E	F	G	H	I	J	K	L	M	N	O	P	Q	R	S	T	U	V	W	X	Y	Z
1	2	3	4	5	6	7	8	9	10	11	12	13	14	15	16	17	18	19	20	21	22	23	24	25	26

DWAYNE W. ANDERSON

(`-**16** x `-**2** = `-**32**)!!!!!~' `-16(`-2) = `-**162** = `-1 + `-62 = `-**63**

`-**16** + `-**32** + `-**43** = `-**91** + `-**3** Presidents = `-**94**!!!!!~'

Two `-**94**'**s** = `-**188**
Three `-**63**'**s** = `-**189**

One `-Off; from being, `-**EXACT**!!!!!~'

`-**189** (-) `-**188** = `-**1** = The English Alphabet = **A** = "**Angel of Death**"!!!!!~'

Apartheid began in `-19**48**; and, ended in `-19**94**!!!!!~' A `-**46** year `-SPAN!!!!!~' *John F. Kennedy/Jacqueline Lee Kennedy/Lyndon B. Johnson/Lady Bird Johnson/Nelson Mandela!!!!!~' `-46 = RECIPROCAL = `-64!!!!!~' `-46 = `-23 x `-2 = `-232 = Reciprocal-Sequenced-Numerology!!!!!~' `-64 = `-2 x `-32 = `-232 = Reciprocal-Sequenced-Numerology!!!!!~'*

`-**44**th President Barack H. Obama (`-**53** years of age in `-**2014**); was born, `-**9** days before the Berlin Wall had begun construction (the `-**13**th of August)!!!!!~ The Berlin Wall was opened in `-19**89** /**RSN** acknowledging `-**53** years since started!!!!~ Vladimir V. Putin (born `-**85** days before `-19**53**) `-**85** = 8 + 5 = `-**13** = `-**9** years older than President Barack H. Obama!!!!!~ The Days `-**85** (Minus) The Age/Year `-**53** = The Number `-**32**!!!!!~ President Barack H. Obama was born in `-19**61**!!!!!~ President Vladimir V. Putin; in `-2014, at the time of this original writing; was, `-**61** years of age!!!!!~ President Barack H. Obama is **6' 1**" in height!!!!!~ President Vladimir V. Putin; and, President Barack H. Obama; are, `-**RECIPROCALS**!!!!!~ There are some `-**63** days (President John F. Kennedy died in `-19**63** / took office in `-19**61**) for this interaction in between their birthdays!!!!!~'

FIRST LADY ELEANOR ROOSEVELT DIED ON **11/7/ FIRST LADY - LADY BIRD JOHNSON** DIED ON **7/11** = **RECIPROCAL-SEQUENCED-NUMEROLOGY/19**62**!!!!!~ FIRST LADY ELEANOR ROOSEVELT** DIED THE VERY SAME YEAR AS MARI**LYN** MONROE IN `-19**62** /-/ JUST SOME `-**94** DAYS AFTER THE

200

DEATH OF MARILYN MONROE!!!!!~ **REVERSED** `-EQUALS `-**270 DAYS!!!!!~'**

PRESIDENT WOODROW WILSON WAS THE **28**th PRESIDENT OF THE UNITED STATES OF AMERICA; WHILE, PRESIDENT GEORGE WASHINGTON WAS THE VERY **1**st _PRESIDENT OF THE UNITED STATES OF AMERICA!!!!!~' `-**28** (-) `-**1** = `-**27**!!!!!~'

There were `-**123** years that lie in between the births; and, deaths of President George Washington; and, President Woodrow Wilson!!!!!~ These two Presidents both died at the tender `-AGE of `-**67**!!!!!~' They both had their very own births; and, deaths alternated with within the exact same two identical months (The Months of - February & December) of each of the others actual own birth; and, death = (**2/12**)!!!!!~' `-**212** = **R**eciprocal-**S**equencing-**N**umerology!!!!!~' `-**32** = **RECIPROCAL** = `-**23**!!!!!~ One was born on `-**32** in `-17**32**; and, the other one died at `-**23** on **2/3**/1924!!!!!~'

`-**1924** = 1(9)2(4) = `-**91** (-) `-**42** = `-**49**

`-**1732** = `-17 + `-**32** = `-**49**

`-**49** = **RECIPROCAL** = `-**94**!!!!!~'

With an `-**E** flipped sideways `-**M**; all `-Three Wives (`-2 Wilson/`-1 Washington) all three of the women had the very same initials!!!!!~' President **W**ilson had a married life of some `-**38** years; while, President **W**ashington had a married life of some `-**40** years!!!!!~' Almost `-**IDENTICAL** in `-**MARRIED** `-**LIFE**!!!!!~' `-**40** + `-**38** = `-**78**!!!!!~' `-**94** (-) `-**78** = `-**16**th President = **Abraham Lincoln**!!!!!~' Who was married to his wife Mary Todd Lincoln for some `-**23** years!!!!!~'

President George Washington died `-**9** years before the birth of President Abraham Lincoln; while, President Woodrow Wilson was born `-**9** Years before the death of President Abraham Lincoln!!!!!~' President Woodrow Wilson was just born in the year that carried the very same number as the `-AGE of `-DEATH of President Abraham

DWAYNE W. ANDERSON

Lincoln (`-**56**) born in `-18**56**!!!!!~' President Woodrow Wilson died just shortly after the turning of `-19**23**!!!!!~' President Woodrow Wilson's 2<sup>nd</sup> wife `-Edith died on his birthday (**12/28**) in `-**1961** at the `-AGE of `-**89**!!!!!~' `-**61** + `-**19** = `-**80**!!!!!~' `-**89** (-) `-**80** = `-**9**!!!!!~' President Woodrow Wilson; and, his wife `-Edith were married for `-**9** years!!!!!~' `-**28** (-) `-**12** = **16**th President = **Abraham Lincoln**!!!!!~'

Explore this further!!!!!~' And now a couple months ago, I have discovered the `-Death Ciphers / `-Death Cypher / The `-Death Formula / The `-GOD `-EQUATIONS; to where you can calculate anyone's "Age of Death" simply by using their "Birthday", "Birth Month"; and, "Year of Birth"!!!!!~' On my `-WEBSITE; go to within, the "PROPHET'S BLOG" to `-SEE the `-EXACT `-CALCULATIONS done of the `-DEATH `-AGES for both the President Mr. John F. Kennedy; and, the First Lady Mrs. Jacqueline Lee Kennedy Onassis!!!!!~'

By the `-WAY, Abraham Lincoln died in `-18**65**!!!!!~' And; at what age did he die?????~' **65** = **RECIPROCAL** = **56**!!!!!~' Abraham Lincoln died at the tender age of `-**56**!!!!!~'

I Hope `-YOU'RE; Enjoying the `-READ!!!!!~' Contact `-ME; for if, `-YOU so `-DESIRE!!!!!~' Dwayne W. Anderson!!!!!~' The "PROPHET"!!!!!~'

©Copyright: Dwayne W. Anderson!!!!!~'

The Prophet!~'
Mediator/Arbitrator: Dwayne W. Anderson
(((Www.TheRealProphetOfDoom.Com)))

202

`-DEATH CIPHERS/CYPHERS FOR LIFE & DEATH!!!~'

COPYRIGHT 06/03/2015 / AUTHOR: DWAYNE W. ANDERSON / THE "PROPHET"!!!!!~' /

The Article on the Website was stating that `-SATAN; and, his `-DEMONS; cannot read our `-MINDS, "so have `-NO `-FEAR"!!!!!~' However, as I explained over the telephone twice in New York; here is my reasoning!!!!!~' The `-BIBLE states that `-GOD; and, `-CHRIST can `-READ our `-MINDS; however, it doesn't say `-ANYTHING about `-SATAN!!!!!~' After three to four hours of meditating; and, reasoning; this is what I came up with!!!!!~' At dinner time; if, we pray to `-GOD without uttering a word; he hears our prayers!!!!!~' Likewise; `-IF, we pray to `-SATAN at dinner time, without uttering a word; and, `-HE can hear our `-PRAYERS, then, `-HE too; can `-READ our `-MINDS!!!!!~' As the Muslims call him; `-SHAITAN!!!!!~ I believe

that `-GOD talks to me with his `-HOLY `-SPIRIT `-directly!!!!!~'
Only when I talk to `-GOD in `-PRAYER; does my `-BODY flinch; or,
pulse!!!!!~' For when I ask if he is `-JEHOVAH talking to `-ME; he
`-PULSES a resounding `-YES!!!!!~' Here is `-SOMETHING `-NEW;
that, I'm `-WORKING `-ON!!!!!~'

Death Ciphers / Death Cypher / Death Formula / `-The `-GOD
`-Equation!!!!!~'

(Example: PRESIDENT JOHN F. KENNEDY & FIRST LADY
JACQUELINE LEE KENNEDY ONASSIS): - *Death Formula* -

PRESIDENT JOHN F. KENNEDY – Birth – 0**5**/**29**/1**91**7 **(46) YEARS
OF AGE AT TIME OF DEATH!!!!!~'**

`-**17** = **RECIPROCAL** = `-**71**

`-71 (-) `-19 = `-**52**

`-52 / `-2 = `-**26**

`-29 (-) `-05 = `-**24**

`-26 (-) `-24 = `-**02**

`-**02** = **RECIPROCAL** = `-**20** = **DAYS IN THE MONTH BEFORE
DEATH!!!!!~'**

`-19 (-) `-17 = `-**02**

`-29 (-) `-05 = `-**24**

`-24 (-) `-02 = `-**22** = **DAY OF DEATH / DAY OF ASSASSINATION!!!!!~'**

`-19 (-) `-17 = `-**02**

`-02 / `-2 = `-**01**

`-29 (-) `-05 = `-**24**

`-24 (-) `-01 = `-**23** = DIED WITHIN `-**23** DAYS OF THE MONTH!!!!!~'

05 + 29 + 19 + 17 = `-**70** = BIRTHDAY `-NUMBER!!!!!~'

`-70 / `-2 = `-**35** = `-**35**th PRESIDENT OF THE UNITED STATES OF AMERICA!!!!!!~'

`-**35** = RECIPROCAL = `-**53** = "WAR OF THE WORLDS"!!!!!~'

`-70 (-) `-17 = `-**53**

JOHN F. KENNEDY MARRIED JACQUELINE LEE KENNEDY IN `-19**53**!!!!!~'

`-29 + `-17 = `-**46** = *EXACT TIME OF AGE AT TIME OF DEATH!!!!!~'*

`-**46** = RECIPROCAL = `-**64**

`-35 + `-29 = `-**64**

7191 (-) 9250 = `-**2059**

`-7191 = `-91 (-) `-17 = `-**74** = RECIPROCAL = `-**47** = *ONE YEAR AWAY FROM EXACT TIME OF DEATH AGE!!!!!~'*

`-7191 = `-17 + `-19 = `-**36** = RECIPROCAL = `-**63** = *YEAR OF DEATH!!!!!~'*

`-29 + `-5 = `-**34** = RECIPROCAL = `-**43** = *THREE YEARS AWAY FROM EXACT TIME OF DEATH AGE!!!!!~'*

`-2059 = 2 + 0 + 5 + 9 = `-16

`-2059 = 2 x 0 x 5 x 9 = `-0

`-16 + `-0 = `-**16**

`-70 + `-16 = `-86

`-86 / `-2 = `-**43** = *THREE YEARS AWAY FROM EXACT TIME OF DEATH AGE!!!!!~'*

`-29 + `-17 = `-**46** = **23** x **2** = `-**232** = *Reciprocal-Sequenced-Numerology-RSN!!!!!~'*

`-91 / `-2 = **45**.**5** = ROUNDED = `-**46** = **23** x **2** = `-**232** = *Reciprocal-Sequenced-Numerology-RSN!!!!!~'*

`-46 / `-2 = `-**23** = *-a Prophetic Number!!!!!~'*

`-16 x `-2 = `-**32** = *-a Prophetic Number!!!!!~'*

`-**23** = RECIPROCAL = `-**32**

JACQUELINE LEE KENNEDY MET JOHN F. KENNEDY FOR WHEN SHE WAS JUST `-**23** YEARS OF AGE!!!!!~'

`-91/ `-2 = **45**.**5** = ROUNDED = `-**46** = *EXACT TIME OF AGE AT TIME OF DEATH!!!!!~'*

`-71 (-) `-19 (-) `-5 = `-**47** = *ONE YEAR AWAY FROM EXACT TIME OF DEATH AGE!!!!!~'*

`-91 (-) `-17 (-) `-29 = `-**45** = *ONE YEAR AWAY FROM EXACT TIME OF DEATH AGE!!!!!~'*

`-29 + `-17 = `-**46** = *EXACT TIME OF AGE AT TIME OF DEATH!!!!!~'*

DEATH – **11**/**22**/19**63** /|\ "**ALPHA** `-**66**"-'!~'

11 + 22 + 19 + 63 = `-**115** / `-**94** = RECIPROCAL = `-**49** / `-**115** (-) `-**49** = `-**66**...!!!!!~'\

`-**94** (-) `-**115** = `-**21** / `-**21** = RECIPROCAL = `-**12**

`-**115** (-) `-**49** = `-**66** / `-**66** = RECIPROCAL = `-**66**

`-21 + `-12 = `-**33** / `-33 + `-132 = `-**165** = (165) = (65 + 1) = `-**66**

`-66 + `-66 = `-**132** / `-165 (-) `-**99** = `-**66**

`-**33** = (-) `-**1** = `-**32** = -a Prophetic Number!!!!!~'

`-**132** = (**1** x **32**) = `-**32** = -a Prophetic Number!!!!!~'

`-**32** + `-**32** = `-**64** = Jacqueline Lee Kennedy Onassis!!!!!~'

`-DUPLICATIVE!!!!!~'

`-**87** = RECIPROCAL = `-**78**

`-21 + `-66 = `-**87** / `-87 + `-78 = `-**165** = (165) = (65 + 1) = `-**66**

`-66 + `-12 = `-**78** / `-165 (-) `-**99** = `-**66**

`-**78** = RECIPROCAL = `-**87**

`-**99** = RECIPROCAL = `-**66** / `-**96** = RECIPROCAL = `-**69** = "The CYCLE of `-LIFE"!!!!!~'

(`-**253**) (-) (`-**83**) Jacqueline Lee Kennedy Onassis **Birthday** `-NUMBER = `-**170** = (**1** x **70**) = `-**70** = John F. Kennedy's **Birthday** `-NUMBER!!!!!~'

(`-**99**) (-) (`-**137**) Jacqueline Lee Kennedy Onassis **Death Day** `-NUMBER = (`-**38**)!!!!!~' (`-**99**) (-) (`-**115**) John F. Kennedy **Death Day** `-NUMBER = (`-**16**)!!!!!~' (`-**38**) + (`-**16**) = (`-**54**)_!!!!!~'

(`-**88**) Jacqueline Lee Kennedy Onassis (+) (`-**66**) John F. Kennedy = `-**154**!!!!!~'

(`-**83**) Birthday `-NUMBER for Jacqueline Lee Kennedy Onassis (-)
(`-**70**) Birthday `-NUMBER for John F. Kennedy = (`-**13**) = **"A VERY PIVOTAL NUMBER"**!!!!!~'

`-**13** = **RECIPROCAL** = `-**31** / `-**31** + `-**1** = `-**32** = -a **Prophetic Number**!!!!!~'

`-**137** (Jacqueline Lee Kennedy Onassis Death Day `-NUMBER) (-) `-**115** (John F. Kennedy Death Day `-NUMBER) = `-**22** = *Encapsulated by the `-NUMBER* `-**23**!!!!!~'

`-**23** = **RECIPROCAL** = `-**32**

"The CYCLE of `-LIFE"!!!!!~'

FIRST LADY JACQUELINE LEE KENNEDY ONASSIS – Birth – 0**7**/**28**/1**92**9 **(64) YEARS OF AGE AT TIME OF DEATH**!!!!!~'

`-**29** = **RECIPROCAL** = `-**92**

`-92 (-) `-19 = `-**73**

`-73 / `-2 = `-**36.5**

`-28 (-) `-07 = `-**21**

`-36.5 (-) `-21 = `-**15.5**

`-**15.5** + `-**3.5** = `-**19** = **ACTUAL DAY OF DEATH**!!!!!~'

`-29 (-) `-19 = `-**10**

`-10 / `-2 = `-**05**

`-28 (-) `-07 = `-**21**

`-21 + `-05 = `-**26**

`-**26** (-) `-**19**-(ACTUAL DAY OF DEATH) = `-**7** = `-**3.5** (x) `-**2**

`-21 (-) `-05 = `-**16** = (**1** / **6** = RECIPROCAL = **9**) = `-**19** = ACTUAL DAY OF DEATH!!!!!~'

07 + 28 + 19 + 29 = `-**83** = BIRTHDAY `-NUMBER!!!!!~'

`-83 (-) `-19 = `-**64** = *EXACT TIME OF AGE AT TIME OF DEATH!!!!!~'*

`-83 / `-2 = `-**41.5**

9291 (-) 8270 = `-**1021**

`-9291 = `-91 (-) `-29 = `-**62** = *TWO YEARS AWAY FROM EXACT TIME OF DEATH AGE!!!!!~'*

`-8270 = `-87 (-) `-20 = `-**67** = *THREE YEARS AWAY FROM EXACT TIME OF DEATH AGE!!!!!~'*

`-8270 = `-80 (-) `-27 = `-**53** = "WAR OF THE WORLDS"!!!!!~'

`-1021 = `-21 + 10 = `-31 x `2 = `-**62** = *TWO YEARS AWAY FROM EXACT TIME OF DEATH AGE!!!!!~'*

`-1021 = 1 + 0 + 2 + 1 = `-4

`-1021 = 1 x 0 x 2 x 1 = `-0

`-4 + `-0 = `-**4**

`-41.5 + `-4 = `-**45.5** = ROUNDED = `-**46** = **23** x **2** = `-**232** = *Reciprocal-Sequenced-Numerology-RSN!!!!!~'*

`-**46** = RECIPROCAL = `-**64** = *EXACT TIME OF AGE AT TIME OF DEATH!!!!!~'*

`-**92** / `-**2** = `-**46** = **23** x **2** = `-**232** = *Reciprocal-Sequenced-Numerology-RSN!!!!!~'*

DWAYNE W. ANDERSON

`-**46** = RECIPROCAL = `-**64** = *EXACT TIME OF AGE AT TIME OF DEATH!!!!!~'*

`-82 (-) `-19 = `-**63** = *ONE YEAR AWAY FROM EXACT TIME OF DEATH AGE!!!!!~'*

`-07 + `-28 + `-29 = `-**64** = *EXACT TIME OF AGE AT TIME OF DEATH!!!!!~'*

`-92 (-) `-28 = `-**64** = *EXACT TIME OF AGE AT TIME OF DEATH!!!!!~'*

`-99 (-) `-28 (-) `-7 = `-**64** = *EXACT TIME OF AGE AT TIME OF DEATH!!!!!~'*

DEATH – 05/19/19**94** / ANOTHER `-Death on the `-NUMBER /`\ `-**94**!!!!!~'

05 + 19 + 19 + 94 = `-**137** / `-**137** (-) `-**94** = `-**43** = RECIPROCAL = -**34** = *Jacqueline's AGE at `-WHAT `-TIME; John F. Kennedy, was `-ASSASSINATED!!!!!~'*

`-**94** (-) `-**137** = `-**43** / `-**43** = RECIPROCAL = `-**34**

`-**137** (-) `-**49** = `-**88** / `-**88** = RECIPROCAL = `-**88**

`-**43** + `-**88** = `-**131** / `-131 + `-122 = `-**253**

`-**88** + `-**34** = `-**122** / `-253 = (2 + 53) = `-**55** = `-**23** + `-**32**

`-**131** = (**1** + **31**) = `-**32** = -a Prophetic Number!!!!!~'

`-**122** = (**1** + **22**) = `-**23** = -a Prophetic Number!!!!!~'

`-**23** = RECIPROCAL = `-**32**

`-**131** (-) `-**122** = `-**9**

`-DUPLICATIVE!!!!!~'

`-43 + `-34 = `-**77** / `-176 + `-77 = `-**253**

`-88 + `-88 = `-**176** / `-253 = (2 + 53) = `-**55** = `-**23** + `-**32**

`-**176** (-) `-**77** = `-**99**

`-**99** = RECIPROCAL = `-**66** / `-**96** = RECIPROCAL = `-**69** = "The CYCLE of `-LIFE"!!!!!~'

(`-**253**) (-) (`-**83**) Jacqueline Lee Kennedy Onassis **Birthday** `-NUMBER = `-**170** = (**1** x **70**) = `-**70** = John F. Kennedy's **Birthday** `-NUMBER!!!!!~'

(`-**99**) (-) (`-**137**) Jacqueline Lee Kennedy Onassis **Death Day** `-NUMBER = (`-**38**)!!!!!~' (`-**99**) (-) (`-**115**) John F. Kennedy **Death Day** `-NUMBER = (`-**16**)!!!!!~' (`-**38**) + (`-**16**) = (`-**54**)_!!!!!~'

(`-**88**) Jacqueline Lee Kennedy Onassis (+) (`-**66**) John F. Kennedy = `-**154**!!!!!~'

(`-**83**) Birthday `-NUMBER for Jacqueline Lee Kennedy Onassis (-) (`-**70**) Birthday `-NUMBER for John F. Kennedy = (`-**13**) = "A VERY PIVOTAL NUMBER"!!!!!~'

`-**13** = RECIPROCAL = `-**31** / `-**31** + `-**1** = `-**32** = -a Prophetic Number!!!!!~'

`-**137** (Jacqueline Lee Kennedy Onassis Death Day `-NUMBER) (-) `-**115** (John F. Kennedy Death Day `-NUMBER) = `-**22** = *Encapsulated by the `-NUMBER `-**23**!!!!!~'*

`-**23** = RECIPROCAL = `-**32**

"The CYCLE of `-LIFE"!!!!!~'

(End of `-EXAMPLE)!~'

Fyi,

Regards, Author,

Dwayne W. Anderson

The "PROPHET"!!!!!~'

©Copyright: Dwayne W. Anderson!!!!!~'

("PROPHET'S BLOG" on `-WEBSITE)

COPYRIGHT 04/23/2015 / AUTHOR: DWAYNE W. ANDERSON / THE "PROPHET"!!!!!~' /

Death Ciphers / Death Cypher / Death Formula / `-The `-GOD `-Equation!!!!!~'

(Example: CHRISTOPHER LEE, WINSTON CHURCHILL; and, GRACE KELLY): *- Death Formula* –

Christopher Lee – Birth – 0**5**/**27**/1**92**2 **(93) YEARS OF AGE AT TIME OF DEATH!!!!!~'**

`-**22** = **RECIPROCAL** = `-**22**

`-22 (-) `-19 = `-**03**

`-03 / `-2 = `-**1.5**

`-27 (-) `-05 = `-**22**

`-22 (-) `-1.5 = `-**20.5**

`-**20.5** = (20**5**) = (**2** + 0 + **5**) = `-**7** = **ACTUAL DAY OF `-DEATH!!!!!~'**

05 + 27 + 19 + 22 = `-**73** = BIRTHDAY `-NUMBER!!!!!~'

`-73 / `-2 = `-**36**.**5**

`-36.5 / `-2 = `-**18**.**25**

`-73 + `-18.25 = `-**91**.**25** = *NEARLY TWO YEARS AWAY FROM EXACT TIME OF DEATH AGE!!!!!~'*

2291 (-) 7250 = `-**4959**

`-75 + `-20 = `-**95** = *TWO YEARS AWAY FROM EXACT TIME OF DEATH AGE!!!!!~'*

`-70 + `-25 = `-**95** = *TWO YEARS AWAY FROM EXACT TIME OF DEATH AGE!!!!!~'*

`-4959 = `-94 + `-95 = `-189 / `-2 = `-**94**.**5** = *NEARLY TWO YEARS AWAY FROM EXACT TIME OF DEATH AGE!!!!!~'*

`-4959 = 4 + 9 + 5 + 9 = `-27

`-4959 = 4 x 9 x 5 x 9 = `-1620

`-1620 / `-27 = `-**60**

`-**92** = **RECIPROCAL** = `-**29**

`-60 + `-29 + `-05 = `-**94** = *ONE YEAR AWAY FROM THE EXACT TIME OF DEATH AGE!!!!!~'*

`-60 + `-27 + `-05 = `-**92** = *ONE YEAR AWAY FROM THE EXACT TIME OF DEATH AGE!!!!!~'*

`-94 + `-92 = `-186 / (`-2) = `-**93** = *EXACT TIME OF AGE AT TIME OF DEATH!!!!!~'*

`-60 + `-29 = `-**89** = *FOUR YEARS AWAY FROM EXACT TIME OF DEATH AGE!!!!!~'*

`-**27** = <u>RECIPROCAL</u> = `-**72**

`-72 + `-22 = `-**94** = *ONE YEAR AWAY FROM THE EXACT TIME OF DEATH AGE!!!!!~'*

`-72 + `-21 = `-**93** = *EXACT TIME OF AGE AT TIME OF DEATH!!!!!~'*

`-72 + `-20 = `-**92** = *ONE YEAR AWAY FROM THE EXACT TIME OF DEATH AGE!!!!!~'*

`-16 = `-1 more `-YEAR; Plus the `-MONTH of `-DEATH!!!!!~'

`-94 + `-92 = `-186 / (`-2) = `-**93** = *EXACT TIME OF AGE AT TIME OF DEATH!!!!!~'*

`-73 + `-20 = `-**93** = *EXACT TIME OF AGE AT TIME OF DEATH!!!!!~'*

`-92 + `-01 = `-**93** = *EXACT TIME OF AGE AT TIME OF DEATH!!!!!~'*

`-72 + `-19 + `-02 = `-**93** = *EXACT TIME OF AGE AT TIME OF DEATH!!!!!~'*

`-92 / `-2 = `-**46**

`-46 + `-27 + `-22 = `-**95** = *TWO YEARS AWAY FROM EXACT TIME OF DEATH AGE!!!!!~'*

`-46 + `-27 + `-20 = `-**93** = *EXACT TIME OF AGE AT TIME OF DEATH!!!!!~'*

Death: 06/07/2015

06 + 07 + 20 + 15 = `-**48** / `-**94** = <u>RECIPROCAL</u> = `-**49**

`-**94** (-) `-**48** = `-**46** / `-**46** = <u>RECIPROCAL</u> = `-**64**

`-**48** (-) `-**49** = `-**01** / `-**01** = <u>RECIPROCAL</u> = `-**10**

`-46 + `-10 = `-**56** / `-56 + `-65 = `-**121** = <u>R</u>eciprocal-<u>S</u>equencing-<u>N</u>umerology!!!!!~'

`-01 + `-64 = `-**65** / `-65 (-) `-56 = `-**9**

`-**56** = <u>RECIPROCAL</u> = `-**65**

`-46 + `-01 = `-**47** / `-47 + `-74 = `-**121** = <u>R</u>eciprocal-<u>S</u>equencing-<u>N</u>umerology!!!!!~'

`-64 + `-10 = `-**74** / `-74 (-) `-47 = `-**27**

`-**47** = <u>RECIPROCAL</u> = `-**74**

`-27 (-) `-9 = `-**18** / `-36 + `-18 = `-**54**

`-27 + `-9 = `-**36**

`-**18** x `-**2** = `-**36**

`-46 + `-64 = `-**110** / `-110 + `-11 = `-**121** = <u>R</u>eciprocal-<u>S</u>equencing-<u>N</u>umerology!!!!!~'

`-01 + `-10 = `-**11**

`-**54** = `-**27** + `-**27** = (**27** x **2**) = `-**272** <u>RSN</u> / `-**27** = (**9** x **3**) = **3**(**9's**) = (**999**) = `-**999**

`-**999** = <u>RECIPROCAL</u> = `-**666** / `-**96** = <u>RECIPROCAL</u> = `-**69** = "The CYCLE of `-LIFE"!!!!!~'

(`-**121**) (-) (`-**48**) Christopher Lee's <u>**Death Day**</u> `-<u>**NUMBER**</u> = <u>**Exactly**</u> (`-**73**) Christopher Lee's <u>**Birthday**</u> `-<u>**NUMBER**</u>!!!!!~' <u>R</u>eciprocal-<u>S</u>equencing-<u>N</u>umerology!!!!!~'

(`-**1922**) Christopher Lee's Birth `-YEAR = `-**19** = **RECIPROCAL** = `-**91** / (`-**91**) (-) (`-**22**) = `-**69** = "The CYCLE of `-LIFE"!!!!!~'

Winston Churchill – Birth – **11**/**30**/**187**4 **(90) YEARS OF AGE AT TIME OF DEATH!!!!!~'**

`-**74** = **RECIPROCAL** = `-**47**

`-47 (-) `-18 = `-**29**

`-29 / `-2 = `-**14.5**

`-30 (-) `-11 = `-**19**

`-19 (-) `-14.5 = `-**4.5**

`-**19** (+) `-**4.5** = `-**23.5** = ROUNDED UP = `-**24** = ACTUAL DAY OF `-DEATH!!!!!~'

`-**29** (-) `-**4.5** = `-**24.5** = ROUNDED DOWN = `-**24** = ACTUAL DAY OF `-DEATH!!!!!~'

`-**74** (-) `-**18** = `-**56**

`-**56** (-) `-**24**-(ACTUAL DAY OF `-DEATH) = `-**32** = -a Prophetic Number!!!!!~'

`-30 + `-11 + `-18 + `-15 = `-**74** /=/ **74**

11 + 30 + 18 + 74 = `-**133** = BIRTHDAY `-NUMBER!!!!!~'

`-133/ `-2 = `-**66.5**

`-66.5 / `-2 = `-**33.25**

`-33.25 + `-43.5 + `-15 = `-**91.75** = *NEAR TWO YEARS AWAY FROM EXACT TIME OF DEATH AGE!!!!!~'*

4781 (-) 0311 = `-**4470**

`-4781 = `-78 + `-14 = `-`-**92** = *TWO YEARS AWAY FROM EXACT TIME OF DEATH AGE!!!!!~'*

`-4781 = `-74 + `-18 = `-`-**92** = *TWO YEARS AWAY FROM EXACT TIME OF DEATH AGE!!!!!~'*

`-4470 = `-47 + `-40 = `-**87** = *THREE YEARS AWAY FROM EXACT TIME OF DEATH AGE!!!!!~'*

`-4470 = 4 + 4 + 7 + 0 = `-15

`-4470 = 4 x 4 x 7 x 0 = `-0

`-15 + `-0 = `-**15**

`-74 + `-15 = `-**89** = *ONE YEAR AWAY FROM THE EXACT TIME OF DEATH AGE!!!!!~'*

`-74 + `-18 = `-**92** = *TWO YEARS AWAY FROM EXACT TIME OF DEATH AGE!!!!!~'*

`-74 + `-11 = `-**85** = *FIVE YEARS AWAY FROM EXACT TIME OF DEATH AGE!!!!!~'*

`-74 + `-03 + `-11 = `-**88** = *TWO YEARS AWAY FROM EXACT TIME OF DEATH AGE!!!!!~'*

`-**74** = **RECIPROCAL** = `-**47**

`-47 + `-18 + `-11 + `-15 = `-**91** = *ONE YEAR AWAY FROM THE EXACT TIME OF DEATH AGE!!!!!~'*

`-47 + `-18 + `-11 + `-15 (-) `-03 = `-**88** = *TWO YEARS AWAY FROM EXACT TIME OF DEATH AGE!!!!!~'*

`-47 + `-11 + `-30 = `-**88** = *TWO YEARS AWAY FROM EXACT TIME OF DEATH AGE!!!!!~'*

`-47 + `-18 + `-30 = `-**95** = *FIVE YEARS AWAY FROM EXACT TIME OF DEATH AGE!!!!!~'*

`-47 + `-18 + `-30 + `-11 (-) `-15 = `-**91** = *ONE YEAR AWAY FROM THE EXACT TIME OF DEATH AGE!!!!!~'*

`-87 / `-2 = `-**43.5**

`-43.5 + `-15 + `-31 = `-**89.5** = *LESS THAN ONE YEAR FROM THE EXACT TIME OF AGE AT TIME OF DEATH!!!!!~'*

`-43.5 = ROUNDED = `-**44**

`-44 + `-15 + `-31 = `-**90** = *EXACT TIME OF AGE AT TIME OF DEATH!!!!!~'*

`-44 + `-15 + `-30 = `-**89** = *ONE YEAR AWAY FROM THE EXACT TIME OF DEATH AGE!!!!!~'*

`-133 (-) `-43.5 = `-**89.5** = *LESS THAN ONE YEAR FROM THE EXACT TIME OF AGE AT TIME OF DEATH!!!!!~'*

`-43.5 + `-30 + `-15 = `-**88.5** = *LESS THAN TWO YEARS FROM THE EXACT TIME OF AGE AT TIME OF DEATH!!!!!~'*

`-81 + `-11 = `-**92** = *TWO YEARS AWAY FROM EXACT TIME OF DEATH AGE!!!!!~'*

`-81 + `-03 + `-11 = `-**95** = *FIVE YEARS AWAY FROM EXACT TIME OF DEATH AGE!!!!!~'*

`-81 + `-10 = `-**91** = *ONE YEAR AWAY FROM THE EXACT TIME OF DEATH AGE!!!!!~'*

`-80 + `-11 = `-**91** = *ONE YEAR AWAY FROM THE EXACT TIME OF DEATH AGE!!!!!~'*

`-87 + `-01 = `-**88** = *TWO YEARS AWAY FROM EXACT TIME OF DEATH AGE!!!!!~'*

`-87 + `-04 = `-**91** = *ONE YEAR AWAY FROM THE EXACT TIME OF DEATH AGE!!!!!~'*

`-87 + `-03 = `-**90** = *EXACT TIME OF AGE AT TIME OF DEATH!!!!!~'*

`-**87** = RECIPROCAL = `-**78**

`-78 + `-10 = `-**88** = *TWO YEARS AWAY FROM EXACT TIME OF DEATH AGE!!!!!~'*

`-78 + `-11 = `-**89** = *ONE YEAR AWAY FROM THE EXACT TIME OF DEATH AGE!!!!!~'*

`-78 + `-14 = `-**92** = *TWO YEARS AWAY FROM EXACT TIME OF DEATH AGE!!!!!~'*

`-78 + `-13 = `-**91** = *ONE YEAR AWAY FROM THE EXACT TIME OF DEATH AGE!!!!!~'*

`-66.5 (-) `-43.5 = `-**23** = -a Prophetic Number!!!!!~'

Death: 01/24/1965

01 + 24 + 19 + 65 = `-**109** / `-**94** = RECIPROCAL = `-**49**

`-**94** (-) `-**109** = `-**15** / `-**15** = RECIPROCAL = `-**51**

`-**109** (-) `-**49** = `-**60** / `-**60** = RECIPROCAL = `-**06**

`-15 + `-06 = `-**21** / `-21 + `-111 = `-**132** = (1 x 32) = `-**32** = -a Prophetic Number!!!!!~'

`-60 + `-51 = `-**111**

`-**132** = (**1** x **32**) = `-**32** = -a Prophetic Number!!!!!~'

`-15 + `-60 = `-**75** / `-57 + `-75 = `-**132** = (1 x 32) = `-**32** = -a Prophetic Number!!!!!~'

`-51 + `-06 = `-**57**

`-**57** = RECIPROCAL = `-**75**

`-**132** = (**1** x **32**) = `-**32** = -a Prophetic Number!!!!!~'

`-15 + `-51 = `-**66** / `-66 + `-66 = `-**132** = (1 x 32) = `-**32** = -a Prophetic Number!!!!!~'

`-60 + `-06 = `-**66**

`-**132** = (**1** x **32**) = `-**32** = -a Prophetic Number!!!!!~'

`-**132** x **3** = `-**396** = **3**(**9's**) = **Emphasized** `-**96** = **RECIPROCAL** = `-**69**!!!!!~'

`-**999** = **RECIPROCAL** = `-**666** / `-**96** = **RECIPROCAL** = `-**69** = "The CYCLE of `-LIFE"!!!!!~'

(`-**132**) (-) (`-**109**) Winston Churchill's Death Date `-NUMBER = `-**23**!= -a Prophetic Number!!!!!~'

(`-**132**) (+) (`-**1**) = (`-**133**) Winston Churchill's **Birthday** `-**NUMBER**!!!!!~'

Grace Kelly was married for when she was `-**26** years of `-AGE; and, was married for some `-**26** `-YEARS!!!!!~' `-**26** x `-**2** = `-**52**!!!!!~' `-**262** = **R**eciprocal-**S**equencing-**N**umerology!!!!!~' Grace Kelly died at the tender `-AGE of `-**52**!!!!!~'

Grace Kelly – Birth – **11**/**12**/19**29** **(52) YEARS OF AGE AT TIME OF DEATH**!!!!!~'

`-**29** = **RECIPROCAL** = `-**92**

`-92 (-) `-19 = `-**73**

`-73 / `-2 = `-**36.5**

`-12 (+) `-11 = `-**23**

`-**36.5** (-) `-**23** = `-**13.5** = ROUNDED DOWN = `-**13** = DAYS IN THE MONTH BEFORE DEATH!!!!!~'

`-**36.5** (-) `-**23** = `-**13.5** = ROUNDED UP = `-**14** = ACTUAL DAY OF `-DEATH!!!!!~'

`-29 (-) `-19 = `-**10** / `-21 (-) `-11 = `-**10** / `-10 + `-05 = `-**15**

`-10 / `-2 = `-**05**

`-10 (+) `-05 = `-**15** = DAYS OF THE MONTH FOR THE DEATH TO OCCUR!!!!!~'

11 + 12 + 19 + 29 = `-**71** = / `-**71** (-) `-**25** = `-**46** = `-**23** x `-**2** = `-**232** = RSN!!!!!~' / BIRTHDAY `-NUMBER!!!!!~'

`-71 / `-2 = `-**35.5**

`-35.5 / `-2 = `-**17.75**

`-35.5 + `-17.75 = `-**53.25** = *NEARLY SIX MONTHS AWAY FROM THE EXACT (EXACT) TIME OF DEATH AGE!!!!!~'*

9291 (-) 2111 = `-**7180**

`-9291 = `-29 + `-19 = `-**48** = *FOUR YEARS AWAY FROM EXACT TIME OF DEATH AGE!!!!!~'*

`-2111 = `-11 + `-12 = `-**23** = -a Prophetic Number!!!!!~'

`-2111 = `-21 + `-11 = `-**32** = -a Prophetic Number!!!!!~'

`-**23** = <u>RECIPROCAL</u> = `-**32**

`-7180 = `-70 (-) `-18 = `-**52** = *EXACT TIME OF AGE AT TIME OF DEATH!!!!!~'*

`-7180 = 7 + 1 + 8 + 0 = `-16

`-7180 = 7 x 1 x 8 x 0 = `-0

`-16 + `-0 = `-**16**

`-71 (-) `-16 = `-**55** = *THREE YEARS AWAY FROM EXACT TIME OF DEATH AGE!!!!!~'*

`-35.5 + `-16 = `-**51**.**5** = *NEARLY ONE YEAR AWAY FROM THE EXACT (EXACT) TIME OF DEATH AGE!!!!!~'*

`-35.5 = ROUNDED = `-36

`-36 + `-16 = `-**52** = *EXACT TIME OF AGE AT TIME OF DEATH!!!!!~'*

`-92 / `-2 = `-**46**

`-**16** = `-1 x `-6 = `-**6**

`-46 + `-6 = `-**52** = *EXACT TIME OF AGE AT TIME OF DEATH!!!!!~'*

`-29 + `-12 + `-11 = `-**52** = *EXACT TIME OF AGE AT TIME OF DEATH!!!!!~'*

`-**29** = <u>RECIPROCAL</u> = `-**92**

`-92 (-) `-19 (-) `-12 (-) `-11 = `-**50** = *TWO YEARS AWAY FROM EXACT TIME OF DEATH AGE!!!!!~'*

`-**12** = <u>RECIPROCAL</u> = `-**21**

`-21 + `-19 + `-11 = `-**51** = *ONE YEAR AWAY FROM THE EXACT TIME OF DEATH AGE!!!!!~'*

`-**19** = **RECIPROCAL** = `-**91**

`-91 (-) `-29 (-) `-11 = `-**51** = *ONE YEAR AWAY FROM THE EXACT TIME OF DEATH AGE!!!!!~'*

`-99 (-) `-21 (-) `-12 (-) `-11 = `-**55** = *THREE YEARS AWAY FROM EXACT TIME OF DEATH AGE!!!!!~'*

`-92 (-) `-19 (-) `-21 = `-**52** = *EXACT TIME OF AGE AT TIME OF DEATH!!!!!~'*

Death: 0**9**/1**4**/1982 / ANOTHER `-Death on the `-NUMBER /`\ `-**94**!!!!!~'

09 + 14 + 19 + 82 = `-**124** / `-**94** = **RECIPROCAL** = `-**49**

`-**94** (-) `-**124** = `-**30** / `-**30** = **RECIPROCAL** = `-**03**

`-**124** (-) `-**49** = `-**75** / `-**75** = **RECIPROCAL** = `-**57**

`-30 + `-57 = `-**87** / `-78 + `-87 = `-**165** = (65 + 1) = `-**66**

`-75 + `-03 = `-**78** / `-165 (-) `-**99** = `-**66**

`-**78** = **RECIPROCAL** = `-**87**

`-30 + `-75 = `-**105** / `-105 + `-60 = `-**165** = (65 + 1) = `-**66**

`-03 + `-57 = `-**60** / `-165 (-) `-**99** = `-**66**

`-30 + `-03 = `-**33** / `-33 + `-132 = `-**165** = (65 + 1) = `-**66**

`-75 + `-57 = `-**132** / `-165 (-) `-**99** = `-**66**

`-99 = RECIPROCAL = `-66 / `-96 = RECIPROCAL = `-69 = "The CYCLE of `-LIFE"!!!!!~'

(`-71) Grace Kelly's Birthday `-NUMBER (+) `-1 = `-72 = RECIPROCAL = `-27!!!!!~' (`-124) Grace Kelly's Death Day `-NUMBER (-) `-72 = `-52 `-YEARS of `-AGE!!!!!~' Her `-AGE of `-DEATH at her `-TIME of `-DEATH!!!!!~'

(`-124) Grace Kelly's Death Date `-NUMBER (-) (`-99) = `-25 = RECIPROCAL = `-52 = the `-EXACT `-AGE of `-DEATH at `-TIME of `-DEATH!!!!!~'

James Horner, Rev. Clementa Pinckney; and, Dick Van Patten are an `-OVERLAY of Christopher Lee, Winston Churchill; and, Grace Kelly!!!!!~'

Film Composer - James Horner – Birth – 08/14/1953 (61) YEARS OF AGE AT TIME OF DEATH!!!!!~'

`-53 = RECIPROCAL = `-35

`-35 (-) `-19 = `-16

`-16 / `-2 = `-08

`-14 (-) `-08 = `-06

`-08 (+) `-06 = `-14

`-14 = RECIPROCAL = `-41

`-41 / `-2 = `-20.5 = ROUNDED UP = `-21 = DAYS IN THE MONTH BEFORE DEATH!!!!!~'

`-14 + `-8 = `-22 = ACTUAL DAY OF `-DEATH!!!!!~'

`-53 (-) `-19 = `-34

`-34 / `-2 = `-**17**

`-14 (-) `-08 = `-**06**

`-17 (+) `-06 = `-**23** = DAYS IN THE MONTH THAT DEATH WILL OCCUR BEFORE!~'

08 + 14 + 19 + 53 = `-**94** = ANOTHER `-Death on the `-NUMBER /'\ `-**94**!!!!!~' / BIRTHDAY `-NUMBER!!!!!~'

`-94 (-) `-16.363636 (-) `-19 = `-**58.636364** = *NEARLY THREE YEARS AWAY FROM EXACT TIME OF DEATH AGE!!!!!~'*

`-94 (-) `-16.363636 (-) `-15 = `-**62.636364** = *NEARLY TWO YEARS AWAY FROM EXACT TIME OF DEATH AGE!!!!!~'*

`-73 / `-2 = `-**47**

`-47 + `-14 = `-**61** = *EXACT TIME OF AGE AT TIME OF DEATH!!!!!~'*

`-36.5 / `-2 = `-**23.5**

`-23.5 + `-08 + `-14 + `-19 = `-**64.5** = *NEARLY FOUR YEARS AWAY FROM EXACT TIME OF DEATH AGE!!!!!~'*

3591 (-) 4180 = `-**589**

`-3591 = `-95 (-) `-31 = `-**64** = *THREE YEARS AWAY FROM THE EXACT TIME OF DEATH AGE!!!!!~'*

`-4180 = `-48 + `-10 = `-**58** = *THREE YEARS AWAY FROM THE EXACT TIME OF DEATH AGE!!!!!~'*

`-4180 = `-40 + `-18 = `-**58** = *THREE YEARS AWAY FROM THE EXACT TIME OF DEATH AGE!!!!!~'*

`-589 = 5 + 8 + 9 = `-22

`-589 = 5 x 8 x 9 = `-360

`-360 / `-22 = `-**16.363636**

`-**53** = **RECIPROCAL** = `-**35**

`-35 + `-16.36 + `-10 = `-**61.36** = *EXACT (EXACT) TIME OF AGE AT TIME OF DEATH (RECIPROCALLY)!!!!!~'*

`-95 (-) `-16 (-) `-18 = `-**61** = *EXACT TIME OF AGE AT TIME OF DEATH!!!!!~'*

`-95 / `-2 = `-**47.5**

`-47.5 + `-14 = `-**61.5** = *EXACT TIME OF AGE AT TIME OF DEATH!!!!!~'*

`-53 + `-08 = `-**61** = *EXACT TIME OF AGE AT TIME OF DEATH!!!!!~'*

`-35 + `-19 + `-08 = `-**62** = *ONE YEAR AWAY FROM THE EXACT TIME OF DEATH AGE!!!!!~'*

`-41 + `-19 = `-**60** = *ONE YEAR AWAY FROM THE EXACT TIME OF DEATH AGE!!!!!~'*

`-43 + `-19 = `-**62** = *ONE YEAR AWAY FROM THE EXACT TIME OF DEATH AGE!!!!!~'*

`-80 (-) `-41 + `-19 = `-**58** = *THREE YEARS AWAY FROM THE EXACT TIME OF DEATH AGE!!!!!~'*

`-80 (-) `-35 + `-14 = `-**59** = *TWO YEARS AWAY FROM EXACT TIME OF DEATH AGE!!!!!~'*

`-80 (-) `-53 + `-19 + `-14 = `-**60** = *ONE YEAR AWAY FROM THE EXACT TIME OF DEATH AGE!!!!!~'*

`-81 (-) `-40 + `-19 = `-**60** = *ONE YEAR AWAY FROM THE EXACT TIME OF DEATH AGE!!!!!~'*

`-81 (-) `-19 = `-**62** = *ONE YEAR AWAY FROM THE EXACT TIME OF DEATH AGE!!!!!~'*

`-80 (-) `-19 = `-**61** = *EXACT TIME OF AGE AT TIME OF DEATH!!!!!~'*

`-90 (-) `-14 (-) `-15 = `-**61** = *EXACT TIME OF AGE AT TIME OF DEATH!!!!!~'*

`-91 (-) `-53 + `-14 + `-08 = `-**60** = *ONE YEAR AWAY FROM THE EXACT TIME OF DEATH AGE!!!!!~'*

`-91 (-) `-41 + `-08 = `-**58** = *THREE YEARS AWAY FROM THE EXACT TIME OF DEATH AGE!!!!!~'*

`-91 (-) `-35 + `-08 = `-**64** = *THREE YEARS AWAY FROM THE EXACT TIME OF DEATH AGE!!!!!~'*

`-53 + `-10 = `-**63** = *TWO YEARS AWAY FROM EXACT TIME OF DEATH AGE!!!!!~'*

`-90 (-) `-14 (-) `-13 = `-**63** = *TWO YEARS AWAY FROM EXACT TIME OF DEATH AGE!!!!!~'*

Death: 06/22/2015 / ANOTHER `-Death on the `-NUMBER /`\ `-**63**!!!!!~'

06 + 22 + 20 + 15 = `-**63**

`-**63** = **RECIPROCAL** = `-**36**

`-**16.363636**

06 + 22 + 20 + 15 = `-**63** / `-**94** = **RECIPROCAL** = `-**49**

`-**94** (-) `-**63** = `-**31** / `-**31** = **RECIPROCAL** = `-**13**

`-**63** (-) `-**49** = `-**14** / `-**14** = RECIPROCAL = `-**41**

`-31 + `-41 = `-**72** / `-27 + `-72 = `-**99**

`-14 + `-13 = `-**27**

`-**27** = RECIPROCAL = `-**72**

`-31 + `-14 = `-**45** / `-45 + `-54 = `-**99**

`-13 + `-41 = `-**54**

`-**45** = RECIPROCAL = `-**54**

`-31 + `-13 = `-**44** / `-55 + `-44 = `-**99**

`-14 + `-41 = `-**55**

`-**55** = `-**23** + `-**32**

(`-**99**) (-) (`-**63**) James Horner's **Death Date** `-NUMBER = RECIPROCAL = `-**36**!!!!!~' (`-**63**) James Horner's **Death Date** `-NUMBER (-) (`-**02**) = the `-EXACT `-AGE of `-DEATH at `-TIME of `-DEATH!!!!!~'

`-**99** = RECIPROCAL = `-**66** / `-**96** = RECIPROCAL = `-**69** = "The CYCLE of `-LIFE"!!!!!~'

(`-**94**) James Horner's **Birthday** `-NUMBER = RECIPROCAL = `-**49**!!!!!~' (`-**63**) James Horner's **Death Date** `-NUMBER = RECIPROCAL = `-**36**!!!!!~' (`-**49**) + (`-**36**) = (`-**85**) = (`-**8** + `-**5**) = `-**13** = "A VERY PIVOTAL NUMBER"!!!!!~' `-**13** = RECIPROCAL = `-**31** / `-**31** + `-**1** = `-**32** = *-a Prophetic Number!!!!!~'*

State Senator / Rev. Clementa Pinckney – Birth – **07/30/197**3 **(41) YEARS OF AGE AT TIME OF DEATH!!!!!~'**

`-**73** = RECIPROCAL = `-**37**

228

`-37 (-) `-19 = `-**18**

`-18 / `-2 = `-**09**

`-30 (-) `-07 = `-**23**

`-23 (+) `-09 = `-**32**

`-**32** = **RECIPROCAL** = `-**23**

`-23 (-) `-09 = `-**14** = **RECIPROCAL** = `-**41** = **ACTUAL AGE OF** `-**DEATH!!!!!~'**

`-23 (-) `-09 = `-**14** = **ADDED TO DAYS IN THE MONTH BEFORE DEATH!!!!!~'**

`-73 (-) `-19 = `-**54** / `-70 (-) `-30 = `-**40** / `-40 (-) `-27 = `- **13** /

`-54 / `-2 = `-**27** / `-**13** + `-**04** = `-**17** = **ACTUAL DAY OF** `-**DEATH!!!!!~'**

`-30 (-) `-07 = `-**23**

`-27 (-) `-23 = `-**04**

`-**14** + `-**04** = `-**18** = **DAYS IN THE MONTH BEFORE DEATH!!!!!~'**

0**7**/3**0**/19**73** / *Began* `-*PUBLIC* `-*OFFICE; at the* `-*AGE, of* (`-**23**)+++_ **!!!!!~'**

07 + 30 + 19 + 73 = `-**129** = **BIRTHDAY** `-**NUMBER!!!!!~'**

`-129/ `-2 = `-**64.5**

`-**23** = **RECIPROCAL** = `-**32**

`-64.5 (-) `-41 = `-**23.5** = **-a Prophetic Number!!!!!~'**

`-64.5 / `-2 = `-**32.25**

`-32.25 + `-07 = `-**39**.**25** = *NEARLY TWO YEARS AWAY FROM EXACT TIME OF DEATH AGE!!!!!~'*

`-32.25 + `-10 = `-**42**.**25** = *JUST OVER ONE YEAR AWAY FROM EXACT TIME OF DEATH AGE!!!!!~'*

3791 (-) 0370 = `-**3421**

`-3791 = `-71 + `-39 = `-`-**32** = *-a Prophetic Number!!!!!~'*

`-0370 = `-70 (-) `-30 = `-**40** = *ONE YEAR AWAY FROM THE EXACT TIME OF DEATH AGE!!!!!~'*

`-3421 = `-32 + `-14 = `-`-**46** = `-**23** x `-**2** = `-**232** = Reciprocal-Sequenced-Numerology!!!!!~'

`-3421 = 3 + 4 + 2 + 1 = `-10

`-3421 = 3 x 4 x 2 x 1 = `-24

`-10 + `-24 = `-**34**

`-34 + `-07 = `-**41** = *EXACT TIME OF AGE AT TIME OF DEATH!!!!!~'*

`-24 (-) `-10 = `-**14**

`-14 + `-30 = `-**44** = *THREE YEARS AWAY FROM THE EXACT TIME OF DEATH AGE!!!!!~'*

`-97 / `-2 = `-48.5

`-48.5 (-) `-07 = `-**41**.**5** = *EXACT TIME OF AGE AT TIME OF DEATH!!!!!~'*

`-30 + `-13 = `-**43** = *TWO YEARS AWAY FROM EXACT TIME OF DEATH AGE!!!!!~'*

`-30 + `-10 = `-**40** = *ONE YEAR AWAY FROM EXACT TIME OF DEATH AGE!!!!!~'*

`-73 (-) `-30 = `-**43** = *TWO YEARS AWAY FROM EXACT TIME OF DEATH AGE!!!!!~'*

`-37 + `-07 = `-**44** = *THREE YEARS AWAY FROM THE EXACT TIME OF DEATH AGE!!!!!~'*

`-70 (-) `-31 + `-03 = `-**42** = *ONE YEAR AWAY FROM THE EXACT TIME OF DEATH AGE!!!!!~'*

`-93 (-) `-17 (-) `-30 (-) `-07 = `-**39** = *TWO YEARS AWAY FROM EXACT TIME OF DEATH AGE!!!!!~'*

`-91 (-) `-73 + `-30 (-) `-07 = `-**41** = *EXACT TIME OF AGE AT TIME OF DEATH!!!!!~'*

`-93 (-) `-71 + `-07 + `-03 = `-**32** = -a Prophetic Number!!!!!~'

Death: 06/17/2015 /|\ `-**94** (-) `-**58** = `-**36** = **RECIPROCAL** = `-**63** = JOHN F. KENNEDY/|

06 + 17 + 20 + 15 = `-**58** = (5 + 8) = `-**13** = **"A VERY PIVOTAL NUMBER"**!!!!!~'

`-**94** (-) `-**63** = `-**31** = **RECIPROCAL** = `-**13** = **"A VERY PIVOTAL NUMBER"**!!!!!~'

06 + 17 + 20 + 15 = `-**58** / `-**94** = **RECIPROCAL** = `-**49**

`-**94** (-) `-**58** = `-**36** / `-**36** = **RECIPROCAL** = `-**63**

`-**58** (-) `-**49** = `-**09** / `-**09** = **RECIPROCAL** = `-**90**

`-36 + `-90 = `-**126** / `-126 + `-72 = `-**198** = (**1** + **98**) = `-**99**

`-09 + `-63 = `-**72**

231

`-**126** / `-**2** = `-**63**

`-**72** / `-**2** = `-**36**

`-**63** = RECIPROCAL = `-**36**

`-36 + `-09 = `-**45** / `-153 + `-45 = `-**198** = (**1** + **98**) = `-**99**

`-63 + `-90 = `-**153**

`-**90** (-) `-**63** = `-**27**

`-**27** = RECIPROCAL = `-**72**

`-36 + `-63 = `-**99** / `-99 + `-99 = `-**198** = (**1** + **98**) = `-**99**

`-09 + `-90 = `-**99**

`-**99** = RECIPROCAL = `-**66** / `-**96** = RECIPROCAL = `-**69** = "The CYCLE of `-LIFE"!!!!!~'

(`-**198**) (-) (`-**129**) Rev. Clementa Pinckney's **Birthday** `-**NUMBER** = `-**69** = "The CYCLE of `-LIFE"!!!!!~' Elected to the South Carolina General Assembly in `-19**96** = RECIPROCAL = `-**69** at age (`-**23**)!!!!!~' "The CYCLE of `-LIFE"!!!!!~'

(`-**99**) (-) (`-**58**) Rev. Clementa Pinckney's **Death Day** `-**NUMBER** = `-**41** `-YEARS of `-AGE!!!!!~' The `-EXACT `-AGE of Rev. Clementa Pinckney at the `-TIME of his `-DEATH!!!!!~'

Actor / Dick Van Patten – Birth – **12**/**09**/19**2**8 (86) YEARS OF AGE AT TIME OF DEATH!!!!!~'

`-**28** = RECIPROCAL = `-**82**

`-82 (-) `-19 = `-**63**

`-63 / `-2 = `-**31.5**

`-**31.5** = <u>RECIPROCAL</u> = `-**13.5**

`-12 (-) `-09 = `-**03**

`-**12** = <u>RECIPROCAL</u> = `-**21**

`-21 (-) `-09 = `-**12**

`-13.5 (+) `-12 = `-**25.5** = ROUNDED DOWN = `-**25** = DIED WITHIN `-**25** DAYS OF THE MONTH!!!!!~'

`-25.5 (-) `-03 = `-**22.5** = ROUNDED DOWN = `-**22** = DAYS IN THE MONTH BEFORE DEATH!!!!!~'

`-25.5 (-) `-03 = `-**22.5** = ROUNDED UP = `-**23** = DAY OF `-DEATH!!!!!~'

`-28 (-) `-19 = `-**09**

`-09 / `-2 = `-**4.5**

`-12 (-) `-09 = `-**03**

`-**03** = <u>RECIPROCAL</u> = `-**30**

`-4.5 (+) `-03 = `-**7.5**

`-30 (-) `-7.5 = `-**22.5** = ROUNDED DOWN = `-**22** = DAYS IN THE MONTH BEFORE DEATH!!!!!~'

`-30 (-) `-7.5 = `-**22.5** = ROUNDED UP = `-**23** = DAY OF `-DEATH!!!!!~'

`-12 (-) `-09 = `-**03**

`-12 (+) `-09 = `-**21**

`-21 + `-03 = `-**24** = DAYS IN THE MONTH BEFORE DEATH!!!!!~'

12 + 09 + 19 + 28 = `-**68** = BIRTHDAY `-NUMBER!!!!!~'

`-**68** = RECIPROCAL = `-**86** = *EXACT TIME OF AGE AT TIME OF DEATH!!!!!~'*

`-68 / `-2 = `-**34**

`-34 / `-2 = `-**17**

`-12 + `-09 + `-19 + `-28 + `-17 = `-**85** = *ONE YEAR AWAY FROM THE EXACT TIME OF DEATH AGE!!!!!~'*

8291 (-) 9021 = `-**730**

`-8291 = `-98 (-) `-12 = `-**86** = *EXACT TIME OF AGE AT TIME OF DEATH!!!!!~'*

`-9021 = `-91 (-) `-02 = `-**89** = *THREE YEARS AWAY FROM THE EXACT TIME OF DEATH AGE!!!!!~'*

`-9021 = `-90 (-) (2 + 1) = `-**87** = *ONE YEAR AWAY FROM THE EXACT TIME OF DEATH AGE!!!!!~'*

`-730 = 7 + 3 + 0 = `-10

`-730 = 7 x 3 x 0 = `-0

`-10 + `-0 = `-**10**

`-**92** = RECIPROCAL = `-**29**

`-29 + `-29 + `-10 = `-**68** = RECIPROCAL = `-**86** = *EXACT TIME OF AGE AT TIME OF DEATH!!!!!~'*

`-29 + `-29 + `-10 + `-18 = `-**86** = *EXACT TIME OF AGE AT TIME OF DEATH!!!!!~'*

`-21 + `-09 + `-19 + `-28 + `-10 = `-**87** = *ONE YEAR AWAY FROM THE EXACT TIME OF DEATH AGE!!!!!~'*

`-92 / `-2 = `-46

`-46 + `-34 + `-08 = `-**88** = *TWO YEARS AWAY FROM EXACT TIME OF DEATH AGE!!!!!~'*

`-99 (-) `-10 = `-`-**89** = *THREE YEARS AWAY FROM THE EXACT TIME OF DEATH AGE!!!!!~'*

`-99 (-) `-12 = `-**87** = *ONE YEAR AWAY FROM THE EXACT TIME OF DEATH AGE!!!!!~'*

`-82 (-) `-19 + `-12 + `-09 = `-**84** = *TWO YEARS AWAY FROM EXACT TIME OF DEATH AGE!!!!!~'*

`-82 (-) `-21 + `-19 + `-09 = `-**89** = *THREE YEARS AWAY FROM THE EXACT TIME OF DEATH AGE!!!!!~'*

`-90 (-) `-21 + `-19 = `-**88** = *TWO YEARS AWAY FROM EXACT TIME OF DEATH AGE!!!!!~'*

`-90 (-) `-21 + `-18 = `-**87** = *ONE YEAR AWAY FROM THE EXACT TIME OF DEATH AGE!!!!!~'*

`-98 (-) `-12 = `-**86** = *EXACT TIME OF AGE AT TIME OF DEATH!!!!!~'*

`-92 (-) `-18 + `-12 = `-**86** = *EXACT TIME OF AGE AT TIME OF DEATH!!!!!~'*

Death: 06/**23**/2015 / ANOTHER `-Death on the `-NUMBER /`\ `-**64**!!!!!~'

06 + 23 + 20 + 15 = `-**64**

`-**64** = <u>RECIPROCAL</u> = `-**46**

235

`-46 = `-23 x `-2 = `-232 = Reciprocal-Sequenced-Numerology!!!!!~'

06 + 23 + 20 + 15 = `-64 / `-94 = RECIPROCAL = `-49

`-94 (-) `-64 = `-30 / `-30 = RECIPROCAL = `-03

`-64 (-) `-49 = `-15 / `-15 = RECIPROCAL = `-51

`-30 + `-51 = `-81 / `-18 + `-81 = `-99

`-15 + `-03 = `-18

`-18 = RECIPROCAL = `-81

`-30 + `-15 = `-45 / `-45 + `-54 = `-99

`-03 + `-51 = `-54

`-45 = RECIPROCAL = `-54

`-30 + `-03 = `-33 / `-66 + `-33 = `-99

`-15 + `-51 = `-66

`-99 = RECIPROCAL = `-66 / `-96 = RECIPROCAL = `-69 = "The CYCLE of `-LIFE"!!!!!~'

(`-68) Dick Van Patten's **Birthday** `-NUMBER (+) (`-64) Dick Van Patten's **Death Date** `-NUMBER = `-132 = (1 x 32) = `-32 = *-a Prophetic Number!!!!!~'* (`-132) (+) (`-99) = (`-231)!!!!!~'

(`-68) Dick Van Patten's **Birthday** `-NUMBER = RECIPROCAL = `-86 (+) (`-64) Dick Van Patten's **Death Date** `-NUMBER = RECIPROCAL = `-46 = `-132 = (1 x 32) = `-32 = *-a Prophetic Number!!!!!~'* (`-132) (+) (`-99) = (`-231)!!!!!~'

(`-99) (-) (`-68) Dick Van Patten's **Birthday** `-NUMBER = `-31 = +1 = `-32 = *-a Prophetic Number!!!!!~'*

James Horner, Rev. Clementa Pinckney; and, Dick Van Patten are an `-<u>OVERLAY</u> of Christopher Lee, Winston Churchill; and, Grace Kelly!!!!!~'

Christopher Lee (`-**93**) (-) James Horner (`-**61**) = `-**32** = **-a Prophetic Number!!!!!~'**

Winston Churchill (`-**90**) (-) Rev. Clementa Pinckney (`-**41**) = `-**49** = <u>**RECIPROCAL**</u> = `-**94** = ANOTHER `-Death on the `-NUMBER /'\ `-**94**!!!!!~'

Dick Van Patten (`-**86**) (-) Grace Kelly (`-**52**) = `-**34** = Jacqueline Kennedy (`-**94**)/Lady Bird Johnson (`-**94**)!!!!!~'

(Boxing Referee) Frank Cappuccino – Birth – 0**2**/0**7**/1**92**9 **(86) YEARS OF AGE AT TIME OF DEATH!!!!!~'**

`-**29** = <u>**RECIPROCAL**</u> = `-**92**

`-92 (-) `-19 = `-**73**

`-73 / `-2 = `-**36.5**

`-07 (-) `-02 = `-**05**

`-**02** = <u>**RECIPROCAL**</u> = `-**20**

`-07 (+) `-20 = `-27

`-36.5 (-) `-27 = `-**9.5** = **ROUNDED DOWN** = `-**09** = **DAYS IN THE MONTH BEFORE DEATH!!!!!~'**

`-29 (-) `-19 = `-**10**

`-10 / `-2 = `-**05**

`-07 (-) `-02 = `-**05**

`-**02** = <u>RECIPROCAL</u> = `-<u>**20**</u>

`-07 (-) `-20 = `-<u>**13**</u>

`-13 (-) `-05 = `-<u>**08**</u> = **DAY OF `-DEATH!!!!!~'**

02 + 07 + 19 + 29 = `-<u>**57**</u> = BIRTHDAY `-NUMBER!!!!!~'

`-57 / `-2 = `-<u>**28**</u>.<u>**5**</u>

`-28.5 / `-2 = `-<u>**14**</u>.<u>**25**</u>

`-57 + `-28.5 = `-<u>**85**</u>.<u>**5**</u> = *NEARLY ONE YEAR AWAY FROM THE EXACT (EXACT) TIME OF DEATH AGE!!!!!~'*

`-57 + `-14.25 + `-16 = `-<u>**87**</u>.<u>**25**</u> = *LESS THAN TWO YEARS FROM THE EXACT TIME OF AGE AT TIME OF DEATH!!!!!~'*

9291 (-) 7020 = `-**2271**

`-9291 = `-99 (-) `-12 = `-<u>**87**</u> = *ONE YEAR AWAY FROM THE EXACT TIME OF DEATH AGE!!!!!~'*

`-7020 = `-70 + `-20 = `-<u>**90**</u> = *FOUR YEARS AWAY FROM EXACT TIME OF DEATH AGE!!!!!~'*

`-2271 = `-72 + `-12 = `-<u>**84**</u> = *TWO YEARS AWAY FROM EXACT TIME OF DEATH AGE!!!!!~'*

`-2271 = 2 + 2 + 7 + 1 = `-12

`-2271 = 2 x 2 x 7 x 1 = `-28

`-28 / `-12 = `-<u>**2**</u>.<u>**3**</u> = `-<u>**23**</u> = -a Prophetic Number!!!!!~'

`-28 (-) `-12 = `-<u>**16**</u>

`-28 + `-12 = `-<u>**40**</u>

'-DEATH CIPHERS/CYPHERS FOR LIFE & DEATH!!!~'

`-92 / `-2 = `-46

`-46 + `-40 = `-**86** = *EXACT TIME OF AGE AT TIME OF DEATH!!!!!~'*

`-92 = RECIPROCAL = `-29

`-29 + `-16 + `-40 = `-**85** = *ONE YEAR AWAY FROM THE EXACT TIME OF DEATH AGE!!!!!~'*

`-29 + `-14.25 + `-40 = `-**83**.**25** = *NEARLY THREE YEARS AWAY FROM THE EXACT TIME OF DEATH AGE!!!!!~'*

`-92 (-) `-07 = `-**85** = *ONE YEAR AWAY FROM THE EXACT TIME OF DEATH AGE!!!!!~'*

`-97 (-) `-09 (-) `-02 = `-**86** = *EXACT TIME OF AGE AT TIME OF DEATH!!!!!~'*

Death: 06/08/2015 / / ANOTHER `-Death on the `-NUMBER /`\ `-**94**!!!!!~'

06 + 08 + 20 + 15 = `-**49** = **RECIPROCAL** = `-**94**

06 + 08 + 20 + 15 = `-**49** / `-**94** = **RECIPROCAL** = `-**49**

`-**94** (-) `-**49** = `-**45** / `-**45** = **RECIPROCAL** = `-**54**

`-**49** (-) `-**49** = `-**00** / `-**00** = **RECIPROCAL** = `-**00**

`-45 + `-00 = `-**45** / `-45 + `-54 = `-**99**

`-00 + `-54 = `-**54**

`-**45** = **RECIPROCAL** = `-**54**

`-45 + `-00 = `-**45** / `-45 + `-54 = `-**99**

`-54 + `-00 = `-**54**

239

`-**45** = RECIPROCAL = `-**54**

`-45 + `-54 = `-**99** / `-99 + `-00 = `-**99**

`-00 + `-00 = `-**00**

`-**55** = `-**23** + `-**32**

`-**99** = RECIPROCAL = `-**66** / `-**96** = RECIPROCAL = `-**69** = "The CYCLE of `-LIFE"!!!!!~'

(`-**57**) Frank Cappuccino's **Birthday `-NUMBER** = RECIPROCAL = (`-**75**) (**+**) (`-**49**) Frank Cappuccino's **Death Date** `-NUMBER = RECIPROCAL = `-**94** = (`-**169**) = (**1** x **69**) = `-**69** = "The CYCLE of `-LIFE"!!!!!~'

(Magician) Harry Houdini – Birth – 0**3**/**24**/18**7**4 **(52) YEARS OF AGE AT TIME OF DEATH!!!!!~'**

`-**74** = RECIPROCAL = `-**47**

`-47 (-) `-18 = `-**29** / `-42 (-) `-30 = `-**12** / `-41.5 (-) `-12 = `-**29.5**

`-29 / `-2 = `-**14.5** / `-**29.5** = ROUNDED UP = `-**30** = DAYS BEFORE DEATH!!!!!~'

`-24 (-) `-03 = `-**21**

`-**14.5** = RECIPROCAL = `-**41.5**

`-**21** = RECIPROCAL = `-**12**

`-41.5 (-) `-12 = `-**29.5** = ROUNDED UP = `-**30** = DAYS IN THE MONTH BEFORE DEATH!!!!!~'

`-74 (-) `-18 = `-**56**

`-56 / `-2 = `-**28**

`-24 (+) `-03 = `-**27**

`-28 (-) `-27 = `-**01** = THE FIRST OF THE MONTH OF `-DEATH!!!!!~'

03 + 24 + 18 + 74 = `-**119** = BIRTHDAY `-NUMBER!!!!!~'

`-119 / `-2 = `-**59.5**

`-59.5 / `-2 = `-**29.75**

`-29.75 / `-2 = `-**14.875**

4781 (-) 4230 = `-**551**

`-4781 = `-87 (-) `-41 = `-**46** = *SIX YEARS AWAY FROM THE EXACT TIME OF DEATH AGE!!!!!~'*

`-4781 = `-71 (-) `-48 = `-**23** = -a Prophetic Number!!!!!~'

`-4230 = `-40 + `-23 = `-**63** = *John F. Kennedy & Marilyn Monroe!!!!!!~'*

`-4230 = `-34 + `-20 = `-**54** = *TWO YEARS AWAY FROM EXACT TIME OF DEATH AGE!!!!!~'*

`-551 = `-55 (-) `-1 = `-**54** = *TWO YEARS AWAY FROM EXACT TIME OF DEATH AGE!!!!!~'*

`-551 = 5 + 5 + 1 = `-11

`-551 = 5 x 5 x 1 = `-25

`-25 + `-11 = `-**36** = *Marilyn Monroe!!!!!~'*

`-25 / `-11 = `-**2.272727**

`-25 (-) `-11 = `-**14**

`-87 / `-2 = `-**43**.**5**

`-43.5 + `-14 = `-57.5

`-57.5 (-) `-52 = `-5.5 = `-5/5

`-57.5 (-) `-03 = `-**54**.**5** = ROUNDED = `-**55** = *THREE YEARS AWAY FROM EXACT TIME OF DEATH AGE!!!!!~'*

`-36 + `-14 = `-**50** = *TWO YEARS AWAY FROM EXACT TIME OF DEATH AGE!!!!!~'*

`-36 + `-14 + `-2.272727 = `-**52**.**272727** = *EXACT (EXACT) TIME OF AGE AT TIME OF DEATH!!!!!~'*

`-36 + `-14 + `-03 = `-**53** = *ONE YEAR AWAY FROM THE EXACT TIME OF DEATH AGE!!!!!~'*

`-74 (-) `-18 (-) `-03 = `-**53** = *ONE YEAR AWAY FROM THE EXACT TIME OF DEATH AGE!!!!!~'*

`-40 + `-13 = `-**53** = *ONE YEAR AWAY FROM THE EXACT TIME OF DEATH AGE!!!!!~'*

`-74 (-) `-24 = `-**50** = *TWO YEARS AWAY FROM EXACT TIME OF DEATH AGE!!!!!~'*

`-78 (-) `-24 = `-**54** = *TWO YEARS AWAY FROM EXACT TIME OF DEATH AGE!!!!!~'*

`-47 + `-03 = `-**50** = *TWO YEARS AWAY FROM EXACT TIME OF DEATH AGE!!!!!~'*

`-42 + `-13 = `-**55** = *THREE YEARS AWAY FROM EXACT TIME OF DEATH AGE!!!!!~'*

`-43 + `-12 = `-**55** = *THREE YEARS AWAY FROM EXACT TIME OF DEATH AGE!!!!!~'*

`-48 + `-03 = `-**51** = *ONE YEAR AWAY FROM THE EXACT TIME OF DEATH AGE!!!!!~'*

`-42 + `-14 (-) `-03 = `-**53** = *ONE YEAR AWAY FROM THE EXACT TIME OF DEATH AGE!!!!!~'*

`-42 + `-10 = `-**52** = *EXACT TIME OF AGE AT TIME OF DEATH!!!!!~'*

`-38 + `-14 = `-**52** = *EXACT TIME OF AGE AT TIME OF DEATH!!!!!~'*

Death: 10/31/19**26** / **Grace Kelly!!!!!~'**

Married in `-18**94**!!!!!~' ANOTHER `-Marriage on the `-NUMBER /'\ `-**94**!!!!!~'

Spouse: Bess Houdini (Married for `-**32** Years / `-18**94** to `-19**26**!!!!!~'

`-**32** = **RECIPROCAL** = `-**23**

10 + 31 + 19 + 26 = `-**86** / `-**94** = **RECIPROCAL** = `-**49**

`-**94** (-) `-**86** = `-**08** / `-**08** = **RECIPROCAL** = `-**80**

`-**86** (-) `-**49** = `-**37** / `-**37** = **RECIPROCAL** = `-**73**

`-08 + `-73 = `-**81** / `-81 + `-117 = `-**198** = (1 + 98) = `-**99**

`-37 + `-80 = `-**117**

`-08 + `-37 = `-**45** / `-153 + `-45 = `-**198** = (1 + 98) = `-**99**

`-80 + `-73 = `-**153**

`-08 + `-80 = `-**88** / `-88 + `-110 = `-**198** = (1 + 98) = `-**99**

`-37 + `-73 = `-**110**

`-**99** = <u>RECIPROCAL</u> = `-**66** / `-**96** = <u>RECIPROCAL</u> = `-**69** = "The CYCLE of `-LIFE"!!!!!~'

(`-**99**) (-) (`-**86**) Harry Houdini's **Death Date** `-NUMBER = `-**13** = "A VERY PIVOTAL NUMBER"!!!!!~' `-**13** = <u>RECIPROCAL</u> = `-**31** / (`-**31**) (+) (`-**1**) = `-**32** = -a Prophetic Number!!!!!~'

(`-**119**) Harry Houdini's **Birthday** `-NUMBER (-) (`-**86**) Harry Houdini's **Death Date** `-NUMBER = `-**33** / (`-**33**) (-) (`-**1**) = `-**32** = -a Prophetic Number!!!!!~'

(`-**119**) Harry Houdini's **Birthday** `-NUMBER (-) (`-**99**) = (`-**20**)!!!!!~' (`-**86**) Harry Houdini's **Death Date** `-NUMBER = <u>RECIPROCAL</u> = (`-**68**) (-) (`-**99**) = (`-**31**)!!!!!~' (`-**31**) (-) (`-**20**) = (`-**11**) = "Yin/Yang" = "The CYCLE of `-LIFE"!!!!!~'

Elvis Presley – Birth – 0**1**/0**8**/19**35** **(42) YEARS OF AGE AT TIME OF DEATH!!!!!~'**

`-**35** = <u>RECIPROCAL</u> = `-**53**

`-53 (-) `-19 = `-**34**

`-34 / `-2 = `-**17**

`-08 (-) `-01 = `-**07**

`-**01** = <u>RECIPROCAL</u> = `-**10**

`-08 (-) `-10 = `-**02**

`-17 (-) `-02 = `-**15** = DAYS IN THE MONTH BEFORE DEATH!!!!!~'

`-35 (-) `-19 = `-**16**

`-16 / `-2 = `-**08**

244

`-08 (+) `-01 = `-**09**

`-08 (+) `-09 = `-**17** = DAYS IN THE MONTH RIGHT AFTER DEATH!!!!!~'

`-08 (-) `-10 = `-**02**

`-08 (-) `-02 = `-**06** = DIE ON A `-**6** OF THE MONTH!!!!!~'

01 + 08 + 19 + 35 = `-**63** = *John F. Kennedy & Marilyn Monroe!!!!!!~'* / BIRTHDAY `-NUMBER!!!!!~'

`-63 / `-2 = `-**31.5** = ROUNDED = `-**32** = -a Prophetic Number!!!!!~'

`-31.5 / `-2 = `-**15.75**

`-15.75 + `-6 (-) `-63 = `-**41.25** = *LESS THAN ONE YEAR RECIPROCALLY FROM THE EXACT (EXACT) TIME OF AGE AT TIME OF DEATH!!!!!~'*

5391 (-) 8010 = `-**2619**

`-5391 = `-93 (-) `-51 = `-**42** = *EXACT TIME OF AGE AT TIME OF DEATH!!!!!~'*

`-2619 = `-26 + `-19 = `-**45** = *THREE YEARS AWAY FROM EXACT TIME OF DEATH AGE!!!!!~'*

`-2619 = `-69 (-) `-21 = `-**48** = *SIX YEARS AWAY FROM THE EXACT TIME OF DEATH AGE!!!!!~'*

`-2619 = 2 + 6 + 1 + 9 = `-18

`-2619 = 2 x 6 x 1 x 9 = `-108

`-108 / `-18 = `-**6**

`-93 / `-2 = `-**46.5**

`-46.5 (-) `-6 = `-**40**.**5** = ROUNDED = `-**41** = *ONE YEAR AWAY FROM THE EXACT TIME OF DEATH AGE!!!!!~'*

`-35 + `-08 = `-**43** = *ONE YEAR AWAY FROM THE EXACT TIME OF DEATH AGE!!!!!~'*

`-35 + `-08 (-) `-01 = `-**42** = *EXACT TIME OF AGE AT TIME OF DEATH!!!!!~'*

`-98 (-) `-53 = `-**45** = *THREE YEARS AWAY FROM EXACT TIME OF DEATH AGE!!!!!~'*

`-**93** = <u>RECIPROCAL</u> = `-**39**

`-39 + `-01 = `-**40** = *TWO YEARS AWAY FROM EXACT TIME OF DEATH AGE!!!!!~'*

`-39 + `-05 = `-**44** = *TWO YEARS AWAY FROM EXACT TIME OF DEATH AGE!!!!!~'*

`-39 + `-05 (-) `-01 = `-**43** = *ONE YEAR AWAY FROM THE EXACT TIME OF DEATH AGE!!!!!~'*

Death: 08/16/1977 /|\ 08 + 16 + 19 + 77 = `-**120** / `-**120** (-) `-**94** = `-**26**!!!!!~'

08 + 16 + 19 + 77 = `-**120** / `-**94** = <u>RECIPROCAL</u> = `-**49**

`-**94** (-) `-**120** = `-**26** / `-**26** = <u>RECIPROCAL</u> = `-**62**

`-**120** (-) `-**49** = `-**71** / `-**71** = <u>RECIPROCAL</u> = `-**17**

`-**26** + `-**17** = `-**43** / `-133 + `-**43** = `-**176** = (17 + 6) = `-**23** = **-a Prophetic Number!!!!!~'**

`-**71** + `-62 = `-**133**

`-26 + `-71 = `-**97** / `-97 + `-79 = `-**176** = (17 + 6) = `-**23** = -a Prophetic Number!!!!!~'

`-62 + `-17 = `-**79**

`-**79** = RECIPROCAL = `-**97**

`-26 + `-62 = `-**88** / `-88 + `-88 = `-**176** = (17 + 6) = `-**23** = -a Prophetic Number!!!!!~'

`-71 + `-17 = `-**88**

`-**99** = RECIPROCAL = `-**66** / `-**96** = RECIPROCAL = `-**69** = "The CYCLE of `-LIFE"!!!!!~'

(`-**176**) (-) (`-**120**) Elvis Presley's **Death Day** `-NUMBER = (`-**56**) = (**5 + 6**) = (`-**11**) = "Yin/Yang" = **"The CYCLE of `-LIFE"!!!!!~'**

(`-**176**) (-) (`-**63**) Elvis Presley's **Birthday** `-NUMBER = (`-**113**) = (**1** x **13**) = (`-**13**) = **"A VERY PIVOTAL NUMBER"!!!!!~'** `-**13** = RECIPROCAL = `-**31** / (`-**31**) (+) (`-**1**) = `-**32** = -a Prophetic Number!!!!!~'

(`-**120**) Elvis Presley's **Death Day** `-NUMBER (+) (`-**63**) Elvis Presley's **Birthday** `-NUMBER = RECIPROCAL = `-**36** = (`-**156**) = (**1** x **56**) = (**56**) = (**5** + **6**) = (`-**11**) = "Yin/Yang" = **"The CYCLE of `-LIFE"!!!!!~'**

(`-**99**) (-) (`-**63**) Elvis Presley's **Birthday** `-NUMBER = RECIPROCAL = `-**36!!!!!~'**

(`-**99**) (-) (`-**120**) Elvis Presley's **Death Day** `-NUMBER = (`-**21**) / (`-**21**) (x) (`-**2**) = (`-**42**) = `-EXACT `-AGE at `-EXACT `-TIME of `-DEATH!!!!!~'

(`-**99**) (-) (`-**120**) Elvis Presley's **Death Day** `-NUMBER = (`-**21**) = RECIPROCAL = (`-**12**)!!!!!~' (`-**99**) (-) (`-**63**) Elvis Presley's **Birthday** `-NUMBER = RECIPROCAL = `-**36!!!!!~'** (`-**36**) (-) (`-**12**) = (`-**24**) = (-) `-**1** = `-**23** = -a Prophetic Number!!!!!~'

`-**32** = <u>RECIPROCAL</u> = `-**23**

State Attorney General - Beau Biden – Birth – 0**2**/**03**/1**96**9 **(46) YEARS OF AGE AT TIME OF DEATH!!!!!~'**

Beau Biden was `-BORN on the very same `-DAY that President Woodrow Wilson had `-DIED on!!!!!~' –(0**2**/0**3**)– *the* `-*NUMBER* `-*23!!!!!~'*

From Beau Biden's `-BIRTH to President Woodrow Wilson's death there is a `-SPAN of some `-**45** years encapsulated by the `-<u>**NUMBER**</u> `-**46** = `-**23** x **2** = `-**232** = <u>R</u>eciprocal-<u>S</u>equencing-<u>N</u>umerology!!!!!~'

`-**69** = <u>RECIPROCAL</u> = `-**96**

`-96 (-) `-19 = `-**77**

`-77 / `-2 = `-**38.5**

`-03 (-) `-02 = `-**01**

`-**03** = <u>RECIPROCAL</u> = `-**30**

`-**02** = <u>RECIPROCAL</u> = `-**20**

`-30 (-) `-20 = `-**10**

`-38.5 (-) `-10 = `-**28.5** = ROUNDED UP = `-**29** = **DAYS IN THE MONTH BEFORE DEATH!!!!!~'**

`-69 (-) `-19 = `-**50**

`-50 / `-2 = `-**25**

`-03 (+) `-02 = `-**05**

`-25 (+) `-05 = `-**30** = **DAY OF `-DEATH!!!!!~'**

02 + 03 + 19 + 69 = `-**93** = ANOTHER `-Death on the `-NUMBER /`\
`-**93**!!!!!~' / BIRTHDAY `-NUMBER!!!!!~'

`-93 / `-2 = `-**46.5** = *EXACT (EXACT) TIME OF AGE AT TIME OF DEATH!!!!!~'*

`-46.5 / `-2 = `-**23.25**

`-23.25 (-) `-69 + `-01 = `-**46.75** = *EXACT (EXACT) TIME OF AGE AT TIME OF DEATH (RECIPROCALLY)!!!!!~'*

9691 (-) 3020 = `-**6671**

`-9691 = `-69 (-) `-19 = `-**50** = *FOUR YEARS AWAY FROM THE EXACT TIME OF DEATH AGE!!!!!~'*

`-9691 = `-99 (-) `-61 = `-**38** = (+) `-**50** = `-88 / `-2 = `-**44** = *TWO YEARS AWAY FROM THE EXACT TIME OF DEATH AGE!!!!!~'*

`-**23** = **RECIPROCAL** = `-**32**

`-9691 = `-91 (-) `-69 = `-**22** = *Encapsulated by the* `-*NUMBER* `-*23!!!!!~'*

`-3020 = (**3**0**2**0) = `-**32** = *-a Prophetic Number!!!!!~'*

`-3020 = `-30 + `-20 = `-**50** = *FOUR YEARS AWAY FROM THE EXACT TIME OF DEATH AGE!!!!!~'*

`-6671 = `-67 (-) `-16 = `-**51** = *FIVE YEARS AWAY FROM THE EXACT TIME OF DEATH AGE!!!!!~'*

`-6671 = 6 + 6 + 7 + 1 = `-20

`-6671 = 6 x 6 x 7 x 1 = `-252

`-252 / `-20 = `-**12.6**

`-**96** = <u>RECIPROCAL</u> = `-**69**

`-69 (-) `-12.6 (-) `-10 = **46.4** = *EXACT (EXACT) TIME OF AGE AT TIME OF DEATH!!!!!~'*

`-96 / `-2 = `-**48**

`-48 (-) `-02 = `-**46** = *EXACT TIME OF AGE AT TIME OF DEATH!!!!!~'*

`-30 + `-19 (-) `-02 = `-**47** = *ONE YEAR AWAY FROM THE EXACT TIME OF DEATH AGE!!!!!~'*

`-96 (-) `-30 (-) `-20 = `-**46** = *EXACT TIME OF AGE AT TIME OF DEATH!!!!!~'*

`-69 (-) `-20 (-) `-03 = `-**46** = *EXACT TIME OF AGE AT TIME OF DEATH!!!!!~'*

`-69 (-) `-19 (-) `-03 = `-**47** = *ONE YEAR AWAY FROM THE EXACT TIME OF DEATH AGE!!!!!~'*

`-69 (-) `-19 (-) `-03 (-) `-02 = `-**45** = *ONE YEAR AWAY FROM THE EXACT TIME OF DEATH AGE!!!!!~'*

`-99 (-) `-61 + `-30 (-) `-20 = **48** = *TWO YEARS AWAY FROM EXACT TIME OF DEATH AGE!!!!!~'*

`-32 + `-16 = **48** = *TWO YEARS AWAY FROM EXACT TIME OF DEATH AGE!!!!!~'*

`-91 (-) `-69 + `-20 + `-03 = `-**45** = *ONE YEAR AWAY FROM THE EXACT TIME OF DEATH AGE!!!!!~'*

`-60 (-) `-21 + `-09 = **48** = *TWO YEARS AWAY FROM EXACT TIME OF DEATH AGE!!!!!~'*

`-36 + `-10 = `-**46** = *EXACT TIME OF AGE AT TIME OF DEATH!!!!!~'*

Death: 05/30/2015 / `-**7**(...)!!!!!~'\ A `-*HEAVENLY* `-*NUMBER!!!!!~'*

05 + 30 + 20 + 15 = `-**70**

`-**70** (-) `-**23.25** = **46.75** = *EXACT (EXACT) TIME OF AGE AT TIME OF DEATH (RECIPROCALLY)!!!!!~'*

`-**94** (-) `-**70** = `-**24** = (-) `-**01** = `-**23** = *-a Prophetic Number!!!!!~'*

05 + 30 + 20 + 15 = `-**70** / `-**94** = RECIPROCAL = `-**49**

`-**94** (-) `-**70** = `-**24** / `-**24** = RECIPROCAL = `-**42**

`-**70** (-) `-**49** = `-**21** / `-**21** = RECIPROCAL = `-**12**

`-**24** + `-**12** = `-**36** / `-63 + `-36 = `-**99**

`-**21** + `-**42** = `-**63**

`-**36** = RECIPROCAL = `-**63**

`-**24** + `-**21** = `-**45** / `-45 + `-54 = `-**99**

`-**42** + `-**12** = `-**54**

`-**45** = RECIPROCAL = `-**54**

`-**24** + `-**42** = `-**66** / `-33 + `-66 = `-**99**

`-**21** + `-**12** = `-**33**

`-**99** = RECIPROCAL = `-**66** / `-**96** = RECIPROCAL = `-**69** = "The CYCLE of `-LIFE"!!!!!~'

(`-**99**) (-) (`-**93**) Beau Biden's **Birthday** `-NUMBER = RECIPROCAL = (`-**39**) = (`-**60**)!!!!!~' (`-**99**) (-) (`-**70**) Beau Biden's **Death Day** `-NUMBER = RECIPROCAL = (`-**07**) = `-**92**!!!!!~' (`-**92**) (+) (`-**60**) = (`-**152**) = (**15** (-) **2**) = (`-**13**) = "A VERY PIVOTAL NUMBER"!!!!!~'

`-**13** = <u>RECIPROCAL</u> = `-**31** / (`-**31**) (+) (`-**1**) = `-**32** = -a Prophetic Number!!!!!~'

(`-**99**) (+) (`-**70**) Beau Biden's **Death Day** `-NUMBER = (`-**169**) = (**1** x **69**) = `-**69** = "The CYCLE of `-LIFE"!!!!!~'

(`-**93**) Beau Biden's **Birthday** `-NUMBER (+) (`-**70**) Beau Biden's **Death Day** `-NUMBER = (`-**163**) = (**1** x **63**) = (`-**63**) = John F. Kennedy = Death at `-**EXACT** same `-**AGE** for `-**BOTH** `-**MEN** at `-AGE (`-**46**)!!!!!~' There are (`-**188**) days that lie in between the Death Dates of these two `-MEN!!!!!~' (`-**188**) = (**1** x **88**) = (`-**88**)_!!!!!~'

(`-**93**) Beau Biden's **Birthday** `-NUMBER (-) (`-**70**) Beau Biden's **Death Day** `-NUMBER = `-**23** = -a Prophetic Number!!!!!~'

Brandon Lee – Birth – 0**2**/0**1**/19**65** **(28) YEARS OF AGE AT TIME OF DEATH!!!!!~'**

`-**65** = <u>RECIPROCAL</u> = `-**56**

`-56 (-) `-19 = `-**37**

`-37 / `-2 = `-**18.5**

`-02 (-) `-01 = `-**01**

`-**02** = <u>RECIPROCAL</u> = `-**20**

`-**01** = <u>RECIPROCAL</u> = `-**10**

`-20 (-) `-10 = `-**10**

`-18.5 (+) `-10 = `-**28.5** = +1 = `-**29.5** = ROUNDED UP = `-**30** = DAYS IN THE MONTH BEFORE DEATH!!!!!~'

`-65 (-) `-19 = `-**46**

`-19 / `-2 = `-**23**

`-**23** = **RECIPROCAL** = `-**32**

`-02 (-) `-01 = `-**01**

`-32 (-) `-01 = `-**31** = **DAY OF `-DEATH!!!!!~'**

02 + 01 + 19 + 65 = `-**87** = BIRTHDAY `-NUMBER!!!!!~'

`-87 / `-2 = `-**43.5**

`-43.5 (-) `-15 = `-**28.5** = *EXACT TIME OF AGE AT TIME OF DEATH!!!!!~'*

`-43.5 (-) `-16 = `-**27.5** = *NEARLY ONE YEAR AWAY FROM THE EXACT TIME OF DEATH AGE!!!!!~'*

`-43.5 / `-2 = `-**21.75**

5691 (-) 1020 = `-**4671**

`-5691 = `-95 (-) `-61 = `-**34** = `- *SIX YEARS AWAY FROM THE EXACT TIME OF DEATH AGE!!!!!~'*

`-1020 = `-10 + `-20 = `-**30** = *TWO YEARS AWAY FROM EXACT TIME OF DEATH AGE!!!!!~'*

`-4671 = `-71 (-) `-46 = `-**25** = *THREE YEARS AWAY FROM EXACT TIME OF DEATH AGE!!!!!~'*

`-4671 = `-47 (-) `-16 = `-**31** = *THREE YEARS AWAY FROM EXACT TIME OF DEATH AGE!!!!!~'*

`-4671 = `-46 (-) `-17 = `-**29** = *ONE YEAR AWAY FROM THE EXACT TIME OF DEATH AGE!!!!!~'*

`-4671 = `-67 (-) `-41 = `-**26** = *TWO YEARS AWAY FROM EXACT TIME OF DEATH AGE!!!!!~'*

`-4671 = `-74 (-) `-61 = `-**13** = **"A VERY PIVOTAL NUMBER!!!!!~'**

`-4671 = 4 + 6 + 7 + 1 = `-18

`-4671 = 4 x 6 x 7 x 1 = `-168

`-168 / `-18 = `-**9.33**

`-9.33 + `-21.75 = `-**31.08** = *THREE YEARS AWAY FROM EXACT TIME OF DEATH AGE!!!!!~'*

`-96 / `-2 = `-**48**

`-48 (-) `-20 = `-**28** = *EXACT TIME OF AGE AT TIME OF DEATH!!!!!~'*

`-**96** = **RECIPROCAL** = `-**69**

`-69 (-) `-48 + `-9.33 = `-**30.33** = *NEARLY TWO YEARS AWAY FROM THE EXACT TIME OF DEATH AGE!!!!!~'*

`-69 (-) `-43.5 = `-**25.5** = *NEARLY THREE YEARS AWAY FROM THE EXACT TIME OF DEATH AGE!!!!!~'*

`-87 (-) `-69 = `-18

`-18 + 9.33 = `-**27.33** = *NEARLY ONE YEAR AWAY FROM THE EXACT (EXACT) TIME OF DEATH AGE!!!!!~'*

`-20 + 09 = `-**29** = *ONE YEAR AWAY FROM THE EXACT TIME OF DEATH AGE!!!!!~'*

`-20 + `-06 = `-**26** = *TWO YEARS AWAY FROM EXACT TIME OF DEATH AGE!!!!!~'*

`-21 + `-06 = `-**27** = *ONE YEAR AWAY FROM THE EXACT TIME OF DEATH AGE!!!!!~'*

`-21 + `-05 = `-`-**26** = *TWO YEARS AWAY FROM EXACT TIME OF DEATH AGE!!!!!~'*

`-20 + `-19 (-) `-10 = `-**29** = *ONE YEAR AWAY FROM THE EXACT TIME OF DEATH AGE!!!!!~'*

`-65 (-) `-19 (-) `-20 = `-**26** = *TWO YEARS AWAY FROM EXACT TIME OF DEATH AGE!!!!!~'*

`-56 (-) `-19 (-) `-10 = `-**27** = *ONE YEAR AWAY FROM THE EXACT TIME OF DEATH AGE!!!!!~'*

`-12 + `-15 = `-**27** = *ONE YEAR AWAY FROM THE EXACT TIME OF DEATH AGE!!!!!~'*

`-12 + `-16 = `-**28** = *EXACT TIME OF AGE AT TIME OF DEATH!!!!!~'*

`-91 (-) `-56 (-) `-10 = `-**25** = *THREE YEARS AWAY FROM EXACT TIME OF DEATH AGE!!!!!~'*

`-91 (-) `-65 = `-**26** = *TWO YEARS AWAY FROM EXACT TIME OF DEATH AGE!!!!!~'*

`-92 (-) `-65 = `-**27** = *ONE YEAR AWAY FROM THE EXACT TIME OF DEATH AGE!!!!!~'*

`-92 (-) `-56 (-) `-10 = `-**26** = *TWO YEARS AWAY FROM EXACT TIME OF DEATH AGE!!!!!~'*

`-90 (-) `-65 = `-**25** = *THREE YEARS AWAY FROM EXACT TIME OF DEATH AGE!!!!!~'*

`-91 (-) `-65 + `-02 = `-**28** = *EXACT TIME OF AGE AT TIME OF DEATH!!!!!~'*

`-69 (-) `-51 + `-10 = `-**28** = *EXACT TIME OF AGE AT TIME OF DEATH!!!!!~'*

255

DWAYNE W. ANDERSON

Death: 0**3**/**31**/19**93** = `-*31* (-) `-*3* = `-**28** = *EXACT TIME OF AGE AT DEATH!!!!!~' jfk*

03 x **31** = `-**93** / ANOTHER `-Death on the `-NUMBER /'\ `-**93**!!!!!~'
`-**313** / **Fatal SHOT/|**

`-**31** = **RECIPROCAL** = `-**13**

Bruce Lee – birth to death – in days that lie in between = `-**235** (Leap Year `-included)!!!!!~'

Brandon Lee – birth to death – in days that lie in between = `-**59** (Leap Year `-included)!!!!!~'

`-**235** + `-59 = `-2**94** = / OTHER `-Deaths on the `-NUMBER /'\ `-**94**!!!!!~'

Bruce Lee – birth to death – in days that lie in between = `-**234** (Leap Year not `-included)!!!!!~' `-**234** = **Prophetic Linear Progression!!!!!~'** `-**23** + `-4 = `-**27**!!!!!~'

Brandon Lee – birth to death – in days that lie in between = `-**58** (Leap Year not `-included)!!!!!~' `-**58** = `-5 + `-8 = `-**13** = **"A VERY PIVOTAL NUMBER"**!!!!!~'

`-**234** + `-58 = `-**292** = **R**eciprocal-**S**equencing-**N**umerology!!!!!~'

Bruce Lee birth – to Brandon Lee death – in days that lie in between = `-**124** (Leap Year `-included)!!!!!~'

Brandon Lee birth – to Bruce Lee death – in days that lie in between = `-**65** / `-**299** (Leap Year `-included)!!!!!~'

`-**299** + `-**124** = `-**423**!!!!!~' `-**423** = **Prophetic Linear Progression!!!!!~'**

Bruce Lee birth – to Brandon Lee death – in days that lie in between = `-**123** (Leap Year not `-included)!!!!!~' `-**123** = **Prophetic Linear Progression!!!!!~'**

256

Brandon Lee birth – to Bruce Lee death – in days that lie in between = `-**65** / `-**298** (Leap Year not `-included)!!!!!~'

`-298 + `-65 = `-**363** = **R**eciprocal-**S**equencing-**N**umerology!!!!!~'

`-123 + `-65 = `-188

`-123 + `-298 = `-421

`-421 + `-188 = `-**60<u>9</u>** = `-**69** = "Yin/Yang" = **"The CYCLE of `-LIFE"!!!!!~'**

03 + 31 + 19 + 93 = `-**146** / `-**94** = **RECIPROCAL** = `-**49**

`-**94** (-) `-**146** = `-**52** / `-**52** = **RECIPROCAL** = `-**25**

`-**146** (-) `-**49** = `-**97** / `-**97** = **RECIPROCAL** = `-**79**

`-52 + `-79 = `-**131** / `-122 + `-131 = `-**253** = (2 + 53) = `-**55** = `-**23** + `-**32**

`-97 + `-25 = `-**122** / `-131 (-) `-122 = `-**9**

`-**131** = (**1** + **31**) = `-**32** = *-a Prophetic Number!!!!!~'*

`-**122** = (**1** + **22**) = `-**23** = *-a Prophetic Number!!!!!~'*

`-52 + `-97 = `-**149** / `-104 + `-149 = `-**253** = (2 + 53) = `-**55** = `-**23** + `-**32**

`-25 + `-79 = `-**104** / `-149 (-) `-104 = `-**45** = **RECIPROCAL** = `-**54** / **45+54** = `-**99**

`-52 + `-25 = `-**77** / `-176 + `-77 = `-**253** = (2 + 53) = `-**55** = `-**23** + `-**32**

`-97 + `-79 = `-**176** / `-176 (-) `-77 = `-**99**

`-**99** = **RECIPROCAL** = `-**66** / `-**96** = **RECIPROCAL** = `-**69** = **"The CYCLE of `-LIFE"!!!!!~'**

(`-**99**) (**+**) (`-**87**) Brandon Lee's **Birthday** `-NUMBER = (`-**186**) = (**86** (**-**) **1**) = (**85**) = (**8** + **5**) = (`-**13**) = "A VERY PIVOTAL NUMBER"!!!!!~'
`-**13** = **RECIPROCAL** = `-**31** / (`-**31**) (**+**) (`-**1**) = `-**32** = -a Prophetic Number!!!!!~'

(`-**146**) Brandon Lee's **Death Day** `-NUMBER (**+**) (`-**87**) Brandon Lee's **Birthday** `-NUMBER = (`-**233**) = (`-**23**) EMPHASIZED!!!!!~'
(`-**46**) **/** (`-**2**) = (`-**23**) +_!!!!!~'

(`-**146**) Brandon Lee's **Death Day** `-NUMBER (**+**) (`-**87**) Brandon Lee's **Birthday** `-NUMBER = **RECIPROCAL** = (`-**78**) = (`-**224**) = (`-**24** + `-**22** / `-**2**) = (`-**23**) = -a Prophetic Number!!!!!~'

(`-**146**) Brandon Lee's **Death Day** `-NUMBER (**+**) (`-**87**) Brandon Lee's **Birthday** `-NUMBER = **RECIPROCAL** = (`-**78**) = (`-**224**) = (`-**24** + `-**22**) = `-**46** = (**1**(**46**)) = (**1** + **46**) = (`-**146**) = Brandon Lee's **Death Day** `-NUMBER!!!!!~'

(`-**146**) Brandon Lee's **Death Day** `-NUMBER (**-**) (`-**87**) Brandon Lee's **Birthday** `-NUMBER = (`-**59**)!!!!!~' (`-**146**) Brandon Lee's **Death Day** `-NUMBER (**-**) (`-**87**) Brandon Lee's **Birthday** `-NUMBER = **RECIPROCAL** = (`-**78**) = (`-**68**)_!!!!!~' (`-**59**) = **RECIPROCAL** = (`-**95**) / (`-**68**) = **RECIPROCAL** = (`-**86**) / (`-**95**) (**+**) (`-**86**) = `-**181** = **R**eciprocal-**S**equenced-Numerology!!!!!~'

KEY CYPHERS - OUR DEATH DATES -VIA- RSN-Reciprocal-Sequenced/Sequencing-Numerology!!!!!~'

DEATH DATE CYPHERS - CODE BREAKERS!!!!!~'

(PROPHET'S) MOM – BIRTH – **11**/**15**/**19**44

`-**44** = **RECIPROCAL** = `-**44**

`-44 (**-**) `-19 = `-**25**

`-DEATH CIPHERS/CYPHERS FOR LIFE & DEATH!!!~'

`-25 / `-2 = `-**12.5**

`-15 (-) `-11 = `-**04**

`-12.5 (+) `-04 = `-**16.5** = ROUNDED DOWN = `-**16** = DAY OF `-DEATH!!!!!~'

`-15 (+) `-11 = `-**26**

`-26 + `-04 = `-**30**

`-44 (-) `-19 = `-**25**

`-25 / `-2 = `-**12.5** = ROUNDED = `-**13**

`-30 (-) `-13 = `-**17** = DAYS IN THE MONTH BEFORE DEATH!!!!!~'

`-15 (-) `-11 = `-4

`-44 (-) `-19 = 25

`-25 / `-2 = `-12.5

`-12.5 + `-4 = `-16.5 = `-EXACT `-DAY of `-DEATH!!!!!~'

1115 = RECIPROCAL = 1511

4419 – 1511 = `-2908

1944 – 1115 = `-829

`-2908 + `-829 = `-3737

4491 – 5111 = `-620 = NEAR AGE OF DEATH!!!!!~'

`-94 (-) `-62 = `-32

'-44 + '-19 = '-63 = AGE AT TIME OF DEATH!!!!!~' THE NUMBER '-**32**!!!!!~'

'-62 = 6 + 2 = '-8

'-62 = 6 x 2 = '-12

620 = 6 + 2 + 0 = '-8

620 = 6 x 2 x 0 = '-0

'-44 + '-11 + '-08 = '-63 = AGE AT TIME OF DEATH!!!!!~'

'-63 (-) '-8 = '-55 = '-23 + '-32

'-8 + '-0 = '-8

'-12 + '-8 = '-20

'-20 / 2 = '-10

'-32 + '-12 + '-8 + '-10 = '-62 = ONE YEAR AWAY FROM AGE OF DEATH!!!!!!~'

TWO APPEARS TWICE = DIVIDE BY '-2 = 6 / 2 = '-3

'-8 x '-12 = '-96 (9-3)(6-3) = '-63 = AGE AT TIME OF DEATH!!!!!~'

'-62 = 6 + 2 + 0 = '-8

'-62 = 6 x 2 x 0 = '-0

08 = YEAR OF DEATH!!!!!~'

11 + 15 + 19 + 44 = '-89 = AGE AT TIME OF DEATH FOR MOTHER'S MOTHER!!!!!~'

'-89 / '-8 = '-11.125

`-DEATH CIPHERS/CYPHERS FOR LIFE & DEATH!!!~'

`-89 = RECIPROCAL = `-98

`-98 (-) `-44 = `-54

`-54 + `-8 = `-62 = ONE YEAR AWAY –NEAR AGE OF DEATH!!!!!~'

`-8 + `-11.125 = `-19.125

`-19.125 / `-2 = `-9.5625

`-54 + `-9.5625 = `-63.5625 = AGE AT TIME OF DEATH!!!!!~'

(RECIPROCAL) IN TIME OF FRACTION (0.5625) – IS THE EXACT TIME OF DEATH!!!!!~'

`-94/2 = `-47

`-47 + `-15 = `-62 = ONE YEAR AWAY –NEAR AGE OF DEATH!!!!!~'

BIRTH – 11/15/1944

11 + 15 + 19 + 44 = `-<u>89</u> = BIRTHDAY `-NUMBER!!!!!~'

DEATH – 04/16/2008 – 10PM / `-<u>48</u> = DEATH DAY `-NUMBER!!!!!~'

04 + 16 + 20 + 08 = `-<u>48</u> / `-<u>94</u> = <u>RECIPROCAL</u> = `-<u>49</u>

`-<u>94</u> (-) `-<u>48</u> = `-<u>46</u> / `-<u>46</u> = <u>RECIPROCAL</u> = `-<u>64</u>

`-<u>48</u> (-) `-<u>49</u> = `-<u>01</u> / `-<u>01</u> = <u>RECIPROCAL</u> = `-<u>10</u>

`-46 + `-10 = `-<u>56</u> / `-56 + `-65 = `-<u>121</u> = <u>R</u>eciprocal-<u>S</u>equencing-<u>N</u>umerology!!!!!~'

`-01 + `-64 = `-<u>65</u> / `-65 (-) `-56 = `-<u>9</u>

`-<u>56</u> = <u>RECIPROCAL</u> = `-<u>65</u>

`-46 + `-01 = `-**47** / `-47 + `-74 = `-**121** = Reciprocal-**S**equencing-**N**umerology!!!!!~'

`-64 + `-10 = `-**74** / `-74 (-) `-47 = `-**27**

`-**47** = **RECIPROCAL** = `-**74**

`-46 + `-64 = `-**110** / `-110 + `-11 = `-**121** = Reciprocal-**S**equencing-**N**umerology!!!!!~'

`-01 + `-10 = `-**11** / `-110 (-) `-11 = `-**99**

`-**55** = `-**23** + `-**32**

`-**54** = `-**27** + `-**27** = (**27** x **2**) = `-**272 RSN** / `-**27** = (**9** x **3**) = **3**(**9's**) = (**999**) = `-**999**

`-**999** = **RECIPROCAL** = `-**666** / `-**96** = **RECIPROCAL** = `-**69** = "The CYCLE of `-LIFE"!!!!!~'

(`-**121**) (-) (`-**89**) MOM'S BIRTHDAY `-NUMBER = `-**32** = -a PROPHETIC NUMBER!!!!!~'

(`-**121**) (-) (`-**48**) MOM'S DEATH DAY `-NUMBER = `-**73**!!!!!~' `-**73** = **RECIPROCAL** = `-**37** !!!!!~' `-**73** + `-**37** = `-**110** = (**11** + **0**) = `-**11** = "The CYCLE of `-LIFE"!!!!!~'

(`-**89**) MOM'S BIRTHDAY `-NUMBER (-) (`-**48**) MOM'S DEATH DAY `-NUMBER = `-**41**!!!!!~' `-**41** = **RECIPROCAL** = `-**14** = `-**41** + `-**14** = `-**55** = `-**23** + `-**32**!!!!~'

(`-**89**) MOM'S BIRTHDAY `-NUMBER (-) (`-**48**) MOM'S DEATH DAY `-NUMBER = `-**41**!!!!!~' `-**41** IS THE YEAR THAT THE `-PROPHET'S FATHER WAS BORN!!!!!~'

(`-**89**) MOM'S BIRTHDAY `-NUMBER (+) (`-**48**) MOM'S DEATH DAY `-NUMBER = `-**137**!!!!!~' `-**137** = (**13** + **7**) = `-**20** = THE DAY THE "PROPHET" WAS BORN!!!!!~'

(`-121) (+) (`-89) MOM'S BIRTHDAY `-NUMBER (+) (`-48) MOM'S DEATH DAY `-NUMBER = `-258!!!!!~'

(`-121) + (`-48) MOM'S DEATH DAY `-NUMBER = `-169 = (1 x 69) = `-69 = "The CYCLE of `-LIFE"!!!!!~'

(PROPHET'S) DAD – BIRTH – 09/01/1941

`-41 = RECIPROCAL = `-14

`-14 (-) `-19 = `-05

`-05 / `-2 = `-2.5

`-09 (-) `-01 = `-08

`-05 (+) `-2.5 (+) `-08 = `-15.5 = ROUNDED UP = `-16 = DAY OF `-DEATH!!!!!~'

`-41 (-) `-19 = `-22

`-22 / `-2 = `-11

`-11 / `-2 = `-5.5

`-09 (+) `-01 = `-10

`-10 (+) `-5.5 = `-15.5 = ROUNDED UP = `-16 = DAY OF `-DEATH!!!!!~'

`-91 = RECIPROCAL = `-19

0901 = RECIPROCAL = `-0109 = `-19

1941 = 41 = RECIPROCAL = `-14

`-19 + `-14 = `-33 / 2 = `-16.5 = 16th OF THE MONTH – ½ DAY OF TIME OF DEATH = `-6AM/6PM!!!!!~'

1491 – 1090 = `-401

`-401 = 4 + 0 + 1 = `-5

`-401 = 4 x 0 x 1 = `-0

`-19 + `-41 = `-60

`-60 + `-5 = `-65 = ONE YEAR AWAY - NEAR AGE OF DEATH!!!!!~'

`-91 (-) `19 = `-72

`-72 (-) `-41 = `-31

`-31 (+) `-5 = `-36

`-**3** x (**2**) = `-6 = THE NUMBER `-**32**!!!!!~'

`-94 / `-2 = `-47

`-47 + `19 = `-66 = AGE AT TIME OF DEATH!!!!!~'

09 + 01 + 19 + 41 = `-70

`-70 (-) 5 = `-65 = ONE YEAR AWAY - NEAR AGE OF DEATH!!!!!~'

09 + 01 + 19 + 41 = `-70 = BIRTHDAY `-NUMBER!!!!!~'

DEATH – 04/16/2008 – 6PM

04 + 16 + 20 + 08 = `-**48** / `-**94** = **RECIPROCAL** = `-**49**

`-**94** (-) `-**48** = `-**46** / `-**46** = **RECIPROCAL** = `-**64**

`-**48** (-) `-**49** = `-**01** / `-**01** = **RECIPROCAL** = `-**10**

`-46 + `-10 = `-**56** / `-56 + `-65 = `-**121** = **R**eciprocal-**S**equencing-**N**umerology!!!!!~'

`-01 + `-64 = `-**65** / `-65 (-) `-56 = `-**9**

`-**56** = **RECIPROCAL** = `-**65**

`-46 + `-01 = `-**47** / `-47 + `-74 = `-**121** = **R**eciprocal-**S**equencing-**N**umerology!!!!!~'

`-64 + `-10 = `-**74** / `-74 (-) `-47 = `-**27**

`-**47** = **RECIPROCAL** = `-**74**

`-46 + `-64 = `-**110** / `-110 + `-11 = `-**121** = **R**eciprocal-**S**equencing-**N**umerology!!!!!~'

`-01 + `-10 = `-**11** / `-110 (-) `-11 = `-**99**

`-**55** = `-**23** + `-**32**

`-**54** = `-**27** + `-**27** = (**27** x **2**) = `-**272 RSN** / `-**27** = (**9** x **3**) = **3**(**9's**) = (**999**) = `-**999**

`-**999** = **RECIPROCAL** = `-**666** / `-**96** = **RECIPROCAL** = `-**69** = "The CYCLE of `-LIFE"!!!!!~'

(`-**121**) (-) (`-**70**) DAD'S BIRTHDAY `-NUMBER = `-**51**!!!!!~' `-**51** = RECIPROCAL = `-**15** !!!!!~' `-**51** + `-**15** = `-**66** = ACTUAL `-AGE AT TIME OF `-DEATH OF `-DAD!!!!!~'

(`-**121**) (+) (`-**70**) DAD'S BIRTHDAY `-NUMBER = (`-**191**) = (**19** + **1**) = `-**20** = THE DAY THE PROPHET WAS BORN!!!!!~' `-**191** = (**91** + **1**) = `-**92** / `-**92** = RECIPROCAL = `-**29** / `-**92** + `-**29** = `-**121**!!!!!~'

(`-**70**) DAD'S BIRTHDAY `-NUMBER = THE YEAR THE "PROPHET" WAS BORN!!!!!~'

PRESIDENT JOHN F. KENNEDY; AND, THE PROPHET'S DAD SHARE THE VERY SAME BIRTHDAY `-NUMBER OF (`-70)!!!!!~' THE DIFFERENCE IN THEIR AGES OF DEATH IS EXACTLY `-20 YEARS!!!!!~ THE `-NUMBER (`-20) SIGNIFIES THE VERY DAY THE "PROPHET" WAS BORN ON!!!!!~' THERE ARE `-145 DAYS (LEAP YEAR INCLUDED) THAT LIE IN BETWEEN THEIR DAYS OF DEATH; OR, DEATH DATES!!!!!~' (`-145) = (1 + 45) = `-46 = `-23 x `-2 = `-232 = RECIPROCAL-SEQUENCED-NUMEROLOGY!!!!!~' THERE ARE `-144 DAYS (NON-LEAP YEAR) THAT LIE IN BETWEEN THEIR DAYS OF DEATH; OR, DEATH DATES!!!!!~' (`-144) = (1 x 44) = `-44 = THE YEAR THE "PROPHET'S" MOTHER WAS BORN!!!!!~'

(`-89) MOM'S BIRTHDAY `-NUMBER (-) (`-48) MOM'S DEATH DAY `-NUMBER = `-41!!!!!~' `-41 IS THE YEAR THAT THE `-PROPHET'S FATHER WAS BORN!!!!!~'

(`-70) DAD'S BIRTHDAY `-NUMBER (-) (`-48) DAD'S DEATH DAY `-NUMBER = `-22 ENCAPSULATED BY THE NUMBER `-23!!!!!~'

(`-121) (+) (`-70) DAD'S BIRTHDAY `-NUMBER (+) (`-48) DAD'S DEATH DAY `-NUMBER = `-239!!!!!~' `-23 & 3(9's) = `-999!!!!!~' "The CYCLE of `-LIFE"!!!!!~'

(`-121) + (`-48) DAD'S DEATH DAY `-NUMBER = `-169 = (1 x 69) = `-69 = "The CYCLE of `-LIFE"!!!!!~'

COPYRIGHT 06/12/2015 / AUTHOR: DWAYNE W. ANDERSON / THE "PROPHET"!!!!!~' /

Subject Title: `-TARGETS for `-EXTRATERRESTRIALS!!!!!~'

Send`-THIS`-ON; to`-ANYONE, that`-MAY be`-INTERESTED!!!!!~'

Look for LIFE on other PLANETS in the following CONSTELLATIONS: (13) Canes Venatici, (23) Circinus; and, (32) Delphinus!!!!!~ For the `-FOLLOWING: (12) Cancer, (33) Dorado; and, (#1) Andromeda; `-THEY, are giving me a FUNNY FEELING; TOO!!!!!!~' Why don't `-YOU; Check them OUT; just as well!!!!!~'

If The COSMOS could be divided into QUADRANTS of CONSTELLATIONS, look for LIFE on OTHER PLANETS; in, QUADRANTS `-23, `-32; and, `-13!!!!!~

A "NEW" `-KIND OF "NUMEROLOGY"; CALLED "PENDULUM FLOW", that I've `-CREATED!!!!!~'

Regards,

Author/Prophet

Dwayne W. Anderson...

"The Real Prophet Of Doom!!!!!~'(...)-'

Through my years in the office & home; and, talking with `-GOD; I created a system in communicating with him!!!!!~' I re-phrase my questions over; and, over again in different ways; which, triggers a different pulse; on the opposite side of my body for a reaction to each particular; and, specific question (exactly the opposite as outlined below)!!!!!~' If I asked a `-QUESTION; and, I got a `-YES; and then, asked the opposite of the `-QUESTION again, the opposite side of my `-BODY will `-RESPOND with a `-NO!!!!!~' I have `-TESTED; and,

`-Test the system `-ALL the `-TIME!!!!!~' I would like to do a `-GOD `-Test as outlined; and, stated below!!!!!~' The apparatus that I'm looking for is quite similar to what is utilized for the testing of sleep apnea!!!!!~' I had tested for my sleep apnea on a home device that I had slept with; and, was diagnosed with!!!!!~' I need a bit more for the `-GOD `-test!!!!!~' People believe in `-PRAYING into the `-THIN clear `-AIR for some `-ENTITY to hear their conversations; and, to actually respond to `-Them; in `-HELPING them with their fervent `-PRAYERS!!!!!~' Throughout `-HISTORY; People have taken `-for what they believe this entity to be; and, in fact something that they themselves cannot even see; and, have approached this `-GODLY `-CREATURE in the `-THIN clear `-AIR!!!!!~' Humans have died for their `-OWN interpretation of this `-GODLY `-CREATURE in the `-THIN clear `-AIR; and, People have killed for their `-OWN interpretation of what is this `-GODLY `-CREATURE in the `-THIN clear `-AIR!!!!!~' They have taken `-BOOKS about the `-GODLY `-CREATURE in the `-THIN clear `-AIR and have shaped their entire lives around `-HIM!!!!!~' I know what the `-GODLY `-CREATURE in the `-THIN clear `-AIR `-IS!!!!!!~' I would like to `-PROVE `-THIS to the `-WORLD!!!!!~' Could you `-HELP `-ME in doing `-this; or, Could you `-HELP me to `-SHED some `-LIGHT on; `-THIS `-SUBJECT of `-LIFE, to the `-COMMUNITY of the `-WORLD!!!!!~' Can `-YOU `-HELP `-ME; to set up; the `-GOD `-TEST!!!!!~' I've attached what I have just created; and, was `-INSPIRED to `-WRITE for this `-MONTH!!!!!~' It's called the Death Ciphers / Death Cypher / The Death Formula / The `-GOD Equation!!!!!!~' You can `-PREDICT someone's age of `-DEATH; simply by using, their `-BIRTHDAY, `-BIRTH `-MONTH; and, Year of `-BIRTH (It really `-WORKS!~')!!!!!~' Please `-READ on; and, please `-RESPOND!!!!!~' Open your `-MIND; and, Dive `-IN; for `-IF YOU so `-DESIRE!!!!!~'

Regards,

Author/Prophet/Engineer

Dwayne W. Anderson!!!!!~'

CIPHER I, CIPHER II; and, CIPHER III / These `-EQUATIONS are something; that I was just inspired to `-WRITE!!!!!~' Predict

`-DEATH CIPHERS/CYPHERS FOR LIFE & DEATH!!!~'

`-ANYONE'S `-DEATH `-AGE (Living; or, Not) simply by using their `-BIRTHDAY, `-BIRTH `-MONTH; and, `-YEAR of `-BIRTH!!!!!~' NOW; `-EVERYONE, can `-PREDICT the `-FUTURE!!!!!~' The "PROPHET" might `-USE you as a `-MESSENGER; for `-If, you so `-DESIRE!!!!!~' Enjoy the `-READ!!!!!~' For `-ARMAGEDDON; I use the `-EXPRESSION, "ARM-AGE-D-DON" = "MR.A-AGE-D-DON!!!!!~' "**ARM**" = **RECIPROCAL** = "**MRA**" <u>Mr. A</u> = <u>Mr. Anderson!!!!!~'</u> <u>AGE</u> = <u>The `-GOD `-EQUATIONS of `-AGE!!!!!~'</u> <u>D-DON = The `-GODFATHER; of, `-SOUL!!!!!~'</u> In `-MY `-DREAMS; `-God; CALLS `-me, a `-***FIRECRACKER!!!!!~'*** `-***EXPLOSIVE /*** `-***ORIGINAL /*** `-***NEW /*** `-***THOUGHTS!!!!!~'***

Man has `-ONLY done according to `-WHAT he `-ONLY `-KNEW!!!!!~'

THE `-<u>BIBLE</u> for `-<u>R</u>ECIPROCAL-<u>S</u>EQUENCING-<u>N</u>UMEROLOGY!!!!!~'

`-The End

Luke **10**:**21** :- In that same hour *he rejoiced in the Holy Spirit*, and said, I thank thee, O Father, Lord of heaven and earth, that *thou didst hide these things from the wise and understanding, and didst reveal them unto babes*: yea, Father; for so it was well-pleasing in thy sight. -(ENGLISH REVISED EDITION - 1885)-

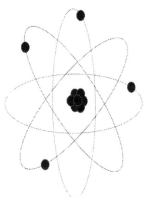

<u>RSN</u>-*Reciprocals*–The`-<u>ATOM</u>!!!!!~'

/|\ The "PROPHET" = Mr. Dwayne W. Anderson!!!!!~' /|

DEATH CIPHERS

FORMULAS - CODE BREAKERS OF LIFE/death (based on the RECIPROCALS of TRIGONOMETRY_)

III